# CAMBRIDGE LIBRARY COLLECTION

*Books of enduring scholarly value*

## Literary Studies

This series provides a high-quality selection of early printings of literary works, textual editions, anthologies and literary criticism which are of lasting scholarly interest. Ranging from Old English to Shakespeare to early twentieth-century work from around the world, these books offer a valuable resource for scholars in reception history, textual editing, and literary studies.

## The Sweet Silvery Sayings of Shakespeare on the Softer Sex

The anonymous 'Old Soldier' who compiled this anthology, published in 1877, states in the preface that he was inspired to make his selection by a passage in The Gentle Life: Essays in Aid of the Formation of Character, by the now large forgotten Victorian essayist James Hain Friswell: 'If a man wanted to make a sugar-sweet book ... let him go through the plays of the great national Poet, and make an extract of those passages wherein he has exalted woman.' In thirty-three sections (four plays are omitted), extensive quotations present examples of 'exalted woman' and give an insight into the taste of the educated middle class in the mid-Victorian period.

Cambridge University Press has long been a pioneer in the reissuing of out-of-print titles from its own backlist, producing digital reprints of books that are still sought after by scholars and students but could not be reprinted economically using traditional technology. The Cambridge Library Collection extends this activity to a wider range of books which are still of importance to researchers and professionals, either for the source material they contain, or as landmarks in the history of their academic discipline.

Drawing from the world-renowned collections in the Cambridge University Library, and guided by the advice of experts in each subject area, Cambridge University Press is using state-of-the-art scanning machines in its own Printing House to capture the content of each book selected for inclusion. The files are processed to give a consistently clear, crisp image, and the books finished to the high quality standard for which the Press is recognised around the world. The latest print-on-demand technology ensures that the books will remain available indefinitely, and that orders for single or multiple copies can quickly be supplied.

The Cambridge Library Collection will bring back to life books of enduring scholarly value across a wide range of disciplines in the humanities and social sciences and in science and technology.

# The Sweet Silvery Sayings of Shakespeare on the Softer Sex

William Shakespeare
Edited by 'An Old Soldier'

Cambridge
University Press

CAMBRIDGE UNIVERSITY PRESS

Cambridge New York Melbourne Madrid Cape Town Singapore São Paolo Delhi

Published in the United States of America by Cambridge University Press, New York

www.cambridge.org
Information on this title: www.cambridge.org/9781108001298



This edition first published 1877
This digitally printed version 2009

ISBN 978-1-108-00129-8

# THE SWEET SILVERY SAYINGS OF SHAKESPEARE ON THE SOFTER SEX.

THE

# SWEET SILVERY SAYINGS OF SHAKESPEARE

## ON THE SOFTER SEX

COMPILED BY AN OLD SOLDIER

HENRY S. KING AND CO. LONDON

1877

"IF a man wanted to make a little sugar-sweet book, which young men in love, and young maidens who are enamoured of their own sex would buy, let him go through the plays of the great national Poet, and make an extract of those passages wherein he has exalted woman."—*Gentle Life.*

"And moreover I know, both from my own sense and from the greatest of all great poets, that there are, and always have been, plenty of women good and gentle, warm-hearted, loving and loveable; very keen, moreover, at seeing the right, be it by reason or otherwise." —*Chapter* 49 *of* "*Lorna Doone,*" *a romance by* R. D. BLACKMORE.

# PREFACE.

IN a far distant dependency, where the howling of the wind, the roar of the surf, and the whistle of wild fowl were night-sounds more familiar to the ear than was the voice of man, I lighted on the passage quoted on the fly-leaf, in Hain Friswell's "Gentle Life."

During the stormy evenings of one long winter I endeavoured to carry out the idea of an author whose works have given an intellectual treat to readers of the present generation. If the selection prove successful, it will meet the requirements suggested; if not, I can only regret that the compilation was not made by a more skilful pen; but none will ever be made by one who has a deeper reverence for the writings of a poet whose knowledge of human passions in all their various phases has never been surpassed.

Often in the dusk of the evening on the banks of the Ganges the river is seen glittering with lights—a pretty superstition of the Indian girls, who commit little frail fire-ships, consisting of a small hollow gourd with oil and lighted wick, to the mighty swift stream; if the floating lamp sinks directly, the omen is disastrous; but if it sails down, still shining, for a considerable distance, then the omen is favourable.

So with this little labour of love. I push it down the stream of criticism, towards, as they say in Spain, the "honoured public."

# CONTENTS.

# SWEET SILVERY SAYINGS OF SHAKESPEARE.

## KING RICHARD III.

### Act I. Scene II.

*Anne.*

SET down, set down your honourable load,—
If honour may be shrouded in a hearse,—
Whilst I a while obsequiously lament
The untimely fall of virtuous Lancaster—
Poor key-cold figure of a holy king!
Pale ashes of the house of Lancaster!
Thou bloodless remnant of that royal blood!
Be it lawful that I invocate thy ghost,
To hear the lamentations of poor Anne,
Wife to thy Edward, to thy slaughter'd son,
Stabb'd by the self-same hand that made these wounds!
Lo, in these windows, that let forth thy life,
I pour the helpless balm of my poor eyes :—
O, cursed be the hand that made these holes!

Cursed the heart, that had the heart to do it!
Cursed the blood, that let this blood from hence!
More direful hap betide that hated wretch,
That makes us wretched by the death of thee,
Than I can wish to adders, spiders, toads,
Or any creeping venom'd thing that lives!
If ever he have child, abortive be it,
Prodigious, and untimely brought to light,
Whose ugly and unnatural aspect
May fright the hopeful mother at the view;
And that be heir to his unhappiness!
If ever he have wife, let her be made
More miserable by the death of him,
Than I am made by my young lord, and thee!—
Come, now, toward Chertsey with your holy load,
Taken from Paul's to be interred there;
And, still as you are weary of the weight,
Rest you, whiles I lament King Henry's corse.

*Gloster.* Stay you, that bear the corse, and set it down.

*Anne.* What black magician conjures up this fiend,
To stop devoted charitable deeds?

*Gloster.* Villains, set down the corse; or, by Saint Paul,
I'll make a corse of him that disobeys.

*Gentleman.* My lord, stand back, and let the coffin pass.

*Gloster.* Unmanner'd dog! stand thou when I command:
Advance thy halberd higher than my breast,
Or, by Saint Paul, I'll strike thee to my foot,
And spurn upon thee, beggar, for thy boldness.
[*The bearers set down the coffin.*

*Anne.* What, do you tremble? are you all afraid?
Alas, I blame you not; for you are mortal,
And mortal eyes cannot endure the devil.—
Avaunt, thou dreadful minister of hell!

Thou hadst but power over his mortal body,
His soul thou canst not have; therefore, be gone.

*Gloster.* Sweet saint, for charity, be not so curst.

*Anne.* Foul devil, for God's sake, hence, and trouble us not;
For thou hast made the happy earth thy hell,
Fill'd it with cursing cries, and deep exclaims.
If thou delight to view thy heinous deeds,
Behold this pattern of thy butcheries:
O, gentlemen, see, see! dead Henry's wounds
Open their congeal'd mouths, and bleed afresh!—
Blush, blush, thou lump of foul deformity;
For 'tis thy presence that exhales this blood
From cold and empty veins, where no blood dwells;
Thy deed, inhuman and unnatural,
Provokes this deluge most unnatural.—
O God, which this blood mad'st, revenge his death!
O earth, which this blood drink'st, revenge his death!
Either, heaven, with lightning strike the murderer dead,
Or, earth, gape open wide, and eat him quick;
As thou dost swallow up this good king's blood,
Which his hell-govern'd arm hath butchered!

* * * * * *

*Gloster.* Thine eyes, sweet lady, have infected mine.

*Anne.* Would they were basilisks, to strike thee dead!

*Gloster.* I would they were, that I might die at once;
For now they kill me with a living death.
Those eyes of thine from mine have drawn salt tears,
Sham'd their aspects with store of childish drops:
These eyes, which never shed remorseful tear,—
Not when my father York and Edward wept,
To hear the piteous moan that Rutland made,
When black-fac'd Clifford shook his sword at him:

Nor when thy warlike father, like a child,
Told the sad story of my father's death ;
And twenty times made pause, to sob, and weep,
That all the standers-by had wet their cheeks,
Like trees bedash'd with rain : in that sad time,
My manly eyes did scorn an humble tear ;
And what these sorrows could not thence exhale,
Thy beauty hath, and made them blind with weeping.
I never su'd to friend, nor enemy ;
My tongue could never learn sweet soothing word ;
But now thy beauty is propos'd my fee,
My proud heart sues, and prompts my tongue to speak.
[*She looks scornfully at him.*
Teach not thy lip such scorn ; for it was made
For kissing, lady, not for such contempt.
If thy revengeful heart cannot forgive,
Lo ! here I lend thee this sharp-pointed sword ;
Which if thou please to hide in this true breast,
And let the soul forth that adoreth thee,
I lay it naked to the deadly stroke,
And humbly beg the death upon my knee.
[*He lays his breast open ; she offers at it with his sword.*
Nay, do not pause ; for I did kill king Henry ;—
But 'twas thy beauty that provoked me.
Nay, now despatch ; 'twas I that stabb'd young Edward :—
[*She again offers at his breast.*
But 'twas thy heavenly face that set me on.
[*She lets fall the sword.*
Take up the sword again, or take up me.

*Anne.* Arise, dissembler : though I wish thy death,
I will not be thy executioner.

*Gloster.* Then bid me kill myself, and I will do it.

### Act IV. Scene I.

*Elizabeth.* Go, go, poor soul, I envy not thy glory ;
To feed my humour, wish thyself no harm.
*Anne.* No ! why ?—When he, that is my husband now,
Came to me, as I follow'd Henry's corse ;
When scarce the blood was well wash'd from his hands,
Which issu'd from my other angel husband,
And that dead saint which then I weeping follow'd ;
O, when, I say, I look'd on Richard's face,
This was my wish,—Be thou, quoth I, accurs'd,
For making me, so young, so old a widow !
And, when thou wed'st, let sorrow haunt thy bed ;
And be thy wife (if any be so mad)
More miserable by the life of thee,
Than thou hast made me by my dear lord's death !
Lo, ere I can repeat this curse again,
Even in so short a space, my woman's heart
Grossly grew captive to his honey words,
And prov'd the subject of mine own soul's curse :
Which ever since hath held mine eyes from rest ;
For never yet one hour in his bed
Did I enjoy the golden dew of sleep,
But with his timorous dreams was still awak'd.
Besides, he hates me for my father Warwick ;
And will, no doubt, shortly be rid of me.
*Elizabeth.* Poor heart, adieu ; I pity thy complaining.
*Anne.* No more than with my soul I mourn for yours.
*Dorset.* Farewell, thou woful welcomer of glory !
*Anne.* Adieu, poor soul, that tak'st thy leave of it !
*Duchess.* Go thou to Richmond, and good fortune guide thee !— [*To Dorset.*

Go thou to Richard, and good angels tend thee!—
[*To Anne.*
Go thou to sanctuary, and good thoughts possess thee!
[*To Q. Elizabeth.*
I to my grave, where peace and rest lie with me!
Eighty odd years of sorrow have I seen,
And each hour's joy wreck'd with a week of teen.
*Elizabeth.* Stay yet; look back, with me, unto the Tower.—
Pity, you ancient stones, those tender babes,
Whom envy hath immur'd within your walls!
Rough cradle for such little pretty ones!
Rude ragged nurse! old sullen playfellow
For tender princes, use my babies well!
So foolish sorrow bids your stones farewell.
[*Exeunt.*

## Act IV. Scene IV.

*Margaret.* I call'd thee then, vain flourish of my fortune;
I call'd thee then, poor shadow, painted queen;
The presentation of but what I was,
The flattering index of a direful pageant,
One heav'd a high, to be hurl'd down below:
A mother only mock'd with two fair babes;
A dream of what thou wast; a garish flag,
To be the aim of every dangerous shot;
A sign of dignity, a breath, a bubble;
A queen in jest, only to fill the scene.
Where is thy husband now? where be thy brothers?
Where be thy two sons? wherein dost thou joy?
Who sues, and kneels, and says—God save the queen?
Where be the bending peers that flatter'd thee?

Where be the thronging troops that follow'd thee?
Decline all this, and see what now thou art.
For happy wife, a most distressed widow;
For joyful mother, one that wails the name;
For one being sued to, one that humbly sues;
For queen, a very caitiff crown'd with care;
For one that scorn'd at me, now scorn'd of me;
For one being fear'd of all, now fearing one;
For one commanding all, obey'd of none.
Thus hath the course of justice wheel'd about,
And left thee but a very prey to time;
Having no more but thought of what thou wert,
To torture thee the more, being what thou art.
Thou didst usurp my place; and dost thou not
Usurp the just proportion of my sorrow?
Now thy proud neck bears half my burden'd yoke;
From which even here I slip my wearied head,
And leave the burden of it all on thee.
Farewell, York's wife,—and queen of sad mischance,—
These English woes shall make me smile in France.

*Elizabeth.* O thou well skill'd in curses, stay a while,
And teach me how to curse mine enemies.

*Margaret.* Forbear to sleep the night, and fast the day;
Compare dead happiness with living woe;
Think that thy babes were fairer than they were,
And he, that slew them, fouler than he is:
Bettering thy loss makes the bad-causer worse;
Revolving this will teach thee how to curse.

* * * * *

*Duchess.* I pr'ythee, hear me speak.

*Richard.* You speak too bitterly.

*Duchess.* Hear me a word;
For I shall never speak to thee again.

*Richard.* So.

*Duchess.* Either thou wilt die, by God's just ordinance
Ere from this war thou turn a conqueror;
Or I with grief and extreme age shall perish,
And never look upon thy face again.
Therefore, take with thee my most heavy curse;
Which, in the day of battle, tire thee more,
Than all the complete armour that thou wear'st!
My prayers on the adverse party fight;
And there the little souls of Edward's children
Whisper the spirits of thine enemies,
And promise them success and victory.
Bloody thou art, bloody will be thy end;
Shame serves thy life, and doth thy death attend.

* * * * *

*Elizabeth.* By nothing; for this is no oath.
Thy George, profan'd, hath lost his holy honour;
Thy garter, blemish'd, pawn'd his knightly virtue;
Thy crown, usurp'd, disgrac'd his kingly glory:
If something thou would'st swear to be believ'd,
Swear then by something that thou hast not wrong'd.

*Richard.* Now by the world,—

*Elizabeth.* 'Tis full of thy foul wrongs.

*Richard.* My father's death,—

*Elizabeth.* Thy life hath that dishonour'd.

*Richard.* Then, by myself,—

*Elizabeth.* Thyself is self—mis-us'd.

*Richard.* Why then, by God,—

*Elizabeth.* God's wrong is most of all.
If thou hadst fear'd to break an oath by him,
The unity, the king thy brother made,
Had not been broken, nor my brother slain.
If thou hadst fear'd to break an oath by him,

The imperial metal, circling now thy head,
Had grac'd the tender temples of my child;
And both the princes had been breathing here,
Which now, two tender bed-fellows for dust,
Thy broken faith hath made a prey for worms.
What canst thou swear by now?

## Act V. Scene IV.

*Richmond.* What men of note are slain on either side?
*Stanley.* John Duke of Norfolk, Walter Lord Ferrers,
Sir Robert Brakenbury, and Sir William Brandon.
*Richmond.* Inter their bodies as becomes their births.
Proclaim a pardon to the soldiers fled,
That in submission will return to us;
And then, as we have ta'en the sacrament,
We will unite the white rose with the red:—
Smile heaven upon this fair conjunction,
That long hath frown'd upon their enmity!—
What traitor hears me, and says not,—Amen?
England hath long been mad, and scarr'd herself;
The brother blindly shed the brother's blood,
The father rashly slaughter'd his own son,
The son, compell'd, been butcher to the sire;
All this divided York and Lancaster,
Divided, in their dire division.—
O, now, let Richmond and Elizabeth,
The true succeeders of each royal house,
By God's fair ordinance conjoin together!
And let their heirs (God, if thy will be so)
Enrich the time to come with smooth-fac'd peace
With smiling plenty, and fair prosperous days!
Abate the edge of traitors, gracious Lord,

That would reduce these bloody days again,
And make poor England weep in streams of blood!
Let them not live to taste this land's increase,
That would with treason wound this fair land's peace!
Now civil wounds are stopp'd, peace lives again;
That she may long live here, God say—Amen!

# ROMEO AND JULIET.

## Act I. Scene IV.

*Benvolio.*

THIS wind, you talk of, blows us from ourselves;
Supper is done, and we shall come too late.
*Romeo.* I fear, too early; for my mind misgives
Some consequence, yet hanging in the stars,
Shall bitterly begin his fearful date
With this night's revels; and expire the term
Of a despised life clos'd in my breast
By some vile forfeit of untimely death;
But he that hath the steerage of my course,
Direct my sail! On, lusty gentlemen.

## Scene V.

*Romeo.* What lady 's that, which doth enrich the hand
Of yonder knight?
*Servant.* I know not, sir.
*Romeo.* O, she doth teach the torches to burn bright!
Her beauty hangs upon the cheek of night

Like a rich jewel in an Ethiop's ear,
Beauty too rich for use, for earth too dear!
So shows a snowy dove trooping with crows
As yonder lady o'er her fellows shows;
The measure done, I'll watch her place of stand,
And, touching hers, make happy my rude hand.
Did my heart love till now? forswear it, sight,
For I ne'er saw true beauty till this night.

*   *   *   *   *

*Romeo.* If I profane with my unworthy hand [*To Juliet*
This holy shrine, the gentle fact is this,—
My lips, two blushing pilgrims, ready stand
To smooth that rough touch with a tender kiss.

*Juliet.* Good pilgrim, you do wrong your hand too much,
Which mannerly devotion shows in this;
For saints have hands that pilgrims' hands do touch,
And palm to palm is holy palmer's kiss.

*Romeo.* Have not saints lips, and holy palmers too?

*Juliet.* Ay, pilgrim, lips that they must use in prayer.

*Romeo.* O then, dear saint, let lips do what hands do;
They pray, grant thou, lest faith turn to despair.

*Juliet.* Saints do not move, though grant for prayer's sake.

*Romeo.* Then move not, while my prayer's effect I take;
Thus from my lips, by yours, my sin is purg'd.
[*Kissing her.*

*Juliet.* Then have my lips the sin that they have took.

*Romeo.* Sin from my lips? O trespass sweetly urg'd.
Give me my sin again.

*Juliet.* You kiss by the book.

*Nurse.* Madam, your mother craves a word with you.

*Romeo.* What is her mother?

*Nurse.* Marry, bachelor,

Her mother is the lady of the house,
And a good lady, and a wise and virtuous:
I nurs'd her daughter, that you talk'd withal.
I tell you,—he that can lay hold of her
Shall have the chinks.

*Romeo.* Is she a Capulet?
O dear account! My life is my foe's debt.

*Benvolio.* Away, begone; the sport is at the best.

*Romeo.* Ay, so I fear; the more is my unrest.

* * * * *

*Juliet.* Come hither, nurse: what is yon gentleman?

*Nurse.* The son and heir of old Tiberio.

*Juliet.* What 's he, that now is going out of door?

*Nurse.* Marry, that, I think, be young Petruchio.

*Juliet.* What 's he, that follows there, that would not dance?

*Nurse.* I know not.

*Juliet.* Go, ask his name:—if he be married
My grave is like to be my wedding bed.

*Nurse.* His name is Romeo, and a Montague;
The only son of your great enemy.

*Juliet.* My only love sprung from my only hate!
Too early seen unknown, and known too late!
Prodigious birth of love it is to me
That I must love a loathed enemy.

* * * * *

## Act II. Scene II.

*Romeo.* He jests at scars, that never felt a wound—
[*Juliet appears above at a window.*
But soft! what light through yonder window breaks?
It is the east, and Juliet is the sun!—

Arise, fair sun, and kill the envious moon,
Who is already sick and pale with grief,
That thou her maid art far more fair than she.
Be not her maid, since she is envious;
Her vestal livery is but sick and green,
And none but fools do wear it; cast it off.—
It is my lady; O, it is my love;
O, that she knew she were!—
She speaks, yet she says nothing; what of that?
Her eye discourses, I will answer it.—
I am too bold, 'tis not to me she speaks:
Two of the fairest stars in all the heavens,
Having some business, do entreat her eyes
To twinkle in their spheres till they return.
What if her eyes were there, they in her head?
The brightness of her cheek would shame those stars
As daylight doth a lamp; her eye in heaven
Would through the airy region stream so bright,
That birds would sing, and think it were not night.
See, how she leans her cheek upon her hand!
O, that I were a glove upon that hand,
That I might touch that cheek!

*Juliet.* Ah me!

*Romeo.* She speaks:—
O, speak again, bright angel! for thou art
As glorious to this night, being o'er my head,
As is a winged messenger of heaven
Unto the white, upturned, wond'ring eyes
Of mortals, that fall back to gaze on him,
When he bestrides the lazy-pacing clouds,
And sails upon the bosom of the air.

*Juliet.* O Romeo, Romeo! wherefore art thou Romeo?
Deny thy father, and refuse thy name:

Or, if thou wilt not, be not sworn my love,
And I 'll no longer be a Capulet.
*Romeo.* Shall I hear more, or shall I speak at this? [*Aside.*
*Juliet.* 'Tis but a name, that is my enemy:—
Thou art thyself, though, not a Montague.
What's Montague? it is nor hand, nor foot,
Nor arm, nor face, nor any other part
Belonging to a man. O, be some other name!
What's in a name? that which we call a rose
By any other name would smell as sweet;
So Romeo would, were he not Romeo call'd,
Retain that dear perfection which he owes
Without that title. Romeo, doff thy name;
And for that name, which is no part of thee,
Take all myself.
*Romeo.* I take thee at thy word;
Call me but love, and I 'll be new baptiz'd.
Henceforth I never will be Romeo.
*Juliet.* What man art thou, that, thus bescreen'd in night,
So stumblest on my counsel?
*Romeo.* By a name
I know not how to tell thee who I am.
My name, dear saint, is hateful to myself
Because it is an enemy to thee;
Had I it written, I would tear the word.
*Juliet.* My ears have not drunk a hundred words
Of that tongue's utterance, yet I know the sound.
Art thou not Romeo, and a Montague?
*Romeo.* Neither, fair saint—if either thee dislike.
*Juliet.* How cam'st thou hither, tell me? and wherefore?
The orchard walls are high, and hard to climb;
And the place death, considering who thou art,

If any of my kinsmen find thee here.
*Romeo.* With love's light wings did I o'erperch these walls,
For stony limits cannot hold love out:
And what love can do, that dares love attempt;
Therefore thy kinsmen are no let to me.
*Juliet.* If they do see thee they will murder thee.
*Romeo.* Alack! there lies more peril in thine eye
Than twenty of their swords; look thou but sweet,
And I am proof against their enmity.
*Juliet.* I would not for the world they saw thee here.
*Romeo.* I have night's cloak to hide me from their sight,
And, but thou love me, let them find me here;
My life were better ended by their hate,
Than death prorogued, wanting of thy love.
*Juliet.* By whose direction found'st thou out this place?
*Romeo.* By love, who first did prompt me to inquire;
He lent me counsel, and I lent him eyes.
I am no pilot; yet, wert thou as far
As that vast shore wash'd with the furthest sea,
I would adventure for such merchandize.
*Juliet.* Thou know'st the mask of night is on my face,
Else would a maiden blush bepaint my cheek,
For that which thou hast heard me speak to-night.
Fain would I dwell on form, fain, fain deny
What I have spoke. But farewell compliment!
Dost thou love me? I know thou wilt say, Ay,
And I will take thy word: yet, if thou swear'st,
Thou may'st prove false; at lovers' perjuries,
They say, Jove laughs. O, gentle Romeo,
If thou dost love, pronounce it faithfully;
Or if thou think'st I am too quickly won,
I'll frown, and be perverse, and say thee nay,

So thou wilt woo; but, else, not for the world.
In truth, fair Montague, I am too fond;
And therefore thou may'st think my 'haviour light,
But, trust me, gentleman, I'll prove more true
Than those that have more cunning to be strange.
I should have been more strange, I must confess,
But that thou overheard'st, ere I was ware,
My true love's passion: therefore pardon me,
And not impute this yielding to light love,
Which the dark night hath so discovered.

*Romeo.* Lady, by yonder blessed moon I swear,
That tips with silver all these fruit-tree tops—

*Juliet.* O, swear not by the moon, the inconstant moon,
That monthly changes in her circled orb,
Lest that thy love prove likewise variable.

*Romeo.* What shall I swear by?

*Juliet.* Do not swear at all:
Or, if thou wilt, swear by thy gracious self,
Which is the god of my idolatry,
And I'll believe thee.

*Romeo.* If my heart's dear love—

*Juliet.* Well, do not swear: although I joy in thee,
I have no joy of this contract to-night;
It is too rash, too unadvis'd, too sudden;
Too like the lightning, which doth cease to be
Ere one can say, It lightens. Sweet, good night!
This bud of love, by summer's ripening breath,
May prove a beauteous flower when next we meet.
Good night, good night! as sweet repose and rest
Come to thy heart, as that within my breast!

*Romeo.* O, wilt thou leave me so unsatisfied?

*Juliet.* What satisfaction canst thou have to-night?

*Romeo.* The exchange of thy love's faithful vow for mine.

*Juliet.* I gave thee mine before thou didst request it:
And yet I would it were to give again.
*Romeo.* Would'st thou withdraw it? For what purpose, love?
*Juliet.* But to be frank, and give it thee again.
And yet I wish but for the thing I have:
My bounty is as boundless as the sea,
My love as deep; the more I give to thee,
The more I have, for both are infinite.
[NURSE *calls within.*
I hear some noise within; Dear love, adieu!—
Anon, good nurse!—Sweet Montague, be true.
Stay but a little, I will come again.
*Romeo.* O blessed, blessed night! I am afeard,
Being in night, all this is but a dream,
Too flattering-sweet to be substantial.
*Juliet.* Three words, dear Romeo, and good night, indeed.
If that thy bent of love be honourable,
Thy purpose marriage, send me word to-morrow,
By one that I'll procure to come to thee,
Where, and what time, thou wilt perform the rite;
And all my fortunes at thy foot I'll lay,
And follow thee my lord throughout the world.
*Nurse* [*within*]. Madam.
*Juliet.* I come, anon.—But if thou mean'st not well,
I do beseech thee—
*Nurse* [*within*]. Madam.
*Juliet.* By-and-by, I come.—
To cease my suit, and leave me to my grief.
To-morrow will I send.
*Romeo.* So thrive my soul—
*Juliet.* A thousand times good night!

*Romeo.* A thousand times the worse, to want thy light.
Love goes towards love, as school-boys from their books ;
But love from love, towards school with heavy looks.

*Juliet.* Hist ! Romeo, hist !—O, for a falconer's voice
To lure this tassel-gentle back again !
Bondage is hoarse, and may not speak aloud ;
Else would I tear the cave where echo lies,
And make her airy tongue more hoarse than mine
With repetition of my Romeo's name.

*Romeo.* It is my soul that calls upon my name :
How silver-sweet sound lovers' tongues by night,
Like softest musick to attending ears !

*Juliet.* Romeo !

*Romeo.* My sweet !

*Juliet.* At what o'clock to-morrow
Shall I send to thee ?

*Romeo.* At the hour of nine.

*Juliet.* I will not fail ; 'tis twenty years till then.
I have forgot why I did call thee back.

*Romeo.* Let me stand here till thou remember it.

*Juliet.* I shall forget, to have thee still stand there,
Rememb'ring how I love thy company.

*Romeo.* And I'll still stay, to have thee still forget,
Forgetting any other home but this.

*Juliet.* 'Tis almost morning ; I would have thee gone,
And yet no further than a wanton's bird,
Who lets it hop a little from her hand,
Like a poor prisoner in his twisted gyves,
And with a silk thread plucks it back again,
So loving-jealous of his liberty.

*Romeo.* I would I were thy bird.

*Juliet.* Sweet, so would I :
Yet I should kill thee with much cherishing.

Good night, good night! parting is such sweet sorrow,
That I shall say good night, till it be morrow. [*Exit.*

*Romeo.* Sleep dwell upon thine eyes, peace in thy breast!—
'Would I were sleep and peace, so sweet to rest!
Hence will I to my ghostly father's cell,
His help to crave, and my dear hap to tell. [*Exit.*

## Scene VI.

*Friar.* So smile the heavens upon this holy act,
That after-hours with sorrow chide us not!

*Romeo.* Amen, amen! but come what sorrow can,
It cannot countervail the exchange of joy
That one short minute gives me in her sight:
Do thou but close our hands with holy words,
Then love-devouring death do what he dare;
It is enough I may but call her mine.

*Friar.* These violent delights have violent ends,
And in their triumph die; like fire and powder,
Which, as they kiss, consume. The sweetest honey
Is loathsome in his own deliciousness,
And in the taste confounds the appetite:
Therefore, love moderately; long love doth so;
Too swift arrives as tardy as too slow.

*Enter* Juliet.

Here comes the lady:—O, so light a foot
Will ne'er wear out the everlasting flint:
A lover may bestride the gossamers
That idle in the wanton summer air,
And yet not fall; so light is vanity.

*Juliet.* Good even to my ghostly confessor.

*Friar.* Romeo shall thank thee, daughter, for us both.
*Juliet.* As much to him, else are his thanks too much.
*Romeo.* Ah, Juliet, if the measure of thy joy
Be heap'd like mine, and that thy skill be more
To blazon it, then sweeten with thy breath
This neighbour air, and let rich musick's tongue
Unfold the imagin'd happiness that both
Receive in either by this dear encounter.
*Juliet.* Conceit, more rich in matter than in words,
Brags of his substance, not of ornament;
They are but beggars that can count their worth;
But my true love is grown to such excess,
I cannot sum up half my sum of wealth.
*Friar.* Come, come with me, and we will make short work;
For, by your leaves, you shall not stay alone,
Till holy church incorporate two in one. [*Exeunt.*

## ACT III. SCENE II.

*Juliet.* Gallop apace, you fiery-footed steeds,
Towards Phœbus' mansion; such a waggoner
As Phaeton would whip you to the west,
And bring in cloudy night immediately.—
Spread thy close curtain, love-performing night!
That run-away's eyes may wink, and Romeo
Leap to these arms, untalk'd of and unseen!—
Lovers can see to do their amorous rites
By their own beauties: or, if Love be blind,
It best agrees with night.—Come, civil night,
Thou sober-suited matron, all in black,
And learn me how to lose a winning match

Play'd for a pair of stainless maidenhoods :
Hood my unmann'd blood bating in my cheeks
With thy black mantle ; till strange love grown bold
Think true love acted, simple modesty.
Come, night ! Come, Romeo ! come, thou day in night !
For thou wilt lie upon the wings of night
Whiter than new snow on a raven's back.
Come, gentle night ; come, loving, black-brow'd night,
Give me my Romeo : and, when he shall die,
Take him and cut him out in little stars,
And he will make the face of heaven so fine
That all the world will be in love with night,
And pay no worship to the garish sun.
O, I have bought the mansion of a love,
But not possess'd it ; and, though I am sold,
Not yet enjoy'd. So tedious is this day,
As is the night before some festival
To an impatient child, that hath new robes
And may not wear them. O, here comes my nurse,
And she brings news ; and every tongue, that speaks
But Romeo's name, speaks heavenly eloquence.—
Now, nurse, what news ? What, hast thou there the cords
That Romeo bade thee fetch ?

## Scene V.

*Juliet.* Wilt thou be gone ? it is not yet near day :
It was the nightingale, and not the lark
That pierc'd the fearful hollow of thine ear ;
Nightly she sings on yon pomegranate tree.
Believe me, love, it was the nightingale.

*Romeo.* It was the lark, the herald of the morn,
No nightingale ; look, love, what envious streaks

Do lace the severing clouds in yonder east;
Night's candles are burnt out, and jocund day
Stands tiptoe on the misty mountain tops;
I must be gone and live, or stay and die.

*Juliet.* Yon light is not daylight, I know it, I:
It is some meteor that the sun exhales,
To be to thee this night a torch-bearer,
And light thee on thy way to Mantua:
Therefore stay yet, thou need'st not to be gone.

*Romeo.* Let me be ta'en, let me be put to death;
I am content, so thou wilt have it so.
I'll say yon grey is not the morning's eye,
'Tis but the pale reflex of Cynthia's brow;
Nor that is not the lark, whose notes do beat
The vaulty heaven so high above our heads.
I have more care to stay, than will to go.
Come, death, and welcome! Juliet wills it so.—
How is 't, my soul? let 's talk, it is not day.

*Juliet.* It is, it is; hie hence, be gone, away;
It is the lark that sings so out of tune,
Straining harsh discords and unpleasing sharps.
Some say, the lark makes sweet division;
This doth not so, for she divideth us.
Some say, the lark and loathed toad change eyes;
O, now I would they had chang'd voices too,
Since arm from arm that voice doth us affray,
Hunting thee hence with hunts-up to the day.
O, now be gone: more light and light it grows.

*Romeo.* More light and light?—more dark and dark our woes.

* * * * *

*Juliet.* Then, window, let day in, and let life out.

*Romeo.* Farewell, farewell! one kiss, and I'll descend.

[ROMEO *descends.*

*Juliet.* Art thou gone so, my love, my lord, my friend?
I must hear from thee every day i' the hour,
For in a minute there are many days:
O! by this count I shall be much in years
Ere I again behold my Romeo.

*Romeo.* Farewell! I will omit no opportunity
That may convey my greetings, love, to thee.

*Juliet.* O, think'st thou, we shall ever meet again?

*Romeo.* I doubt it not; and all these woes shall serve
For sweet discourses in our time to come.

*Juliet.* O God! I have an ill-divining soul.[1]
Methinks I see thee, now thou art below,
As one dead in the bottom of a tomb;
Either my eyesight fails, or thou look'st pale.

*Romeo.* And trust me, love, in my eye so do you:
Dry sorrow drinks our blood. Adieu—adieu!

*Juliet.* O fortune, fortune! all men call thee fickle:
If thou art fickle, what dost thou with him
That is renown'd for faith? Be fickle, fortune;
For then, I hope, thou wilt not keep him long,
But send him back.

* * * * *

*Juliet.* O God! O nurse, how shall this be prevented?
My husband is on earth, my faith in heaven;
How shall that faith return again to earth,
Unless that husband send it me from heaven
By leaving earth? Comfort me, counsel me.
Alack, alack, that heaven should practise stratagems
Upon so soft a subject as myself!—
What say'st thou? hast thou not a word of joy?
Some comfort, nurse.

*Nurse.* 'Faith, here 'tis: Romeo
Is banished; and all the world to nothing,

That he dares ne'er come back to challenge you;
Or, if he do, it needs must be by stealth.
Then, since the case so stands as now it doth,
I think it best you married with the county.
O, he's a lovely gentleman!
Romeo's a dishclout to him; an eagle, madam,
Hath not so green, so quick, so fair an eye,
As Paris hath. Beshrew my very heart,
I think you are happy in this second match,
For it excels your first: or if it did not,
Your first is dead, or 'twere as good he were,
As living here and you no use of him.

*Juliet.* Speakest thou from thy heart?

*Nurse.* From my soul too;
Or else beshrew them both.

*Juliet.* Amen!

*Nurse.* To what?

*Juliet.* Well, thou hast comforted me marvellous much.
Go in, and tell my lady I am gone,
Having displeas'd my father, to Laurence' cell,
To make confession, and to be absolv'd.

*Nurse.* Marry, I will; and this is wisely done. [*Exit.*

*Juliet.* Ancient damnation! O most wicked fiend!
Is it more sin—to wish me thus forsworn,
Or to dispraise my lord with that same tongue
Which she hath prais'd him with above compare
So many thousand times?—Go, counsellor;
Thou and my bosom henceforth shall be twain.—
I'll to the friar, to know his remedy;
If all else fail, myself have power to die.

## ACT IV. SCENE I.

*Juliet.* O, bid me leap, rather than marry Paris,
From off the battlements of yonder tower;
Or walk in thievish ways; or bid me lurk
Where serpents are; chain me with roaring bears;
Or shut me nightly in a charnel-house,
O'er-cover'd quite with dead men's rattling bones,
With reeky shanks, and yellow, chapless sculls;
Or bid me go into a new-made grave,
And hide me with a dead man in his shroud:
Things that, to hear them told, have made me tremble;
And I will do it without fear or doubt,
To live an unstain'd wife to my sweet love.

## ACT IV. SCENE III.

*Juliet.* Farewell!—Heaven knows when we shall meet again.
I have a faint cold fear thrills through my veins,
That almost freezes up the heat of life:
I'll call them back again to comfort me.—
Nurse!—What should she do here?
My dismal scene I needs must act alone.—
Come, phial,—
What if this mixture do not work at all?
Must I of force be married to the county?
No, no;—this shall forbid it:—lie thou there.
[*Laying down a dagger.*
What if it be a poison, which the friar
Subtly hath minister'd to have me dead,
Lest in this marriage he should be dishonour'd,
Because he married me before to Romeo?

I fear it is: and yet, methinks, it should not,
For he hath still been tried a holy man:
I will not entertain so bad a thought.
How if, when I am laid into the tomb,
I wake before the time that Romeo
Come to redeem me? there's a fearful point!
Shall I not then be stifled in the vault,
To whose foul mouth no healthsome air breathes in,
And there die strangled ere my Romeo comes?
Or, if I live, is it not very like,
The horrible conceit of death and night,
Together with the terror of the place,—
As in a vault, an ancient receptacle,
Where, for these many hundred years, the bones
Of all my buried ancestors are pack'd;
Where bloody Tybalt, yet but green in earth,
Lies festering in his shroud, where, as they say,
At some hours in the night spirits resort;—
Alack, alack! is it not like, that I,
So early waking, what with loathsome smells,
And shrieks like mandrake's torn out of the earth,
That living mortals, hearing them, run mad—
O! if I wake, shall I not be distraught,
Environed with all these hideous fears?
And madly play with my forefathers' joints,
And pluck the mangled Tybalt from his shroud?
And, in this rage, with some great kinsman's bone,
As with a club, dash out my desperate brains?
O, look! methinks I see my cousin's ghost
Seeking out Romeo, that did spit his body
Upon a rapier's point:—stay, Tybalt, stay!
Romeo, I come! this do I drink to thee.

[*She throws herself on the bed.*

## Act V. Scene I.

*Romeo.* If I may trust the flattering eye of sleep,
My dreams presage some joyful news at hand.
My bosom's lord sits lightly in his throne,
And, all this day, an unaccustom'd spirit
Lifts me above the ground with cheerful thoughts.
I dreamt my lady came and found me dead
(Strange dream! that gives a dead man leave to think),
And breath'd such life with kisses in my lips,
That I reviv'd and was an emperour.
Ah me! how sweet is love itself possess'd,
When but love's shadows are so rich in joy!

*Enter* Balthasar.

News from Verona!—How now, Balthasar?
Dost thou not bring me letters from the friar?
How doth my lady? Is my father well?
How fares my Juliet? That I ask again;
For nothing can be ill, if she be well.
*Balthasar.* Then she is well, and nothing can be ill;
Her body sleeps in Capels' monument,
And her immortal part with angels lives;
I saw her laid low in her kindred's vault,
And presently took post to tell it you.
O pardon me for bringing these ill news,
Since you did leave it for my office, sir.
*Romeo.* Is it even so? then I defy you, stars!
Thou know'st my lodging: get me ink and paper,
And hire post horses; I will hence to-night.
*Balthasar.* Pardon me, sir, I will not leave you thus:

Your looks are pale and wild, and do import
Some misadventure.
*Romeo.* Tush, thou art deceiv'd;
Leave me, and do the thing I bid thee do.
Hast thou no letters to me from the friar?
*Balthasar.* No, my good lord.
*Romeo.* No matter. Get thee gone
And hire those horses; I'll be with thee straight.
Well, Juliet, I will lie with thee to-night.
Let 's see for means. O mischief! thou art swift
To enter in the thoughts of desperate men!
I do remember an Apothecary—
And hereabouts he dwells—whom late I noted
In tatter'd weeds, with overwhelming brows,
Culling of simples; meagre were his looks,
Sharp misery had worn him to the bones,
And in his needy shop a tortoise hung,
An alligator stuff'd, and other skins
Of ill-shaped fishes; and about his shelves
A beggarly account of empty boxes,
Green earthen pots, bladders, and musty seeds,
Remnants of packthread, and old cakes of roses,
Were thinly scatter'd, to make up a show.
Noting this penury, to myself I said—
An if a man did need a poison now,
Whose sale is present death in Mantua,
Here lives a caitiff wretch would sell it him.
O, this same thought did but fore-run my need;
And this same needy man must sell it me.
As I remember, this should be the house.
Being holy day, the beggar's shop is shut.
What, ho! Apothecary!

* * * * *

*Apothecary.* Put this in any liquid thing you will,
And drink it off; and, if you had the strength
Of twenty men, it would despatch you straight.

*Romeo.* There is thy gold; worse poison to men's souls,
Doing more murders in this loathsome world,
Than these poor compounds that thou may'st not sell:
I sell thee poison, thou hast sold me none.
Farewell; buy food, and get thyself in flesh.—
Come, cordial, and not poison; go with me
To Juliet's grave, for there must I use thee.

## Act V. Scene III.

*Paris.* Sweet flower, with flowers I strew thy bridal bed.
Sweet tomb, that in thy circuit dost contain
The perfect model of eternity;
Fair Juliet, that with angels dost remain,
Accept this latest favour at my hands,
That living honour'd thee, and, being dead,
With funeral praises do adorn thy tomb!
The boy gives warning, something doth approach.
What cursed foot wanders this way to-night
To cross my obsequies, and true love's rite?
What, with a torch! muffle me, night, awhile.

* * * * *

*Romeo.* Thou detestable maw, thou womb of death,
Gorg'd with the dearest morsel of the earth,
Thus I enforce thy rotten jaws to open,
And in despite I'll cram thee with more food.

*Paris.* This is that banish'd, haughty Montague
That murder'd my love's cousin—with which grief
It is supposed the fair creature died—
And here is come to do some villainous shame

To the dead bodies; I will apprehend him.
Stop thy unhallow'd toil, vile Montague;
Can vengeance be pursu'd further than death?
Condemned villain, I do apprehend thee;
Obey, and go with me; for thou must die.
*Romeo.* I must, indeed; and therefore came I hither.—
Good, gentle youth, tempt not a desperate man;
Fly hence and leave me.—Think upon these gone;
Let them affright thee.—I beseech thee, youth,
Heap not another sin upon my head,
By urging me to fury;—O, be gone!
By heaven, I love thee better than myself,
For I come hither arm'd against myself;
Stay not, be gone; live, and hereafter say
A madman's mercy bade thee run away.
*Paris.* I do defy thy conjurations,
And do attach thee as a felon here.
*Romeo.* Wilt thou provoke me? then have at thee, boy.
*Paris.* O, I am slain! If thou be merciful,
Open the tomb, lay me with Juliet.— [*Dies.*
*Romeo.* In faith, I will.—Let me peruse this face;—
Mercutio's kinsman, noble county Paris.
What said my man, when my betossed soul
Did not attend him as we rode? I think,
He told me, Paris should have married Juliet;
Said he not so? or did I dream so?
Or am I mad, hearing him talk of Juliet,
To think it was so?—O, give me thy hand,
One writ with me in sour misfortune's book!
I'll bury thee in a triumphant grave—
A grave? O, no; a lantern, slaughter'd youth,
For here lies Juliet, and her beauty makes
This vault a feasting presence full of light.

Death, lie thou there, by a dead man interr'd.
How oft, when men are at the point of death,
Have they been merry? which their keepers call
A lightning before death. O, how may I
Call this a lightning?—O my love! my wife!
Death, that hath suck'd the honey of thy breath,
Hath had no power yet upon thy beauty.
Thou art not conquer'd; beauty's ensign yet
Is crimson in thy lips, and in thy cheeks,
And death's pale flag is not advanced there.—
Tybalt, liest thou there in thy bloody sheet?
O, what more favour can I do to thee,
Than with that hand that cut thy youth in twain,
To sunder his that was thine enemy?
Forgive me, cousin! Ah, dear Juliet,
Why art thou yet so fair? Shall I believe
That unsubstantial death is amorous,
And that the lean, abhorred monster keeps
Thee here in dark, to be his paramour?
For fear of that, I will stay with thee,
And never from this palace of dim night
Depart again; here, here, will I remain
With worms that are my chamber-maids. O here
Will I set up my everlasting rest,
And shake the yoke of inauspicious stars
From this world-wearied flesh.—Eyes, look your last;
Arms, take your last embrace! and lips, O you,
The doors of breath, seal with a righteous kiss
A dateless bargain to engrossing death!
Come, bitter conduct! come, unsavoury guide!
Thou desperate pilot, now at once run on
The dashing rocks thy sea-sick, weary bark!
Here 's to my love!—(*drinks*). O, true apothecary!

Thy drugs are quick.—Thus with a kiss I die. [*Dies.*

* * * * *

*Juliet.* O comfortable Friar! where is my lord?
I do remember well where I should be,
And there I am:—Where is my Romeo?

*Friar.* I hear some noise.—Lady, come from that nest
Of death, contagion, and unnatural sleep;
A greater power than we can contradict
Hath thwarted our intents; come, come away!
Thy husband in thy bosom there lies dead;
And Paris too: come, I'll dispose of thee
Among a sisterhood of holy nuns.
Stay not to question, for the watch is coming;
Come, go, good Juliet,—I dare stay no longer.

*Juliet.* Go, get thee hence, for I will not away.—
What's here? a cup, clos'd in my true love's hand?
Poison, I see, hath been his timeless end:—
O churl! drink all; and leave no friendly drop
To help me after? I will kiss thy lips;
Haply, some poison yet doth hang on them
To make me die with a restorative. [*Kisses him.*
Thy lips are warm!

1*st Watch* [*within*]. Lead, boy:—Which way?

*Juliet.* Yea, noise? then I'll be brief.—O happy dagger!
This is thy sheath [*stabs herself*]; there rest and let me die.
[*Falls on Romeo's body and dies.*

* * * * *

*Prince.* This letter doth make good the Friar's words,
Their course of love, the tidings of her death:
And here he writes—that he did buy a poison
Of a poor 'pothecary, and wherewithal
Came to this vault to die, and lie with Juliet.—
Where be these enemies? Capulet! Montague!—

D

See, what a scourge is laid upon your hate,
That heaven finds means to kill your joys with love!
And I, for winking at your discords too,
Have lost a brace of kinsmen;—all are punished.
*Capulet.* O brother Montague, give me thy hand;
This is my daughter's jointure, for no more
Can I demand.
*Montague.* But I can give thee more:
For I will raise her statue in pure gold:
That while Verona by that name is known,
There shall no figure at such rate be set
As that of true and faithful Juliet.—
*Capulet.* As rich shall Romeo by his lady lie,
Poor sacrifices of our enmity!
*Prince.* A glooming peace this morning with it brings;
The sun for sorrow will not show his head.
Go hence, to have more talk of these sad things;
Some shall be pardon'd and some punished.
For never was a story of more woe
Than this of Juliet and her Romeo.

## JULIUS CÆSAR.

M. BRUTUS, *Roman Conspirator.* PORTIA, *Wife to Brutus.*

### ACT II. SCENE I.

*Portia.*

BRUTUS, my lord!

*Brutus.* Portia, what mean you? Wherefore rise you now?
It is not for your health, thus to commit
Your weak condition to the raw, cold morning.

*Portia.* Nor for yours neither. You have ungently, Brutus,
Stole from your bed. And yesternight, at supper,
You suddenly rose, and walk'd about,
Musing, and sighing, with your arms across;
And when I ask'd you what the matter was,
You star'd upon me with ungentle looks:
I urg'd you further: then you scratch'd your head,
And too impatiently stamp'd with your foot:
Yet I insisted, yet you answer'd not;
But, with an angry wafture of your hand,
Gave sign for me to leave you. So I did,
Fearing to strengthen that impatience

Which seem'd too much enkindled ; and, withal,
Hoping it was but an effect of humour,
Which sometime hath his hour with every man.
It will not let you eat, nor talk, nor sleep ;
And could it work so much upon your shape
As it hath much prevail'd on your condition,
I should not know you, Brutus. Dear my lord,
Make me acquainted with your cause of grief.

*Brutus.* I am not well in health, and that is all.

*Portia.* Brutus is wise, and were he not in health,
He would embrace the means to come by it.

*Brutus.* Why, so I do.—Good Portia, go to bed.

*Portia.* Is Brutus sick ? and is it physical
To walk unbraced, and suck up the humours
Of the dank morning ? What, is Brutus sick ?
And will he steal out of his wholesome bed
To dare the vile contagion of the night,
And tempt the rheumy and unpurged air
To add unto his sickness ? No, my Brutus :
You have some sick offence within your mind,
Which, by the right and virtue of my place,
I ought to know of : And, upon my knees,
I charm you, by my once commended beauty,
By all your vows of love, and that great vow
Which did incorporate and make us one,
That you unfold to me, yourself, your half,
Why you are heavy, and what men to-night
Have had resort to you : for here have been
Some six or seven, who did hide their faces
Even from the darkness.

*Brutus.* Kneel not, gentle Portia.

*Portia.* I should not need, if you were gentle Brutus.
Within the bond of marriage, tell me, Brutus,

Is it expected, I should know no secrets
That appertain to you? Am I yourself,
But, as it were, in sort, or limitation;
To keep with you at meals, comfort your bed,
And talk to you sometimes? Dwell I but in the suburbs
Of your good pleasure? If it be no more,
Portia is Brutus' harlot, not his wife.

*Brutus.* You are my true and honourable wife;
As dear to me, as are the ruddy drops
That visit my sad heart.

*Portia.* If this were true, then should I know this secret.
I grant, I am a woman; but, withal,
A woman that Lord Brutus took to wife:
I grant, I am a woman; but, withal,
A woman well reputed—Cato's daughter.
Think you, I am no stronger than my sex,
Being so father'd and so husbanded?
Tell me your counsels, I will not disclose them:
I have made strong proof of my constancy,
Giving myself a voluntary wound
Here, in the thigh: Can I bear that with patience,
And not my husband's secrets?

*Brutus.* O ye gods,
Render me worthy of this noble wife!
Hark, hark! one knocks: Portia, go in awhile;
And by-and-by thy bosom shall partake
The secret of my heart;
All my engagements I will construe to thee,
All the charactery of my sad brows.—
Leave me with haste.

## Scene II.

*Calphurnia.* What mean you, Cæsar? Think you to walk forth?
You shall not stir out of your house to-day.
*Cæsar.* Cæsar shall forth: The things that threaten'd me,
Ne'er look'd but on my back; when they shall see
The face of Cæsar, they are vanished.
*Calphurnia.* Cæsar, I never stood on ceremonies,
Yet now they fright me. There is one within,
Besides the things that we have heard and seen,
Recounts most horrid sights seen by the watch:
A lioness hath whelped in the streets,
And graves have yawn'd, and yielded up their dead;
Fierce, fiery warriors fight upon the clouds,
In ranks, and squadrons, and right form of war,
Which drizzled blood upon the Capitol;
The noise of battle hurtled in the air,
Horses did neigh, and dying men did groan,
And ghosts did shriek and squeal about the streets.
O Cæsar! these things are beyond all use,
And I do fear them.
*Cæsar.* What can be avoided,
Whose end is purpos'd by the mighty gods?
Yet Cæsar shall go forth: for these predictions
Are to the world in general, as to Cæsar.
*Calphurnia.* When beggars die, there are no comets seen;
The heavens themselves blaze forth the death of princes.
*Cæsar.* Cowards die many times before their death;
The valiant never taste of death but once.

Of all the wonders that I yet have heard,
It seems to me most strange that men should fear;
Seeing that death, a necessary end,
Will come, when it will come.

* * * * *

*Calphurnia.* Alas, my lord,
Your wisdom is consum'd in confidence.
Do not go forth to-day: call it my fear,
That keeps you in the house, and not your own.
We'll send Mark Antony to the senate-house;
And he shall say, you are not well to-day.
Let me, upon my knee, prevail in this.

*Cæsar.* Mark Antony shall say, I am not well:
And, for thy humour, I will stay at home.—

## Act II. Scene IV.

*Portia.* I pr'ythee, boy, run to the senate-house;
Stay not to answer me, but get thee gone.
Why dost thou stay?

*Lucius.* To know my errand, madam.

*Portia.* I would have had thee there, and here again,
Ere I can tell thee what thou should'st do there.
O constancy, be strong upon my side!
Set a huge mountain 'tween my heart and tongue!
I have a man's mind, but a woman's might.
How hard it is for women to keep counsel!—
Art thou here yet?

*Lucius.* Madam, what should I do?
Run to the Capitol, and nothing else?
And so return to you, and nothing else?

*Portia.* Yes, bring me word, boy, if thy lord look well,

For he went sickly forth : and take good note
What Cæsar doth, what suitors press to him.
Hark, boy ! what noise is that ?

*Lucius.* I hear none, madam.

*Portia.* Pr'ythee, listen well ;
I heard a bustling rumour, like a fray,
And the wind brings it from the Capitol.

*Lucius.* Sooth, madam, I hear nothing.

*Enter* Soothsayer.

*Portia.* Come hither, fellow ;
Which way hast thou been ?

*Soothsayer.* At mine own house, good lady.

*Portia.* What is 't o'clock ?

*Soothsayer.* About the ninth hour, lady.

*Portia.* Is Cæsar yet gone to the Capitol ?

*Soothsayer.* Madam, not yet : I go to take my stand
To see him pass on to the Capitol.

*Portia.* Thou hast some suit to Cæsar, hast thou not ?

*Soothsayer.* That I have, lady : If it will please Cæsar
To be so good to Cæsar, as to hear me,
I shall beseech him to befriend himself.

*Portia.* Why, know'st thou any harm's intended towards him ?

*Soothsayer.* None that I know will be, much that I fear may chance.
Good morrow to you.

* * * * *

*Portia.* I must go in.—Ah me ! how weak a thing
The heart of woman is ! O Brutus !
The heavens speed thee in thine enterprise !
Sure, the boy heard me :—Brutus hath a suit,
That Cæsar will not grant.—O, I grow faint.—

Run, Lucius, and commend me to my lord ;
Say, I am merry : come to me again,
And bring me word what he doth say to thee.

ACT V. SCENE V.

*Antony.* This was the noblest Roman of them all.
All the conspirators, save only he,
Did that they did in envy of great Cæsar ;
He only, in a general honest thought
And common good to all, made one of them.
His life was gentle ; and the elements
So mix'd in him, that Nature might stand up
And say to all the world, This was a man!
*Octavius.* According to his virtue let us use him
With all respect, and rites of burial ;
Within my tent his bones to-night shall lie
Most like a soldier, order'd honourably.—
So, call the field to rest, and let 's away,
To part the glories of this happy day.

# TROILUS AND CRESSIDA.

TROILUS, *Son of Priam.* CRESSIDA, *Daughter to Calchas.*

## ACT I. SCENE I.

*Troilus.*

O PANDARUS! I tell thee, Pandarus,—
When I do tell thee, There my hopes lie
drown'd,
Reply not in how many fathoms deep
They lie indrench'd. I tell thee, I am mad
In Cressid's love; Thou answer'st, She is fair;
Pour'st in the open ulcer of my heart
Her eyes, her hair, her cheek, her gait, her voice;
Handlest in thy discourse, O, that her hand,
In whose comparison all whites are ink,
Writing their own reproach; to whose soft seizure
The cygnet's down is harsh, and spirit of sense
Hard as the palm of ploughman! This thou tell'st me,
As true thou tell'st me, when I say—I love her;
But, saying thus, instead of oil and balm
Thou lay'st in every gash that love hath given me
The knife that made it.

* * * * *

*Troilus.* Peace, you ungracious clamours! peace, rude
sounds!

Fools on both sides! Helen must needs be fair,
When with your blood you daily paint her thus.
I cannot fight upon this argument;
It is too starv'd a subject for my sword.
But, Pandarus—O gods, how you do plague me!
I cannot come to Cressid, but by Pandar,
And he 's as tetchy to be woo'd to woo,
As she is stubborn-chaste against all suit.
Tell me, Apollo, for thy Daphne's love,
What Cressid is, what Pandar, and what we?
Her bed is India; there she lies, a pearl:
Between our Ilium, and where she resides,
Let it be call'd the wild and wandering flood;
Ourself, the merchant; and this sailing Pandar
Our doubtful hope, our convoy, and our bark.

## Scene II.

*Cressida.* Words, vows, griefs, tears, and love's full sacrifice
He offers in another's enterprise;
But more in Troilus thousand fold I see
Than in the glass of Pandar's praise may be;
Yet hold I off. Women are angels, wooing;
Things won are done, joy's soul lies in the doing;
That she belov'd knows nought, that knows not this,—
Men prize the thing ungain'd more than it is:
That she was never yet, that ever knew
Love got so sweet, as when desire did sue:
Therefore this maxim out of love I teach,—
Achievement is command: ungain'd, beseech;
Then though my heart's content firm love doth bear,
Nothing of that shall from mine eyes appear.

## Act II. Scene II.

*Troilus.* Why, there you touch'd the life of our design:
Were it not glory that we more affected
Than the performance of our heaving spleens,
I would not wish a drop of Trojan blood
Spent more in her defence. But, worthy Hector,
She is a theme of honour and renown,
A spur to valiant and magnanimous deeds,
Whose present courage may beat down our foes,
And fame, in time to come, canonize us;
For, I presume, brave Hector would not lose
So rich advantage of a promis'd glory,
As smiles upon the forehead of this action,
For the wide world's revenue.

## Act III. Scene I.

*Paris.* They are come from field; let us to Priam's hall,
To greet the warriors. Sweet Helen, I must woo you
To help unarm our Hector: his stubborn buckles,
With these your white enchanting fingers touch'd,
Shall more obey, than to the edge of steel
Or force of Greekish sinews; you shall do more
Than all the island kings, disarm great Hector.
*Helen.* 'Twill make us proud to be his servant, Paris.
Yea, what he shall receive of us in duty,
Give us more palm in beauty than we have;
Yea, overshines ourself.
*Paris.* Sweet, above thought I love thee.

### Scene II.

*Troilus.* I am giddy ; expectation whirls me round.
The imaginary relish is so sweet
That it enchants my sense ; what will it be,
When that the watery palate tastes indeed
Love's thrice-reputed nectar? death, I fear me ;
Swooning destruction ; or some joy too fine,
Too subtle-potent, tun'd too sharp in sweetness
For the capacity of my ruder powers :
I fear it much ; and I do fear besides
That I shall lose distinction in my joys ;
As doth a battle, when they charge on heaps
The enemy flying.

* * * * *

*Troilus.* Even such a passion doth embrace my bosom ;
My heart beats thicker than a feverous pulse ;
And all my powers do their bestowing lose,
Like vassalage at unawares encountering
The eye of majesty.

* * * * *

*Cressida.* Boldness comes to me now, and brings me heart :—
Prince Troilus, I have lov'd you night and day
For many weary months.

*Troilus.* Why was my Cressid then so hard to win?

*Cressida.* Hard to seem won; but I was won, my lord,
With the first glance that ever—Pardon me :—
If I confess much, you will play the tyrant.
I love you now ; but not, till now, so much
But I might master it :—in faith, I lie ;
My thoughts were like unbridled children, grown

Too headstrong for their mother: See, we fools!
Why have I blabb'd? who shall be true to us,
When we are so unsecret to ourselves?
But, though I lov'd you well, I woo'd you not;
And yet, good faith, I wish'd myself a man;
Or that we women had men's privilege
Of speaking first. Sweet, bid me hold my tongue;
For, in this rapture, I shall surely speak
The thing I shall repent. See, see, your silence,
Cunning in dumbness, from my weakness draws
My very soul of counsel: Stop, my mouth.

*Troilus.* And shall, albeit sweet musick issues thence.

*Pandarus.* Pretty, i' faith.

*Cressida.* My lord, I do beseech you pardon me;
'Twas not my purpose, thus to beg a kiss.
I am asham'd;—O heavens! what have I done?—
For this time will I take my leave, my lord.

* * * * *

*Cressida.* Perchance, my lord, I show more craft than love;
And fell so roundly to a large confession
To angle for your thoughts: But you are wise;
Or else you love not; For to be wise, and love,
Exceeds man's might; that dwells with gods above.

*Troilus.* O, that I thought it could be in a woman,
(As, if it can, I will presume in you,)
To feed for aye her lamp and flames of love;
To keep her constancy in plight and youth,
Outliving beauty's outward, with a mind
That doth renew swifter than blood decays!
Or, that persuasion could but thus convince me,—
That my integrity and truth to you
Might be affronted with the match and weight

Of such a winnow'd purity in love;
How were I then uplifted! but, alas,
I am as true as truth's simplicity,
And simpler than the infancy of truth.

*Cressida.* In that I'll war with you.

*Troilus.* O virtuous fight,
When right with right wars who shall be most right!
True swains in love shall, in the world to come,
Approve their truths by Troilus: when their rhymes,
Full of protest, of oath, and big compare,
Want similes, truth tir'd with iteration,—
As true as steel, as plantage to the moon,
As sun to day, as turtle to her mate,
As iron to adamant, as earth to the centre,—
Yet, after all comparisons of truth,
As truth's authentick author to be cited,
As true as Troilus shall crown up the verse,
And sanctify the numbers.

*Cressida.* Prophet may you be!
If I be false, or swerve a hair from truth,
When time is old and hath forgot itself,
When water-drops have worn the stones of Troy,
And blind oblivion swallow'd cities up,
And mighty states characterless are grated
To dusty nothing; yet let memory,
From false to false, among false maids in love,
Upbraid my falsehood! when they have said—as false
As air, as water, wind, or sandy earth,
As fox to lamb, as wolf to heifer's calf,
Pard to the hind, or stepdame to her son;
Yea, let them say, to stick the heart of falsehood,
As false as Cressid.

## Act IV. Scene II.

*Troilus.* Dear, trouble not yourself; the morn is cold.
*Cressida.* Then, sweet my lord, I'll call mine uncle down;
He shall unbolt the gates.
*Troilus.* Trouble him not;
To bed, to bed: Sleep kill those pretty eyes,
And give as soft attachment to thy senses,
As infant's empty of all thought!
*Cressida.* Good morrow then.
*Troilus.* 'Pr'ythee now, to bed.
*Cressida.* Are you aweary of me?
*Troilus.* O Cressida! but that the busy day,
Wak'd by the lark, hath rous'd the ribald crows,
And dreaming night will hide our joys no longer,
I would not from thee.
*Cressida.* Night hath been too brief.
*Troilus.* Beshrew the witch! with venomous wights she stays,
As tediously as hell; but flies the grasps of love,
With wings more momentary-swift than thought.
You will catch cold, and curse me.
*Cressida.* Pr'ythee, tarry;—
You men will never tarry.—
O foolish Cressid!—I might have still held off,
And then you would have tarried. Hark, there's one up.
*Pandarus.* [*Within.*] What, are all the doors open here?
*Troilus.* It is your uncle.

* * * * *

*Cressida.* I will not, uncle: I have forgot my father;

I know no touch of consanguinity;
No kin, no love, no blood, no soul so near me
As the sweet Troilus.—O you gods divine!
Make Cressid's name the very crown of falsehood
If ever she leave Troilus!—Time, force, and death,
Do to this body what extremes you can;
But the strong base and building of my love
Is as the very centre of the earth,
Drawing all things to it.—I'll go in, and weep.

## Scene IV.

*Cressida.* Why tell you me of moderation?
The grief is fine, full, perfect, that I taste,
And violenteth in a sense as strong
As that which causeth it: How can I moderate it?
If I could temporize with my affection
Or brew it to a weak and colder palate,
The like allayment could I give my grief:
My love admits no qualifying dross:
No more my grief, in such a precious loss.

* * * * *

*Troilus.* Cressid, I love thee in so strain'd a purity,
That the blest gods—as angry with my fancy,
More bright in zeal than the devotion which
Cold lips blow to their deities,—take thee from me.
*Cressida.* Have the gods envy?
*Pandarus.* Ay, ay, ay, ay; 'tis too plain a case.
*Cressida.* And is it true, that I must go from Troy?
*Troilus.* A hateful truth.
*Cressida.* What, and from Troilus too?
*Troilus.* From Troy, and Troilus.
*Cressida.* Is it possible?

*Troilus.* And suddenly; where injury of chance
Puts back leave-taking, jostles roughly by
All time of pause, rudely beguiles our lips
Of all rejoindure, forcibly prevents
Our lock'd embrasures, strangles our dear vows
Even in the birth of our own labouring breath;
We two, that with so many thousand sighs
Did buy each other, must poorly sell ourselves
With the rude brevity and discharge of one.
Injurious time now, with a robber's haste,
Crams his rich thievery up, he knows not how:
As many farewells as be stars in heaven,
With distinct breath and consign'd kisses to them,
He fumbles up into a loose adieu;
And scants us with a single famish'd kiss
Distasted with the salt of broken tears.

*Æneas.* My lord! is the lady ready?

*Troilus.* Hark! you are call'd: some say, the Genius so
Cries, Come! to him that instantly must die.—
Bid them have patience; she shall come anon.

*Cressida.* I must then to the Greeks?

*Troilus.* No remedy.

*Cressida.* A woeful Cressid 'mongst the merry Greeks!
When shall we see again?

*Troilus.* Hear me, my love: Be thou but true of heart.—

*Cressida.* I true! how now? what wicked deem is this?

*Troilus.* Nay, we must use expostulation kindly
For it is parting from us:
I speak not, be thou true, as fearing thee;
For I will throw my glove to death himself,
That there's no maculation in thy heart;
But, be thou true, say I, to fashion in

My sequent protestation; be thou true,
And I will see thee.

*Cressida.* O, you shall be expos'd, my lord, to dangers
As infinite as imminent! but, I'll be true.

*Troilus.* And I'll grow friend with danger. Wear this sleeve.

*Cressida.* And you this glove. When shall I see you?

*Troilus.* I will corrupt the Grecian sentinels,
To give thee nightly visitation.
But yet, be true.

*Cressida.* O heavens!—be true, again?

*Troilus.* Hear why I speak it, love;
The Grecian youths are full of quality;
They're loving, well compos'd, with gifts of nature flowing,
And swelling o'er with arts and exercise;
How novelty may move, and parts with person,
Alas! a kind of godly jealousy
(Which, I beseech you, call a virtuous sin)
Makes me afeard.

*Cressida.* O heavens! you love me not.

*Troilus.* Die I a villain then!
In this I do not call your faith in question,
So mainly as my merit: I cannot sing,
Nor heel the high lavolt, nor sweeten talk,
Nor play at subtle games; fair virtues all,
To which the Grecians are most prompt and pregnant:
But I can tell, that in each grace of these
There lurks a still and dumb-discoursive devil,
That tempts most cunningly: but be not tempted.

*Cressida.* Do you think, I will?

*Troilus.* No.
But something may be done, that we will not:
And sometimes we are devils to ourselves,

When we will tempt the frailty of our powers,
Presuming on their changeful potency.

*Æneas.* [*Within.*] Nay, good my lord,—

*Troilus.* Come, kiss; and let us part.

*Paris.* [*Within.*] Brother Troilus!

*Troilus.* Good brother, come you hither,
And bring Æneas, and the Grecian, with you.

*Cressida.* My lord, will you be true?

*Troilus.* Who I? Alas, it is my vice, my fault:
While others fish with craft for great opinion,
I with great truth catch mere simplicity;
Whilst some with cunning gild their copper crowns,
With truth and plainness I do wear mine bare.
Fear not my truth; the moral of my wit
Is—plain, and true,—there 's all the reach of it.—
Welcome, Sir Diomed! here is the lady,
Which for Antenor we deliver you:
At the port, lord, I'll give her to thy hand;
And, by the way, possess thee what she is.
Entreat her fair; and, by my soul, fair Greek,
If e'er thou stand at mercy of my sword,
Name Cressid, and thy life shall be as safe
As Priam is in Ilion.

*Diomed.* Fair lady Cressid,
So please you, save the thanks this prince expects:
The lustre in your eye, heaven in your cheek,
Pleads your fair usage; and to Diomed
You shall be mistress, and command him wholly.

*Troilus.* Grecian, thou dost not use me courteously,
To shame the zeal of my petition to thee,
In praising her: I tell thee, lord of Greece,
She is as far high-soaring o'er thy praises
As thou unworthy to be call'd her servant.

I charge thee, use her well, even for my charge;
For, by the dreadful Pluto, if thou dost not,
Though the great bulk Achilles be thy guard,
I'll cut thy throat.

* * * * *

*Troilus.* Come, to the port.—I'll tell thee, Diomed,
This brave shall oft make thee to hide thy head.—
Lady, give me your hand; and, as we walk,
To our own selves bend we our needful talk.

### Scene V.

*Agamemnon.* What Trojan is that same that looks so heavy?

*Ulysses.* The youngest son of Priam, a true knight;
Not yet mature, yet matchless; firm of word;
Speaking in deeds, and deedless in his tongue;
Not soon provok'd, nor, being provok'd, soon calm'd;
His heart and hand both open, and both free;
For what he has, he gives, what thinks, he shows;
Yet gives he not till judgment guide his bounty,
Nor dignifies an impair thought with breath:
Manly as Hector, but more dangerous;
For Hector, in his blaze of wrath, subscribes
To tender objects; but he, in heat of action,
Is more vindicative than jealous love;
They call him Troilus; and on him erect
A second hope, as fairly built as Hector.
Thus says Æneas; one that knows the youth
Even to his inches, and, with private soul,
Did in great Ilion thus translate him to me.

* * * * *

*Troilus.* My lord Ulysses, tell me, I beseech you,

In what place of the field doth Calchas keep?
*Ulysses.* At Menelaus' tent, most princely Troilus:
There Diomed doth feast with him to-night;
Who neither looks upon the heaven, nor earth,
But gives all gaze and bent of amorous view
On the fair Cressid.
*Troilus.* Shall I, sweet lord, be bound to you so much,
After we part from Agamemnon's tent,
To bring me thither?
*Ulysses.* You shall command me, sir.
As gentle tell me, of what honour was
This Cressida in Troy? Had she no lover there
That wails her absence?
*Troilus.* O, sir, to such as boasting show their scars,
A mock is due—Will you walk on, my lord?
She was belov'd, she lov'd; she is, and doth:
But, still, sweet love is food for fortune's tooth.

## ACT V. SCENE II.

*Ulysses.* May worthy Troilus be half attach'd
With that which here his passion doth express?
*Troilus.* Ay, Greek: and that shall be divulged well
In characters as red as Mars his heart
Inflam'd with Venus: never did young man fancy
With so eternal and so fix'd a soul.
Hark, Greek;—As much as I do Cressid love,
So much by weight hate I her Diomed:
That sleeve is mine, that he 'll bear on his helm;
Were it a casque compos'd by Vulcan's skill,
My sword should bite it; not the dreadful spout
Which shipmen do the hurricano call

Constring'd in mass by the almighty sun,
Shall dizzy with more clamour Neptune's ear
In his descent, than shall my prompted sword
Falling on Diomed.
O Cressid! O false Cressid! false, false, false!
Let all untruths stand by thy stained name,
And they'll seem glorious.

SCENE III.

*Andromache.* When was my lord so much ungently temper'd
To stop his ears against admonishment?
Unarm, unarm, and do not fight to-day.
*Hector.* You train me to offend you; get you in:
By all the everlasting gods, I'll go.
*Andromache.* My dreams will, sure, prove ominous to the day.
*Hector.* No more, I say.
*Cassandra.* Where is my brother Hector?
*Andromache.* Here, sister; arm'd, and bloody in intent;
Consort with me in loud and dear petition,
Pursue we him on knees; for I have dream'd
Of bloody turbulence, and this whole night
Hath nothing been but shapes and forms of slaughter.
*Cassandra.* O, it is true.
*Hector.* Ho! bid my trumpet sound!
*Cassandra.* No notes of sally, for the heavens, sweet brother.
*Hector.* Begone, I say: the gods have heard me swear.
*Cassandra.* The gods are deaf to hot and peevish vows;
They are polluted offerings, more abhorr'd
Than spotted livers in the sacrifice.

*Andromache.* O! be persuaded: Do not count it holy
To hurt by being just: it is as lawful,
For we would give much, to use violent thefts,
And rob in the behalf of charity.

*Cassandra.* It is the purpose that makes strong the vow;
But vows to every purpose must not hold:
Unarm, sweet Hector.

*Hector.* Hold you still, I say;
Mine honour keeps the weather of my fate;
Life every man holds dear; but the dear man
Holds honour far more precious-dear than life.—

*Enter* TROILUS.

How now, young man? mean'st thou to fight to-day?

*Andromache.* Cassandra, call my father to persuade.

*Hector.* No, 'faith, young Troilus; doff thy harness, youth,
I am to-day i' the vein of chivalry:
Let grow thy sinews till their knots be strong,
And tempt not yet the brushes of the war.
Unarm thee, go; and doubt thou not, brave boy,
I'll stand to-day, for thee, and me, and Troy.

*Troilus.* Brother, you have a vice of mercy in you
Which better fits a lion, than a man.

*Hector.* What vice is that, good Troilus? chide me for it.

*Troilus.* When many times the captive Grecians fall
Even in the fan and wind of your fair sword,
You bid them rise and live.

*Hector.* O! 'tis fair play.

*Troilus.* Foul play, by heaven, Hector.

*Hector.* How now? How now?

*Troilus.* For the love of all the gods,
Let 's leave the hermit Pity with our mother;
And when we have our armours buckled on,
The venom'd vengeance ride upon our swords;
Spur them to ruthful work, rein them from ruth.
*Hector.* Fye, savage, fye!
*Troilus.* Hector, then 'tis wars.
*Hector.* Troilus, I would not have you fight to-day.
*Troilus.* Who should withhold me?
Not fate, obedience, nor the hand of Mars
Beckoning with fiery truncheon my retire;
Not Priamus and Hecuba on knees,
Their eyes o'ergalled with recourse of tears;
Nor you, my brother, with your true sword drawn,
Oppos'd to hinder me, should stop my way,
But by my ruin.

# ANTONY AND CLEOPATRA.[2]

MARCUS ANTONIUS, *Triumvir.*
CLEOPATRA, *Queen of Egypt.*
DOMITIUS ENOBARBUS, *Friend of Antony.*
AGRIPPA, *Friend of Cæsar.*
OCTAVIA, *Sister to Cæsar and wife to Antony.*
CHARMIAN *and* IRAS, *Attendants on Cleopatra.*

## ACT I. SCENE II.

*2nd Messenger.*

FULVIA thy wife is dead.
*Antony.* Where died she?
*2nd Messenger.* In Sicyon:
Her length of sickness, with what else more serious
Importeth thee to know, this bears. [*Gives a letter.*
*Antony.* Forbear me.—
There 's a great spirit gone! Thus did I desire it:
What our contempts do often hurl from us,
We wish it ours again; the present pleasure,
By revolution lowering, does become
The opposite of itself: she 's good, being gone;
The hand could pluck her back, that shov'd her on.
I must from this enchanting queen break off;
Ten thousand harms, more than the ills I know,
My idleness doth hatch.—How now! Enobarbus!

### Act II. Scene II.

*Enobarbus.* When she first met Mark Antony, she pursed up his heart upon the river Cydnus.

*Agrippa.* There she appeared indeed; or my reporter devised well for her.

*Enobarbus.* I will tell you:
The barge she sat in, like a burnish'd throne,
Burn'd on the water: the poop was beaten gold;
Purple the sails, and so perfumed, that
The winds were love-sick with them: the oars were silver;
Which to the tune of flutes kept stroke, and made
The water, which they beat, to follow faster,
As amorous of their strokes. For her own person,
It beggar'd all description: she did lie
In her pavilion (cloth of gold, of tissue),
O'er-picturing that Venus, where we see
The fancy out-work nature: on each side her
Stood pretty dimpled boys, like smiling Cupids,
With divers coloured fans, whose wind did seem
To glow the delicate cheeks which they did cool,
And what they undid, did.
Her gentlewomen, like the Nereides,
So many mermaids, tended her i' the eyes
And made their bends adoring: at the helm
A seeming mermaid steers: the silken tackle
Swell with the touches of those flower-soft hands
That yarely frame the office. From the barge
A strange invisible perfume hits the sense
Of the adjacent wharfs. The city cast
Her people out upon her; and Antony,

Enthron'd in the market-place, did sit alone,
Whistling to the air; which, but for vacancy,
Had gone to gaze on Cleopatra too,
And made a gap in nature.

*Agrippa.* Rare Egyptian!

*Enobarbus.* Upon her landing, Antony sent to her,
Invited her to supper; she replied,
It should be better, he became her guest;
Which she entreated: Our courteous Antony,
Whom ne'er the word of No woman heard speak,
Being barber'd ten times o'er, goes to the feast;
And, for his ordinary, pays his heart
For what his eyes eat only.

## Act III. Scene II.

*Antony.* No further, sir.

*Cæsar.* You take from me a great part of myself.
Use me well in it.—Sister, prove such a wife
As my thoughts make thee, and as my furthest band
Shall pass on thy approof.—Most noble Antony,
Let not the piece of virtue, which is set
Betwixt us, as the cement of our love
To keep it builded, be the ram, to batter
The fortress of it; for better might we
Have loved without this mean, if on both parts
This be not cherish'd.

*Antony.* Make me not offended
In your distrust.

*Cæsar.* I have said.

*Antony.* You shall not find,
Though you be therein curious, the least cause
For what you seem to fear: so, the gods keep you,

And make the hearts of Romans serve your ends!
We will here part.

*Cæsar.* Farewell, my dearest sister, fare thee well.
The elements be kind to thee, and make
Thy spirits all of comfort! fare thee well.

*Octavia.* My noble brother!

*Antony.* The April 's in her eyes: it is love's spring,
And these the showers to bring it on. Be cheerful.

*Octavia.* Look well to my husband's house; and, sir—

*Cæsar.* What,
Octavia?

*Octavia.* I'll tell you in your ear.

*Antony.* Her tongue will not obey her heart,[3] nor can
Her heart inform her tongue; the swan's down feather
That stands upon the swell at full of tide,
And neither way inclines.

## Act III. Scene III.

*Cleopatra.* Did'st thou behold Octavia?

*Messenger.* Ay, dread queen.

*Cleopatra.* Where?

*Messenger.* Madam, in Rome.
I look'd her in the face, and saw her led
Between her brother and Mark Antony.

*Cleopatra.* Is she as tall as me?[4]

*Messenger.* She is not, madam.

*Cleopatra.* Didst hear her speak? Is she shrill-tongu'd or low?

*Messenger.* Madam, I heard her speak; she is low-voic'd.

*Cleopatra.* That's not so good.—He cannot like her long.

*Charmian.* Like her? O, Isis! 'tis impossible.

*Cleopatra.* I think so, Charmian; dull of tongue and dwarfish!
What majesty is in her gait? Remember,
If e'er thou look'dst on majesty.

*Messenger.* She creeps;
Her motion and her station are as one;
She shows a body, rather than a life;
A statue, than a breather.

*Cleopatra.* Is this certain?

*Messenger.* Or I have no observance.

*Charmian.* Three in Egypt
Cannot make better note.

*Cleopatra.* He 's very knowing,
I do perceive 't. There 's nothing in her yet.
The fellow has sound judgment.

*Charmian.* Excellent.

*Cleopatra.* Guess at her years, I pr'ythee.

*Messenger.* Madam,
She was a widow.

*Cleopatra.* Widow? Charmian, hark.

*Messenger.* And I do think she 's thirty.

*Cleopatra.* Bear'st thou her face in mind? is 't long or round?

*Messenger.* Round, even to faultiness.

*Cleopatra.* For the most part, too,
They are foolish that are so. Her hair, what colour?

*Messenger.* Brown, madam; and her forehead is as low
As she would wish it.

*Cleopatra.* There is gold for thee;
Thou must not take my former sharpness ill.
I will employ thee back again: I find thee
More fit for business. Go, make thee ready;
Our letters are prepar'd.

*Charmian.* A proper man.

*Cleopatra.* Indeed, he is so: I repent me much
That I so harry'd him. Why, methinks, by him
The creature 's no such thing.

*Charmian.* O, nothing, madam.

*Cleopatra.* The man hath seen some majesty, and should know.

*Charmian.* Hath he seen majesty? Isis else defend.
And serving you so long!

*Cleopatra.* I have one thing more to ask him yet, good Charmian,
But 'tis no matter; thou shalt bring him to me
Where I will write. All may be well enough.

*Charmian.* I warrant you, madam.

## Act IV. Scene XIII.

*Antony.* The miserable change now at my end
Lament nor sorrow at: but please your thoughts
In feeding them with those my former fortunes
Wherein I liv'd, the greatest prince o' the world,
The noblest: and do now not basely die,
Nor cowardly; put off my helmet to
My countryman, a Roman, by a Roman
Valiantly vanquish'd. Now, my spirit is going;
I can no more. [*Dies.*

*Cleopatra.* Noblest of men, woo't die?
Hast thou no care of me? Shall I abide
In this dull world, which in thy absence is
No better than a sty? O see, my women,
The crown o' the earth doth melt. My lord!
O, wither'd is the garland of the war,
The soldier's pole is fallen; young boys and girls

Are level now with men: the odds is gone,
And there is nothing left remarkable
Beneath the visiting moon. [*She faints.*

*Charmian.* O, quietness, lady!

*Iras.* She is dead too, our sovereign.

*Charmian.* Lady!

*Iras.* Madam!

*Charmian.* O, madam, madam, madam!

*Iras.* Royal Egypt!
Empress!

*Charmian.* Peace, peace, Iras.

*Cleopatra.* No more, but e'en a woman; and commanded
By such poor passion as the maid that milks,
And does the meanest chares. It were for me
To throw my sceptre at the injurious gods,
To tell them that this world did equal theirs,
Till they had stolen our jewel. All 's but naught;
Patience is sottish; and impatience does
Become a dog that 's mad. Then is it sin
To rush into the secret house of death
Ere death dare come to us? How do you, women?
What, what? Good cheer! Why, how now, Charmian?
My noble girls! Ah, women, women! look,
Our lamp is spent, it 's out:—Good sirs, take heart:—
[*To the guard below.*
We 'll bury him: and then, what 's brave, what 's noble,
Let 's do it after the high Roman fashion,
And make death proud to take us. Come away:
This case of that huge spirit now is cold.
Ah, women, women! come; we have no friend
But resolution, and the briefest end.
[*Exeunt, those above bearing off Antony's body.*

ACT V. SCENE II.

*Cleopatra.* My desolation does begin to make
A better life: 'Tis paltry to be Cæsar;
Not being fortune, he 's but fortune's knave,
A minister of her will; And it is great[5]
To do that thing that ends all other deeds;
Which shackles accidents, and bolts up change;
Which sleeps, and never palates more the dung;
The beggar's nurse and Cæsar's.

* * * * *

*Cleopatra.* Why, that 's the way
To fool their preparation, and to conquer
Their most absurd intents.—Now, Charmian?—
Show me, my women, like a queen;—Go fetch
My best attires; I am again for Cydnus,
To meet Mark Antony: Sirrah, Iras, go.—
Now, noble Charmian, we'll despatch indeed:
And, when thou hast done this chare, I'll give thee leave
To play till doomsday.—Bring our crown and all:
Wherefore 's this noise?

* * * * *

*Re-enter* IRAS, *with robe, crown, &c.*

*Cleopatra.* Give me my robe, put on my crown; I have
Immortal longings in me: Now no more
The juice of Egypt's grape shall moist this lip:—
Yare, yare, good Iras; quick.—Methinks, I hear
Antony call; I see him rouse himself
To praise my noble act; I hear him mock
The luck of Cæsar, which the gods give men
To excuse their after wrath: Husband, I come:

Now to that name my courage prove my title!
I am fire, and air; my other elements
I give to baser life.—So,—have you done?
Come then, and take the last warmth of my lips.
Farewell, kind Charmian; Iras, long farewell.
[*Kisses them. Iras falls and dies.*
Have I the aspick in my lips? Dost fall?
If thou and nature can so gently part,
The stroke of death is as a lover's pinch,
Which hurts, and is desir'd. Dost thou lie still?
If thus thou vanishest, thou tell'st the world
It is not worth leave-taking.

*Charmian.* Dissolve, thick cloud, and rain; that I may say
The gods themselves do weep!

*Cleopatra.* This proves me base;
If she first meet the curled Antony,
He'll make demand of her; and spend that kiss,
Which is my heaven to have. Come, mortal wretch,
[*To the Asp, which she applies to her breast.*
With thy sharp teeth this knot intrinsicate
Of life at once untie: poor venomous fool,
Be angry, and despatch.—O, could'st thou speak!
That I might hear thee call great Cæsar, ass
Unpolicied!

*Charmian.* O Eastern Star!

*Cleopatra.* Peace, peace!
Dost thou not see my baby at my breast,
That sucks the nurse asleep?

*Charmian.* O break! O break!

*Cleopatra.* As sweet as balm, as soft as air, as gentle,—
O Antony!—Nay, I will take thee too;—
[*Applying another Asp to her arm.*

What should I stay— [*Falls on a bed and dies.*

*Charmian.* In this wild world?—So, fare thee well.—
Now boast thee, death! in thy possession lies
A lass unparallel'd.—Downy windows, close:
And golden Phœbus never be beheld
Of eyes again so royal! Your crown's awry;
I'll mend it, and then play.

*Enter the* Guard, *rushing in.*

*1st. Guard.* Where is the queen?

*Charmian.* Speak softly, wake her not.

*1st. Guard.* Cæsar hath sent.

*Charmian.* Too slow a messenger.
[*Applies the Asp.*
O come; apace, despatch; I partly feel thee.

*1st. Guard.* Approach, ho! All's not well; Cæsar's beguiled.

*2nd. Guard.* There's Dolabella sent from Cæsar;—call him.

*1st. Guard.* What work is here?—Charmian, is this well done?

*Charmian.* It is well done, and fitting for a princess
Descended of so many royal kings.
Ah, soldier! [*Dies.*

*Enter* DOLABELLA.

*Dolabella.* How goes it here?

*2nd. Guard.* All dead.

*Dolabella.* Cæsar, thy thoughts
Touch their effects in this: Thyself art coming
To see perform'd the dreaded act, which thou
So sought'st to hinder.

*Within.* A way there, way for Cæsar!

*Enter* Cæsar, *and attendants.*

*Dolabella.* O sir, you are too sure an augurer;
That you did fear, is done.
*Cæsar.* Bravest at the last;
She levell'd at our purposes, and, being royal,
Took her own way.—The manner of their deaths?
I do not see them bleed.
*Dolabella.* Who was last with them?
*1st. Guard.* A simple countryman, that brought her figs;
This was his basket.
*Cæsar.* Poison'd then.
*1st. Guard.* O Cæsar,
This Charmian lived but now; she stood, and spake;
I found her trimming up the diadem
On her dead mistress; tremblingly she stood,
And on the sudden dropp'd.
*Cæsar.* O noble weakness!—
If they had swallow'd poison, 'twould appear
By external swelling, but she looks like sleep,
As she would catch another Antony
In her strong toil of grace.
*Dolabella.* Here, on her breast,
There is a vent of blood, and something blown:
The like is on her arm.
*1st. Guard.* This is an aspick's trail: and these fig leaves
Have slime upon them, such as the aspick leaves
Upon the caves of Nile.
*Cæsar.* Most probable
That so she died; for her physician tells me,
She hath pursu'd conclusions infinite

Of easy ways to die.—Take up her bed;
And bear her women from the monument:—
She shall be buried by her Antony:
No grave upon the earth shall clip in it
A pair so famous. High events as these
Strike those that make them: and their story is
No less in pity, than his glory, which
Brought them to be lamented. Our army shall,
In solemn show, attend this funeral;
And then to Rome.—Come, Dolabella, see
High order in this great solemnity.

# HAMLET.

CLAUDIUS, *King of Denmark.*
HAMLET, *Son to the former, and nephew to the present King.*
LAERTES, *Son to Polonius, Lord Chamberlain.*
GERTRUDE, *Queen of Denmark, and mother to Hamlet.*
OPHELIA, *Daughter to Polonius.*

## ACT III. SCENE I.

*Ophelia.*

O WHAT a noble mind is here o'erthrown!
The courtier's, scholar's, soldier's eye, tongue, sword:
The expectancy and rose of the fair state,
The glass of fashion, and the mould of form,
The observ'd of all observers! quite, quite down!
And I, of ladies most deject and wretched,
That suck'd the honey of his musick vows,
Now see that noble and most sovereign reason,
Like sweet bells jangled, out of tune and harsh;
That unmatch'd form and feature of blown youth,
Blasted with ecstasy: O, woe is me!
To have seen what I have seen, see what I see!

## ACT IV. SCENE V.

*Laertes.* How now! what noise is that?

O heat, dry up my brains! tears seven times salt,
Burn out the sense and virtue of mine eye!—
By heaven, thy madness shall be paid with weight,
Till our scale turn the beam. O rose of May!
Dear maid, kind sister, sweet Ophelia!—
O heavens! is 't possible, a young maid's wits
Should be as mortal as an old man's life?
Nature is fine in love; and, where 'tis fine,
It sends some precious instance of itself
After the thing it loves.

* * * * *

Hadst thou thy wits, and didst persuade revenge,
It could not move thus.

*Ophelia.* You must sing, Down-a-down, an you call him a-down-a. O, how the wheel becomes it! it is the false steward, that stole his master's daughter.

*Laertes.* This nothing 's more than matter.

*Ophelia.* There 's rosemary, that 's for remembrance; 'pray you, love, remember: and there is pansies, that 's for thoughts.

*Laertes.* A document in madness; thoughts and remembrance fitted.

*Ophelia.* There 's fennel for you, and columbines:—there 's rue for you; and here 's some for me:—we may call it, herb of grace o' Sundays:—O! you must wear your rue with a difference.—There 's a daisy:—I would give you some violets; but they withered all, when my father died:—They say, he made a good end.—

## Act IV. Scene VII.

*Queen.* There is a willow grows ascaunt the brook,
That shows his hoar leaves in the glassy stream:

Therewith fantastick garlands did she make
Of crow-flowers, nettles, daisies, and long purples,
That liberal shepherds give a grosser name,
But our cold maids do dead men's fingers call them:
There on the pendent boughs her coronet weeds
Clambering to hang, an envious sliver broke;
When down her weedy trophies, and herself,
Fell in the weeping brook. Her clothes spread wide;
And, mermaid-like, awhile they bore her up:
Which time, she chanted snatches of old tunes;
As one incapable of her own distress,
Or like a creature native and indu'd
Unto that element: but long it could not be,
Till that her garments, heavy with their drink,
Pull'd the poor wretch from her melodious lay
To muddy death.

*Laertes.* Too much of water hast thou, poor Ophelia,
And therefore I forbid my tears: But yet
It is our trick; nature her custom holds,
Let shame say what it will: when these are gone,
The woman will be out.—Adieu, my lord!
I have a speech of fire, that fain would blaze,
But that this folly drowns it.

*King.* Let 's follow, Gertrude:
How much I had to do to calm his rage!
Now fear I, this will give it start again;
Therefore, let 's follow. [*Exeunt.*

## ACT V. SCENE I.

1*st. Priest.* Her obsequies have been as far enlarg'd
As we have warranty: Her death was doubtful;

And, but that great command o'ersways the order,
She should in ground unsanctified have lodg'd
Till the last trumpet; for charitable prayers,
Shards, flints, and pebbles, should be thrown on her,
Yet here she is allow'd her virgin crants,
Her maiden strewments, and the bringing home
Of bell and burial.

*Laertes.* Must there no more be done?

1*st. Priest.* No more be done!
We should profane the service of the dead
To sing a requiem, and such rest to her
As to peace-parted souls.

*Laertes.* Lay her i' the earth;—
And from her fair and unpolluted flesh
May violets spring!—I tell thee, churlish priest,
A ministering angel shall my sister be,
When thou liest howling.

*Hamlet.* What! the fair Ophelia?

*Queen.* Sweets to the sweet: Farewell![6]
[*Scattering flowers.*
I hop'd, thou shouldst have been my Hamlet's wife;
I thought, thy bride-bed to have deck'd, sweet maid,
And not t' have strew'd thy grave.

*Laertes.* O, treble woe
Fall ten times treble on that cursed head
Whose wicked deed thy most ingenious sense
Depriv'd thee of!—Hold off the earth awhile,
Till I have caught her once more in mine arms.
[*Leaps into the grave.*
Now pile your dust upon the quick and dead;
Till of this flat a mountain you have made,
To o'ertop old Pelion, or the skyish head
Of blue Olympus.

*Hamlet* [*advancing*]. What is he, whose grief
Bears such an emphasis? whose phrase of sorrow
Conjures the wand'ring stars, and makes them stand
Like wonder-wounded hearers? this is I,
Hamlet the Dane. [*Leaps into the grave.*

*Laertes.* The devil take thy soul!
[*Grappling with him.*

*Hamlet.* Thou pray'st not well.
I pr'ythee, take thy fingers from my throat;
For, though I am not splenetive and rash,
Yet have I in me something dangerous
Which let thy wisdom fear.—Hold off thy hand.

*King.* Pluck them asunder.

*Queen.* Hamlet! Hamlet!

*All.* Gentlemen,—

*Horatio.* Good my lord, be quiet.

*Hamlet.* Why, I will fight with him upon this theme
Until my eyelids will no longer wag.

*Queen.* O my son! what theme?

*Hamlet.* I lov'd Ophelia; forty thousand brothers
Could not, with all their quantity of love,
Make up my sum.—What wilt thou do for her?

*King.* O, he is mad, Laertes.

*Queen.* For love of God, forbear him.

*Hamlet.* 'Zounds, show me what thou'lt do:
Woul't weep? woul't fight? woul't fast? woul't tear thyself?
Woul't drink up Esil? eat a crocodile?
I'll do't.—Dost thou come here to whine?
To outface me with leaping in her grave?
Be buried quick with her, and so will I:
And, if thou prate of mountains, let them throw
Millions of acres on us; till our ground,
Singeing his pate against the burning zone,

Make Ossa like a wart! Nay, an thou'lt mouth,
I'll rant as well as thou.
*Queen.* This is mere madness:
And thus awhile the fit will work on him;
Anon, as patient as the female dove,
When that her golden couplets are disclosed,
His silence will sit drooping.
*Hamlet.* Hear you, sir;
What is the reason that you use me thus?
I lov'd you ever: But it is no matter;
Let Hercules himself do what he may,
The cat will mew, and dog will have his day.

# CYMBELINE.[7]

CYMBELINE, *King of Britain.*
LEONATUS POSTHUMOUS, *Husband to Imogen.*
PISANIO, *Servant to Posthumus.*
IACHIMO, *Friend to Philario.*
IMOGEN, *Daughter to Cymbeline by former Queen.*
HELEN, *Woman to Imogen.*

## ACT I. SCENE II.

*Imogen.*

O, DISSEMBLING courtesy! How fine this tyrant
Can tickle where she wounds!—My dearest husband,
I something fear my father's wrath; but nothing
(Always reserv'd my holy duty) what
His rage can do on me: You must be gone;
And I shall here abide the hourly shot
Of angry eyes; not comforted to live,
But that there is this jewel in the world,
That I may see again.

*Posthumus.* My queen! my mistress!
O, lady, weep no more; lest I give cause

To be suspected of more tenderness
Than doth become a man ! I will remain
The loyal'st husband that did e'er plight troth ;
My residence in Rome at one Philario's,
Who to my father was a friend, to me
Known but by letter ; thither write, my queen,
And with mine eyes I'll drink the words you send,
Though ink be made of gall.

* * * * *

*Posthumus.* Should we be taking leave
As long a term as yet we have to live,
The loathness to depart would grow : Adieu !
*Imogen.* Nay, stay a little ;
Were you but riding forth to air yourself,
Such parting were too petty. Look here, love :
This diamond was my mother's ; take it, heart ;
But keep it till you woo another wife,
When Imogen is dead.
*Posthumus.* How ! how ! another ?
You gentle gods, give me but this I have,
And sear up my embracements from a next
With bonds of death ! Remain, remain thou here
[*Putting on the ring.*
While sense can keep it on. And sweetest, fairest,
As I my poor self did exchange for you,
To your so infinite loss ; so, in our trifles
I still win of you : For my sake, wear this ;
It is a manacle of love ; I'll place it
Upon this fairest prisoner.
[*Putting a bracelet on her arm.*
*Imogen.* O, the gods !
When shall we see again ?

* * * * *

*Imogen.* Sir,
It is your fault that I have lov'd Posthumus:
You bred him as my playfellow; and he is
A man, worth any woman; overbuys me
Almost the sum he pays.

*Cymbeline.* What!—art thou mad?

*Imogen.* Almost, sir: Heaven restore me! 'Would I were
A neat-herd's daughter! and my Leonatus
Our neighbour shepherd's son!

## Scene IV.

*Imogen.* I would thou grew'st unto the shores o' the haven,
And question'dst every sail: if he should write,
And I not have it, 'twere a paper lost
As offer'd mercy is. What was the last
That he spake to thee?

*Pisanio.* 'Twas, his queen, his queen!

*Imogen.* Then wav'd his handkerchief?

*Pisanio.* And kiss'd it, madam.

*Imogen.* Senseless linen! happier therein than I!—
And that was all?

*Pisanio.* No, madam; for so long
As he could make me with this eye or ear
Distinguish him from others, he did keep
The deck, with glove, or hat, or handkerchief,
Still waving, as the fits and stirs of his mind
Could best express how slow his soul sail'd on,
How swift his ship.

*Imogen.* Thou should'st have made him
As little as a crow, or less, ere left

To after-eye him.

*Pisanio.* Madam, so I did.

*Imogen.* I would have broke mine eye-strings; crack'd them, but
To look upon him; till the diminution
Of space had pointed him sharp as my needle:
Nay, follow'd him, till he had melted from
The smallness of a gnat to air; and then
Have turn'd mine eye and wept.—But, good Pisanio,
When shall we hear from him?

*Pisanio.* Be assur'd, madam,
With his next vantage.

*Imogen.* I did not take my leave of him, but had
Most pretty things to say: ere I could tell him,
How I would think on him, at certain hours,
Such thoughts, and such; or I could make him swear
The shes of Italy should not betray
Mine interest, and his honour; or have charg'd him,
At the sixth hour of morn, at noon, at midnight,
To encounter me with orisons, for then
I am in heaven for him; or ere I could
Give him that parting kiss, which I had set
Betwixt two charming words, comes in my father,
And, like the tyrannous breathing of the north,
Shakes all our buds from growing.

SCENE V.—*Rome.*

*Iachimo.* I dare, thereon, pawn the moiety of my estate to your ring; which, in my opinion, o'ervalues it something: But I make my wager rather against your confidence, than her reputation: and, to bar your offence herein too, I durst attempt it against any lady in the world.[8]

* * * * *

*Posthumus.* What lady would you choose to assail?

*Iachimo.* Yours; whom in constancy, you think, stands so safe. I will lay you ten thousand ducats to your ring, that, commend me to the court where your lady is, with no more advantage than the opportunity of a second conference, and I will bring from thence that honour of hers, which you imagine so reserved.

### Scene VII.

*Imogen.* A father cruel, and a step-dame false;
A foolish suitor to a wedded lady,
That hath her husband banish'd: O, that husband!
My supreme crown of grief! and those repeated
Vexations of it! Had I been thief-stolen,
As my two brothers, happy! but most miserable
Is the desire that's glorious: Blessed be those,
How mean soe'er, that have their honest wills,
Which seasons comfort.—Who may this be? Fye!

*Enter* Pisanio *and* Iachimo.

*Pisanio.* Madam, a noble gentleman of Rome
Comes from my lord with letters.

*Iachimo.* Change you, madam?
The worthy Leonatus is in safety,
And greets your highness dearly. [*Presents a letter.*

*Imogen.* Thanks, good sir:
You are kindly welcome.

*Iachimo.* All of her, that is out of door, most rich. [*Aside.*
If she be furnish'd with a mind so rare,

She is alone the Arabian bird; and I
Have lost the wager. Boldness be my friend
Arm me, audacity, from head to foot!
Or, like the Parthian, I shall flying fight;
Rather, directly fly.

## Act II. Scene II.

*Imogen.* Who's there? my woman Helen?
*Lady.* Please you, madam.
*Imogen.* What hour is it?
*Lady.* Almost midnight, madam.
*Imogen.* I have read three hours then: mine eyes are weak:—
Fold down the leaf where I have left: To bed:
Take not away the taper, leave it burning;
And if thou canst awake by four o' the clock,
I pr'ythee, call me. Sleep hath seiz'd me wholly.
[*Exit Lady.*
To your protection I commend me, gods!
From fairies, and the tempters of the night,
Guard me, beseech ye!
[*Sleeps. Iachimo, from the trunk.*
*Iachimo.* The crickets sing, and man's o'er-labour'd sense
Repairs itself by rest: Our Tarquin thus
Did softly press the rushes, ere he waken'd
The chastity he wounded.—Cytherea,
How bravely thou becom'st thy bed! fresh lily!
And whiter than the sheets! That I might touch!
But kiss; one kiss!—Rubies unparagon'd,
How dearly they do't!—'Tis her breathing that
Perfumes the chamber thus: The flame o' the taper
Bows toward her; and would underpeep her lids,

To see the enclosed lights, now canopied
Under these windows: White and azure, lac'd
With blue of heaven's own tinct.—But my design?
To note the chamber:—I will write all down:—
Such, and such, pictures:—There the window:—Such
The adornment of her bed;—The arras, figures,
Why, such, and such:—And the contents o' the story,—
Ay, but some natural notes about her body,
Above ten thousand meaner moveables
Would testify, to enrich mine inventory:
O sleep, thou ape of death, lie dull upon her!
And be her sense but as a monument,
Thus in a chapel lying!—Come off, come off;—
[*Taking off her bracelet.*
As slippery, as the Gordian knot was hard!—
'Tis mine; and this will witness outwardly,
As strongly as the conscience does within,
To the madding of her lord. On her left breast
A mole cinque-spotted, like the crimson drops
I' the bottom of a cowslip.[9] Here's a voucher,
Stronger than ever law could make: this secret
Will force him think I have pick'd the lock, and ta'en
The treasure of her honour. No more.—To what end?
Why should I write this down, that 's riveted,
Screw'd to my memory? She hath been reading late
The tale of Tereus; here the leaf's turn'd down,
Where Philomel gave up;—I have enough:
To the trunk again, and shut the spring of it.
Swift, swift, you dragons of the night!—that dawning
May bare the raven's eye: I lodge in fear;
Though this a heavenly angel, hell is here. [*Clock strikes.*
One, two, three,—Time, time!
[*Goes into the trunk. The scene closes.*

## Scene III.

*Imogen.* I am sprighted with a fool;
Frighted, and anger'd worse;—Go, bid my woman
Search for a jewel, that too casually
Hath left mine arm; it was thy master's: 'shrew me,
If I would lose it for a revenue
Of any king's in Europe. I do think,
I saw 't this morning: Confident I am,
Last night 'twas on mine arm; I kiss'd it:
I hope, it be not gone, to tell my lord
That I kiss aught but he.

## Act III. Scene I.

*Queen.* That opportunity
Which then they had to take from us, to resume
We have again.—Remember, sir, my liege,
The kings your ancestors; together with
The natural bravery of your isle; which stands
As Neptune's park, ribbed and paled in
With rocks unscaleable, and roaring waters;
With sands, that will not bear your enemies' boats,
But suck them up to the top-mast. A kind of conquest
Cæsar made here; but made not here his brag
Of, came, and saw, and overcame; with shame
(The first that ever touch'd him), he was carried
From off our coast, twice beaten; and his shipping,
(Poor ignorant baubles!) on our terrible seas,
Like egg-shells mov'd upon their surges, crack'd
As easily 'gainst our rocks: for joy whereof,

The fam'd Cassibelan, who was once at point
(O giglot fortune !) to master Cæsar's sword,
Made Lud's town with rejoicing fires bright,
And Britons strut with courage.

*Cloten.* Come, there's no more tribute to be paid. Our kingdom is stronger than it was at that time; and, as I said, there is no more such Cæsars: other of them may have crooked noses; but, to owe such straight arms, none.

*Cymbeline.* Son, let your mother end.

*Cloten.* We have yet many among us can gripe as hard as Cassibelan: I do not say, I am one; but I have a hand.—Why tribute? why should we pay tribute? If Cæsar can hide the sun from us with a blanket, or put the moon in his pocket, we will pay him tribute for light: else, sir, no more tribute, pray you now.

## Scene II.

*Pisanio.* How! of adultery? wherefore write you not
What monster 's her accuser?—Leonatus!
O, master! what a strange infection
Is fallen into thy ear? What false Italian
(As poisonous tongu'd, as handed) hath prevail'd
On thy too ready hearing?—Disloyal? No:
She 's punish'd for her truth; and undergoes,
More goddess-like than wife-like, such assaults
As would take in some virtue.—O, my master!
Thy mind to her is now as low, as were
Thy fortunes.—How! that I should murder her?
Upon the love, and truth, and vows, which I
Have made to thy command?—I, her?—her blood?
If it be so to do good service, never

Let me be counted serviceable. How look I,
That I should seem to lack humanity,
So much as this fact comes to? Do't: the letter
[*Reading.*
That I have sent her, by her own command
Shall give thee opportunity:—O damn'd paper!
Black as the ink that's on thee! Senseless bauble,
Art thou a feodary for this act, and look'st
So virgin-like without? Lo, here she comes.

*Enter* IMOGEN.

I am ignorant in what I am commanded.

*Imogen.* How now, Pisanio?

*Pisanio.* Madam, here is a letter from my lord.

*Imogen.* Who? thy lord? that is my lord? Leonatus?
O, learn'd indeed were that astronomer,
That knew the stars, as I his characters;
He'd lay the future open.—You good gods,
Let what is here contain'd relish of love,
Of my lord's health, of his content,—yet not,
That we two are asunder, let that grieve him,—
(Some griefs are medicinable;) that is one of them,
For it doth physick love;—of his content,
All but in that!—Good wax, thy leave:—Bless'd be,
You bees, that make these locks of counsel! Lovers,
And men in dangerous bonds, pray not alike;
Though forfeiters you cast in prison, yet
You clasp young Cupid's tables.—Good news, gods!
[*Reads.*

Justice, and your father's wrath, should he take me in his dominion, could not be so cruel to me as you, O the dearest of creatures, would not even renew me with your eyes. Take notice, that I am in Cambria, at Milford-Haven. What your own love will, out of this, advise you, follow. So, he wishes you all happiness, that remains loyal to his vow, and your, increasing in love,

Leonatus Posthumus.

O, for a horse with wings!—Hear'st thou, Pisanio?
He is at Milford-Haven: Read, and tell me
How far 'tis thither. If one of mean affairs
May plod it in a week, why may not I
Glide thither in a day?—Then, true Pisanio,
(Who long'st, like me, to see thy lord; who long'st,—
O, let me 'bate,—but not like me;—yet long'st,—
But in a fainter kind:—O, not like me;
For mine's beyond beyond,) say, and speak thick,
(Love's counsellor should fill the bores of hearing,
To the smothering of the sense,) how far it is
To this same blessed Milford: And, by the way,
Tell me how Wales was made so happy, as
To inherit such a haven: But, first of all,
How we may steal from hence; and, for the gap
That we shall make in time, from our hence-going,
And our return, to excuse:—but first, how get hence:
Why should excuse be born or e'er begot?
We'll talk of that hereafter. Pr'ythee, speak,
How many score of miles may we well ride
'Twixt hour and hour?

*Pisanio.* One score, 'twixt sun and sun,
Madam, 's enough for you; and too much too.

*Imogen.* Why, one that rode to his execution, man,
Could never go so slow: I have heard of riding wagers,
Where horses have been nimbler than the sands
That run i' the clock's behalf:—But this is foolery:
Go, bid my woman feign a sickness; say

She'll home to her father: and provide me, presently,
A riding suit; no costlier than would fit
A franklin's housewife.

*Pisanio.* Madam, you're best consider.

*Imogen.* I see before me, man, nor here, nor here,
Nor what ensues; but have a fog in them,
That I cannot look through. Away, I pr'ythee;
Do as I bid thee: There's no more to say;
Accessible is none but Milford way. [*Exeunt.*

## Act III. Scene IV.

*Imogen.* Thou told'st me, when we came from horse, the place
Was near at hand:—Ne'er long'd my mother so
To see me first, as I have now:—Pisanio! Man!
Where is Posthumus? What is in thy mind,
That makes thee stare thus? Wherefore breaks that sigh
From the inward of thee? One, but painted thus,
Would be interpreted a thing perplex'd
Beyond self-explication: Put thyself
Into a haviour of less fear, ere wildness
Vanquish my staider senses. What's the matter?
Why tender'st thou that paper to me, with
A look untender? If it be summer news,
Smile to't before: if winterly, thou need'st
But keep that countenance still.—My husband's hand!
That drug-damn'd Italy hath out-craftied him,
And he's at some hard point.—Speak, man; thy tongue
May take off some extremity, which to read
Would be even mortal to me.

*Pisanio.* Please you, read;
And you shall find me, wretched man, a thing

The most disdain'd of fortune.

* * * * *

*Pisanio.* What shall I need to draw my sword? the paper
Hath cut her throat already.—No, 'tis slander;
Whose edge is sharper than the sword; whose tongue
Outvenoms all the worms of Nile; whose breath
Rides on the posting winds, and doth belie
All corners of the world: kings, queens, and states,
Maids, matrons, nay, the secrets of the grave
This viperous slander enters.—What cheer, madam?

*Imogen.* False to his bed! What is it, to be false?
To lie in watch there, and to think on him?
To weep 'twixt clock and clock? if sleep charge nature,
To break it with a fearful dream of him,
And cry myself awake? that's false to his bed?
Is it?

*Pisanio.* Alas, good lady!

*Imogen.* I false! Thy conscience witness:—Iachimo,
Thou didst accuse him of incontinency;
Thou then look'dst like a villain; now, methinks,
Thy favour's good enough.—Some jay of Italy,
Whose mother was her painting, hath betray'd him:
Poor I am stale, a garment out of fashion;
And, for I am richer than to hang by the walls,
I must be ripp'd:—to pieces with me!—O,
Men's vows are women's traitors! All good seeming,
By thy revolt, O husband, shall be thought
Put on for villainy; not born, where't grows;
But worn, a bait for ladies.

*Pisanio.* Good madam, hear me.

*Imogen.* True honest men being heard, like false Æneas,
Were, in his time, thought false: and Sinon's weeping
Did scandal many a holy tear; took pity

From most true wretchedness: So, thou, Posthumus,
Wilt lay the leaven on all proper men;
Goodly, and gallant, shall be false and perjur'd,
From thy great fail.—Come, fellow, be thou honest:
Do thou thy master's bidding: when thou see'st him,
A little witness my obedience: Look!
I draw the sword myself: take it; and hit
The innocent mansion of my love, my heart:
Fear not; 'tis empty of all things, but grief:
Thy master is not there; who was, indeed,
The riches of it: Do his bidding; strike.
Thou may'st be valiant in a better cause;
But now thou seem'st a coward.

*Pisanio.* Hence, vile instrument!
Thou shalt not damn my hand.

*Imogen.* Why, I must die;
And if I do not by thy hand, thou art
No servant of thy master's: Against self-slaughter
There is a prohibition so divine,
That cravens my weak hand. Come, here's my heart;
Something's afore't:—Soft, soft; we'll no defence:
Obedient as the scabbard.—What is here?
The scriptures of the loyal Leonatus,
All turn'd to heresy? Away, away,
Corrupters of my faith! you shall no more
Be stomachers to my heart! Thus may poor fools
Believe false teachers: Though those that are betray'd
Do feel the treason sharply, yet the traitor
Stands in worse case of woe.
And thou, Posthumus, thou that didst set up
My disobedience 'gainst the king my father,
And make me put into contempt the suits
Of princely fellows, shalt hereafter find

It is no act of common passage, but
A strain of rareness: and I grieve myself,
To think, when thou shalt be disedg'd by her
That now thou tir'st on, how thy memory
Will then be pang'd by me.—Pr'ythee, despatch:
The lamb entreats the butcher: Where 's thy knife?
Thou art too slow to do thy master's bidding,
When I desire it too.

*Pisanio.* O gracious lady,
Since I receiv'd command to do this business,
I have not slept one wink.

*Imogen.* Do 't, and to bed then.

*Pisanio.* I'll wake mine eye-balls blind first.

*Imogen.* Wherefore then
Didst undertake it? Why hast thou abus'd
So many miles with a pretence? this place?
Mine action, and thine own? our horses' labour?
The time inviting thee? the perturb'd court,
For my being absent; whereunto I never
Purpose return? Why hast thou gone so far,
To be unbent, when thou hast ta'en thy stand,
The elected deer before thee?

*Pisanio.* But to win time
To lose so bad employment: in the which
I have consider'd of a course; Good lady,
Hear me with patience.

*Imogen.* Talk thy tongue weary; speak:
I have heard, I am a strumpet; and mine ear,
Therein false struck, can take no greater wound,
Nor tent to bottom that. But speak.

*Pisanio.* Then, madam,
I thought you would not back again.

*Imogen.* Most like;

Bringing me here to kill me.
*Pisanio.* Not so, neither:
But if I were as wise as honest, then
My purpose would prove well. It cannot be,
But that my master is abus'd:
Some villain, ay, and singular in his art,
Hath done you both this cursed injury.
*Imogen.* Some Roman courtezan.
*Pisanio.* No, on my life.
I'll give but notice you are dead, and send him
Some bloody sign of it; for 'tis commanded
I should do so: You shall be miss'd at court,
And that will well confirm it.
*Imogen.* Why, good fellow,
What shall I do the while? Where bide? How live?
Or in my life what comfort, when I am
Dead to my husband?
*Pisanio.* If you'll back to the court,—
*Imogen.* No court, no father; nor no more ado
With that harsh, noble, simple, nothing:
That Cloten, whose love-suit hath been to me
As fearful as a seige.
*Pisanio.* If not at court,
Then not in Britain must you bide.
*Imogen.* Where then?
Hath Britain all the sun that shines? Day, night,
Are they not but in Britain? I' the world's volume
Our Britain seems as of it, but not in it;
In a great pool, a swan's nest; Pr'ythee, think
There 's livers out of Britain.
*Pisanio.* I am most glad
You think of other place. The embassador
Lucius the Roman, comes to Milford Haven

To-morrow: Now, if you could wear a mind
Dark as your fortune is; and but disguise
That, which, to appear itself, must not yet be,
But by self-danger; you should tread a course
Pretty, and full of view: yea, haply, near
The residence of Posthumus: so nigh, at least,
That though his actions were not visible, yet
Report should render him hourly to your ear,
As truly as he moves.

*Imogen.* O, for such means!
Though peril to my modesty, not death on 't,
I would adventure.

*Pisanio.* Well then, here 's the point:
You must forget to be a woman; change
Command into obedience; fear and niceness
(The handmaids of all women, or, more truly,
Woman its pretty self) to a waggish courage;
Ready in gibes, quick-answer'd, saucy, and
As quarrellous as the weasel: nay, you must
Forget that rarest treasure of your cheek,
Exposing it (but, O, the harder heart!
Alack no remedy!) to the greedy touch
Of common-kissing Titan; and forget
Your laboursome and dainty trims, wherein
You made great Juno angry.

*Imogen.* Nay, be brief:
I see into thy end, and am almost
A man already.

*Pisanio.* First, make yourself but like one,
Fore-thinking this, I have already fit
('Tis in my cloak-bag) doublet, hat, hose, all
That answer to them: Would you, in their serving,
And with what imitation you can borrow

From youth of such a season, 'fore noble Lucius
Present yourself, desire his service, tell him
Wherein you are happy (which you'll make him know,
If that his head have ear in musick), doubtless,
With joy he will embrace you; for he's honourable,
And, doubling that, most holy. Your means abroad
You have me, rich; and I will never fail
Beginning, nor supplyment.

*Imogen.* Thou art all the comfort
The gods will diet me with. Pr'ythee, away:
There's more to be consider'd; but we'll even
All that good time will give us: This attempt
I am soldier to, and will abide it with
A prince's courage. Away, I pr'ythee.

*Pisanio.* Well, madam, we must take a short farewell;
Lest, being miss'd, I be suspected of
Your carriage from the court. My noble mistress,
Here is a box; I had it from the queen;
What's in 't is precious; if you are sick at sea,
Or stomach-qualm'd at land, a dram of this
Will drive away distemper.—To some shade,
And fit you to your manhood:—May the gods
Direct you to the best!

*Imogen.* Amen: I thank thee. [*Exeunt.*

## SCENE VI.

*Imogen.* I see, a man's life is a tedious one:
I have tir'd myself; and for two nights together
Have made the ground my bed. I should be sick,
But that my resolution helps me.—Milford,
When from the mountain-top Pisanio show'd thee,

Thou wast within a ken: O Jove! I think,
Foundations fly the wretched: such, I mean,
Where they should be reliev'd. Two beggars told me,
I could not miss my way: Will poor folks lie,
That have afflictions on them; knowing 'tis
A punishment, or trial? Yes; no wonder,
When rich ones scarce tell true: To lapse in fulness
Is sorer, than to lie for need; and falsehood
Is worse in kings, than beggars.—My dear lord!
Thou art one o' the false ones: Now I think on thee,
My hunger's gone; but even before, I was
At point to sink for food.—But what is this?
Here is a path to it: 'Tis some savage hold:
I were best not call; I dare not call: yet famine,
Ere clean it o'erthrow nature, makes it valiant.
Plenty, and peace, breeds cowards; hardness ever
Of hardiness is mother.—Ho! Who 's here?
If any thing that 's civil, speak; if savage,
Take, or lend.—Ho!—No answer? then I'll enter.
Best draw my sword; and if mine enemy
But fear the sword like me, he'll scarcely look on't.
Such a foe, good heavens! [*She goes into the cave.*

## Act IV. Scene II.

*Belarius.* You are not well [*To Imogen*]: remain here: in the cave:
We'll come to you after hunting.

*Arviragus.* Brother, stay here:
Are we not brothers? [*To Imogen.*

*Imogen.* So man and man should be;
But clay and clay differs in dignity,
Whose dust is both alike. I am very sick.

*Guiderius.* Go you to hunting. I'll abide with him.

*Imogen.* So sick I am not;—yet I am not well:
But not so citizen a wanton, as
To seem to die, ere sick: So please you leave me;
Stick to your journal course: the breach of custom
Is breach of all. I am ill; but your being by me
Cannot amend me: Society is no comfort
To one not sociable: I'm not very sick,
Since I can reason of it. Pray you, trust me here:
I'll rob none but myself; and let me die,
Stealing so poorly.

*Guiderius.* I love thee; I have spoke it:
How much the quantity, the weight as much,
As I do love my father.

*Belarius.* What? how? how?

*Arviragus.* If it be sin to say so, sir, I yoke me
In my good brother's fault: I know not why
I love this youth; and I have heard you say,
Love's reason 's without reason; the bier at door,
And a demand who is 't shall die, I'd say,
My father, not this youth.

*Belarius.* O noble strain!
O worthiness of nature! breed of greatness! [*Aside.*
Cowards father cowards, and base things sire base:
Nature hath meal, and bran; contempt, and grace.
I am not their father; yet who this should be,
Doth miracle itself, lov'd before me.—
'Tis the ninth hour o' the morn.

*Arviragus.* Brother, farewell.

*Imogen.* I wish ye sport.

*Arviragus.* Your health.—So please you, sir.

*Imogen* (*aside*). These are kind creatures: Gods, what lies I have heard!

Our courtiers say, all's savage, but at court :
Experience, O, thou disprov'st report !
The imperious seas breed monsters ; for the dish,
Poor tributary rivers as sweet fish.
I am sick still ; heart-sick :—Pisanio,
I'll now taste of thy drug.
*Guiderius.* I could not stir him :
He said, he was gentle, but unfortunate ;
Dishonestly afflicted, but yet honest.
*Arviragus.* Thus did he answer me : yet said, hereafter
I might know more.

* * * * *

With fairest flowers,
Whilst summer lasts, and I live here, Fidele,
I'll sweeten thy sad grave : Thou shalt not lack
The flower, that 's like thy face, pale primrose ; nor
The azur'd hare-bell, like thy veins ; no, nor
The leaf of eglantine, whom not to slander,
Out-sweeten'd not thy breath : the ruddock would,
With charitable bill (O bill, sore-shaming
Those rich-left heirs, that let their fathers lie
Without a monument !) bring thee all this ;
Yea, and furr'd moss besides, when flowers are none,
To winter-ground thy corse.

### Act V. Scene I.

*Posthumus.* Yea, bloody cloth, I 'll keep thee ; for I wish'd
Thou should'st be colour'd thus. You married ones
If each of you would take this course, how many
Must murder wives much better than themselves,
For wrying but a little ?—O, Pisanio !

Every good servant does not all commands:
No bond, but to do just ones.—Gods! if you
Should have ta'en vengeance on my faults, I never
Had liv'd to put on this: so had you saved
The noble Imogen to repent; and struck
Me, wretch, more worth your vengeance. But, alack,
You snatch some hence for little faults; that's love,
To have them fall no more: You some permit
To second ills with ills, each elder worse;
And make them dread it to the doer's thrift.
But Imogen is your own: Do your best wills,
And make me bless'd to obey!—I am brought hither
Among the Italian gentry, and to fight
Against my lady's kingdom: 'Tis enough
That, Britain, I have kill'd thy mistress; peace!
I'll give no wound to thee. Therefore, good heavens,
Hear patiently my purpose: I'll disrobe me
Of these Italian weeds, and suit myself
As does a Briton peasant: so I'll fight
Against the part I come with; so I'll die
For thee, O Imogen, even for whom my life
Is, every breath, a death; and thus, unknown,
Pitied nor hated, to the face of peril
Myself I'll dedicate. Let me make men know
More valour in me, than my habits show.
Gods, put the strength o' the Leonati in me!
To shame the guise o' the world, I will begin
The fashion, less without, and more within.

## Scene II.

*Iachimo.* The heaviness and guilt within my bosom
Takes off my manhood: I have belied a lady,

The princess of this country, and the air on 't
Revengingly enfeebles me; Or could this carl,
A very drudge of nature's, have subdu'd me
In my profession? Knighthoods and honours, borne
As I wear mine, are titles but of scorn.
If that thy gentry, Britain, go before
This lout, as he exceeds our lords, the odds
Is, that we scarce are men, and you are gods.

### Scene V.

*Iachimo.* That paragon, thy daughter,—
For whom my heart drops blood, and my false spirits
Quail to remember,—Give me leave; I faint.
*Cymbeline.* My daughter! what of her? Renew thy strength:
I had rather thou should'st live while nature will,
Than die ere I hear more: strive man, and speak.
*Iachimo.* Upon a time (unhappy was the clock
That struck the hour!) it was in Rome (accurs'd
The mansion where!) 't was at a feast, (O 'would
Our viands had been poison'd! or, at least,
Those which I heav'd to head!) the good Posthumus.
(What should I say? he was too good, to be
Where ill men were; and was the best of all
Amongst the rar'st of good ones), sitting sadly,
Hearing us praise our loves of Italy
For beauty that made barren the swell'd boast
Of him that best could speak: for feature, laming
The shrine of Venus, or straight-pight Minerva,
Postures beyond brief nature; for condition,
A shop of all the qualities that man

Loves woman for; besides, that hook of wiving,
Fairness which strikes the eye:—

* * * * *

*Posthumus.* Ay, so thou dost,
Italian fiend! Ah me, most credulous fool,
Egregious murderer, thief, anything
That's due to all the villains past, in being,
To come!—O, give me cord, or knife, or poison,
Some upright justicer! Thou king, send out
For torturers ingenious: it is I
That all the abhorred things o' the earth amend,
By being worse than they. I am Posthumus,
That kill'd thy daughter:—villain-like, I lie;
I caus'd a lesser villain than myself,
A sacrilegious thief, to do't:—the temple
Of virtue was she; yea, and she herself.
Spit, and throw stones, cast mire upon me, set
The dogs o' the street to bay me: every villain
Be call'd, Posthumus Leonatus; and
Be villainy less than 'twas!—O Imogen!
My queen, my life, my wife! O Imogen,
Imogen, Imogen!

*Imogen.* Peace, my lord; hear, hear—

*Posthumus.* Shall's have a play of this? Thou scornful page,
There lie thy part. [*Striking her; she falls.*

*Pisanio.* O, gentlemen, help, help,
Mine, and your mistress:—O, my Lord Posthumus!
You ne'er kill'd Imogen till now:—Help, help!—
Mine honour'd lady!

* * * * *

*Imogen.* Why did you throw your wedded lady from you?

Think, that you are upon a rock ; and now
Throw me again. [*Embracing him.*

*Posthumus.* Hang there like fruit, my soul,
Till the tree die !

* * * * *

*Cymbeline.* The forlorn soldier, that so nobly fought,
He would have well becom'd this place, and grac'd
The thankings of a king.

*Posthumus.* I am, sir,
The soldier that did company these three
In poor beseeming ; 'twas a fitment for
The purpose I then follow'd ;—That I was he,
Speak, Iachimo ; I had you down, and might
Have made you finish.

*Iachimo.* I am down again : [*Kneeling.*
But now my heavy conscience sinks my knee,
As then your force did. Take that life, 'beseech you,
Which I so often owe : but, your ring first ;
And here the bracelet of the truest princess,
That ever swore her faith.

*Posthumus.* Kneel not to me ;
The power that I have on you, is to spare you ;
The malice towards you, to forgive you : Live,
And deal with others better.

# COMEDY OF ERRORS.

## Act II. Scene I.

*Adriana.*

NEITHER my husband, nor the slave returned,
That in such haste I sent to seek his master!
Sure, Luciana, it is two o'clock.
*Luciana.* Perhaps, some merchant hath invited him,
And from the mart he 's somewhere gone to dinner;
Good sister, let us dine, and never fret:
A man is master of his liberty:
Time is their master; and, when they see time,
They'll go, or come: If so, be patient, sister.
*Adriana.* Why should their liberty than ours be more?
*Luciana.* Because their business still lies out o' door.
*Adriana.* Look, when I serve him so, he takes it ill.
*Luciana.* O, know, he is the bridle of your will.
*Adriana.* There 's none, but asses, will be bridled so.
*Luciana.* Why, headstrong liberty is lash'd with woe.
There 's nothing, situate under Heaven's eye,
But hath his bound, in earth, in sea, in sky:
The beasts, the fishes, and the winged fowls,
Are their males' subjects, and at their controls:

Men, more divine, the masters of all these,
Lords of the wide world, and wild watry seas,
Indued with intellectual sense and souls,
Of more pre-eminence than fish and fowls,
Are masters to their females, and their lords:
Then let your will attend on their accords.

*Adriana.* This servitude makes you to keep unwed.

*Luciana.* Not this, but troubles of the marriage bed.

*Adriana.* But, were you wedded, you would bear some sway.

*Luciana.* Ere I learn love, I'll practise to obey.

*Adriana.* How if your husband start some other where?

*Luciana.* Till he come home again, I would forbear.

*Adriana.* Patience, unmov'd, no marvel though she pause;
They can be meek, that have no other cause.
A wretched soul, bruis'd with adversity,
We bid be quiet, when we hear it cry;
But were we burden'd with like weight of pain,
As much, or more, we should ourselves complain:
So thou, that hast no unkind mate to grieve thee,
With urging helpless patience would'st relieve me:
But, if thou live to see like right bereft,
This fool-begg'd patience in thee will be left.

*Luciana.* Well, I will marry one day, but to try;—
Here comes your man, now is your husband nigh.

# KING LEAR.

## Act I. Scene I.

*Cordelia.*

GOOD my lord
You have begot me, bred me, lov'd me: I
Return those duties back as are right fit,
Obey you, love you, and most honour you.
Why have my sisters husbands, if they say,
They love you, all? Haply, when I shall wed,
That lord, whose hand must take my plight, shall carry
Half my love with him, half my care, and duty:
Sure, I shall never marry like my sisters,
To love my father all.

* * * * *

*France.* This is most strange!
That she, that even but now was your best object,
The argument of your praise, balm of your age,
Most best, most dearest, should in this trice of time
Commit a thing so monstrous, to dismantle
So many folds of favour! Sure, her offence
Must be of such unnatural degree,
That monsters it, or your fore-vouch'd affection

Fall into taint: which to believe of her
Must be a faith, that reason without miracle
Could never plant in me.

*Cordelia.* I yet beseech your majesty
(If for I want that glib and oily art,
To speak and purpose not; since what I well intend,
I'll do 't before I speak), that you make known
It is no vicious blot, murder, or foulness,
No unchaste action, or dishonour'd step,
That hath depriv'd me of your grace and favour:
But even for want of that, for which I am richer;
A still-soliciting eye, and such a tongue
That I am glad I have not, though not to have it,
Hath lost me in your liking.

*Lear.* Better thou
Hadst not been born, than not to have pleas'd me better.

*France.* Is it but this? a tardiness in nature,
Which often leaves the history unspoke,
That it intends to do?—My Lord of Burgundy,
What say you to the lady? Love is not love,
When it is mingled with respects, that stand
Aloof from the entire point. Will you have her?
She is herself a dowry.

* * * * *

*France.* Fairest Cordelia, that art most rich, being poor;
Most choice, forsaken; and most lov'd, despised!
Thee and thy virtues here I seize upon:
Be it lawful, I take up what's cast away.
Gods, gods! 'tis strange, that from their cold'st neglect
My love should kindle to inflam'd respect.—
Thy dowerless daughter, king, thrown to my chance,
Is queen of us, of ours, and our fair France:
Not all the dukes of wat'rish Burgundy

Shall buy this unpriz'd precious maid of me.—
Bid them farewell, Cordelia, though unkind :
Thou losest here, a better where to find.

* * * * *

*France.* Bid farewell to your sisters.
*Cordelia.* The jewels of our father, with wash'd eyes
Cordelia leaves you ; I know you what you are :
And, like a sister, am most loath to call
Your faults, as they are nam'd. Use well our father :
To your professed bosoms I commit him :
But yet, alas ! stood I within his grace,
I would prefer him to a better place.
So farewell to you both.

## Act IV. Scene VII.

*Cordelia.* O thou good Kent, how shall I live, and work,
To match thy goodness ? My life will be too short,
And every measure fail me.
*Kent.* To be acknowledg'd, madam, is o'erpaid.
All my reports go with the modest truth ;
Nor more, nor clipp'd, but so.
*Cordelia.* Be better suited :
These weeds are memories of those worser hours ;
I prythee, put them off.
*Kent.* Pardon me, dear madam ;
Yet to be known, shortens my made intent :
My boon I make it, that you know me not,
Till time and I think meet.
*Cordelia.* Then be it so, my good lord.—How does the king ?
*Physician.* Madam, sleeps still.

*Cordelia.* O you kind gods,
Cure this great breach in his abused nature !
The untun'd and jarring senses, O, wind up
Of this child-changed father !

*Physician.* So please your majesty,
That we may wake the king? he hath slept long.

*Cordelia.* Be govern'd by your knowledge, and proceed
I' the sway of your own will. Is he array'd?

*Gentleman.* Ay, madam, in the heaviness of his sleep,
We put fresh garments on him.

*Physician.* Be by, good madam, when we do awake him;
I doubt not of his temperance.

*Cordelia.* Very well.

*Physician.* Please you, draw near.—Louder the musick there.

*Cordelia.* O my dear father! Restoration, hang
Thy medicine on my lips; and let this kiss
Repair those violent harms, that my two sisters
Have in thy reverence made !

*Kent.* Kind and dear princess !

*Cordelia.* Had you not been their father, these white flakes
Had challeng'd pity of them. Was this a face
To be expos'd against the warring winds?
To stand against the deep dread-bolted thunder?
In the most terrible and nimble stroke
Of quick, cross lightning? to watch (poor perdu !)
With this thin helm? Mine enemy's dog,
Though he had bit me, should have stood that night
Against my fire; And wast thou fain, poor father,
To hovel thee with swine, and rogues forlorn,
In short and musty straw? Alack, alack !
'Tis wonder, that thy life and wits at once

Had not concluded all.—He wakes; speak to him.

*Physician.* Madam, do you; 'tis fittest.

*Cordelia.* How does my royal lord? How fares your majesty?

*Lear.* You do me wrong, to take me out o' the grave:—
Thou art a soul in bliss; but I am bound
Upon a wheel of fire, that mine own tears
Do scald like molten lead.

*Cordelia.* Sir, do you know me?

*Lear.* You are a spirit, I know; When did you die?

*Cordelia.* Still, still, far wide!

*Physician.* He's scarce awake; let him alone awhile.

*Lear.* Where have I been?—Where am I?—Fair daylight?
I am mightily abus'd.—I should even die with pity,
To see another thus.—I know not what to say.—
I will not swear, these are my hands:—let's see;
I feel this pin prick. 'Would, I were assur'd
Of my condition.

*Cordelia.* O, look upon me, sir,
And hold your hands in benediction o'er me;—
No, sir, you must not kneel.

*Lear.* Pray, do not mock me:
I am a very foolish fond old man,
Fourscore and upward; and, to deal plainly,
I fear, I am not in my perfect mind.
Methinks, I should know you, and know this man:
Yet I am doubtful: for I am mainly ignorant
What place this is; and all the skill I have
Remembers not these garments; nor I know not
Where I did lodge last night: Do not laugh at me;
For, as I am a man, I think this lady
To be my child Cordelia.

*Cordelia.* And so I am, I am.

*Lear.* Be your tears wet? Yes, 'faith. I pray, weep not:
If you have poison for me, I will drink it.
I know, you do not love me; for your sisters
Have, as I do remember, done me wrong:
You have some cause, they have not.

*Cordelia.* No cause, no cause.

*Lear.* Am I in France?

*Kent.* In your own kingdom, sir.

*Lear.* Do not abuse me.

*Physician.* Be comforted, good madam: the great rage,
You see, is cur'd in him: [and yet it is danger
To make him even o'er the time he has lost.]
Desire him to go in; trouble him no more,
Till further settling.

*Cordelia.* Will't please your highness walk?

*Lear.* You must bear with me:
Pray now, forget and forgive: I am old, and foolish.

## Act V. Scene III.

*Lear.* Howl, howl, howl, howl!—O, you are men of stones;
Had I your tongues and eyes, I'd use them so
That heaven's vault should crack:—O, she is gone for ever!—
I know when one is dead, and when one lives;
She 's dead as earth:—Lend me a looking glass;
If that her breath will mist or stain the stone
Why, then she lives.

*Kent.* Is this the promis'd end?

*Edgar.* Or image of that horror?

*Albany.* Fall, and cease!
*Lear.* This feather stirs; she lives! if it be so,
It is a chance that does redeem all sorrows
That ever I have felt.
*Kent.* O my good master!
*Lear.* Pr'ythee, away.
*Edgar.* 'Tis noble Kent, your friend.
*Lear.* A plague upon you, murderers, traitors all!
I might have sav'd her; now she 's gone for ever!—
Cordelia, Cordelia, stay a little. Ha!
What is 't thou say'st?—Her voice was ever soft,
Gentle, and low; an excellent thing in woman:—
I kill'd the slave that was a hanging thee.

## KING JOHN.

### Act III. Scene I.

*Lewis.*

FATHER, to arms!

*Blanche.* Upon thy wedding day?[11]
Against the blood that thou hast married?
What, shall our feast be kept with slaughter'd men?
Shall braying trumpets, and loud churlish drums,—
Clamours of hell,—be measures to our pomp?
O husband, hear me!—ah, alack, how new
Is husband in my mouth? even for that name,
Which till this time my tongue did ne'er pronounce,
Upon my knee I beg, go not to arms
Against mine uncle.

* * * * *

*Blanche.* The sun's o'ercast with blood: Fair day, adieu!
Which is the side that I must go withal?
I am with both: each army hath a hand;
And, in their rage, I having hold of both,
They whirl asunder, and dismember me.

Husband, I cannot pray that thou may'st win;
Uncle, I needs must pray that thou may'st lose;
Father, I may not wish the fortune thine;
Grandam, I will not wish thy wishes thrive:
Whoever wins, on that side shall I lose;
Assured loss, before the match be play'd.

## Act III. Scene IV.

*Pandulph.* Lady, you utter madness, and not sorrow.
*Constance.* Thou art not holy to belie me so;
I am not mad: this hair I tear is mine;
My name is Constance: I was Geffrey's wife;
Young Arthur is my son, and he is lost:
I am not mad:—I would to heaven, I were!
For then, 'tis like I should forget myself:
O, if I could, what grief should I forget!—
Preach some philosophy to make me mad,
And thou shalt be canoniz'd, cardinal:
For, being not mad, but sensible of grief,
My reasonable part produces reason
How I may be deliver'd of these woes,
And teaches me to kill or hang myself:
If I were mad, I should forget my son;
Or madly think, a babe of clouts were he:
I am not mad; too well, too well I feel
The different plague of each calamity.
*K. Philip.* Bind up those tresses; O, what love I note
In the fair multitude of those her hairs!
Where but by chance a silver drop hath fallen,
Even to that drop ten thousand wiry friends
Do glew themselves in sociable grief;

Like true, inseparable, faithful loves,
Sticking together in calamity.

*Constance.* To England, if you will.

*K. Philip.* Bind up your hairs.

*Constance.* Yes, that I will; and wherefore will I do it?
I tore them from their bonds; and cried aloud,
O that these hands could so redeem my son
As they have given these hairs their liberty!
But now I envy at their liberty,
And will again commit them to their bonds,
Because my poor child is a prisoner.—
And, father cardinal, I have heard you say,
That we shall see and know our friends in heaven:
If that be true, I shall see my boy again;
For, since the birth of Cain, the first male child,
To him that did but yesterday suspire,
There was not such a gracious creature born,
But now will canker sorrow eat my bud,
And chase the native beauty from his cheek,
And he will look as hollow as a ghost;
As dim and meagre as an ague's fit;
And so he'll die; and, rising so again,
When I shall meet him in the court of heaven
I shall not know him: therefore never, never
Must I behold my pretty Arthur more.

*Pandulph.* You hold too heinous a respect of grief.

*Constance.* He talks to me, that never had a son.

*K. Philip.* You are as fond of grief, as of your child.

*Constance.* Grief fills the room up of my absent child,
Lies in his bed, walks up and down with me;
Puts on his pretty looks, repeats his words,
Remembers me of all his gracious parts,
Stuffs out his vacant garments with his form;

Then, have I reason to be fond of grief.
Fare you well: had you such a loss as I,
I could give better comfort than you do.—
I will not keep this form upon my head,
[*Tearing off her head-dress.*
When there is such disorder in my wit.
O Lord! my boy, my Arthur, my fair son!
My life, my joy, my food, my all the world!
My widow-comfort, and my sorrow's cure!
*K. Philip.* I fear some outrage, and I'll follow her.

# CORIOLANUS.

## Act III. Scene II.

*Volumnia.*

YOU are too absolute;
Though therein you can never be too noble,
But when extremities speak. I have heard
you say,
Honour and policy, like unsever'd friends,
I' the war do grow together: Grant that, and tell me,
In peace, what each of them by th' other lose,
That they combine not there.

*Coriolanus.* Tush, tush!

*Menenius.* A good demand.

*Volumnia.* If it be honour, in your wars, to seem
The same you are not (which, for your best ends,
You adopt your policy), how is it less, or worse,
That it shall hold companionship in peace
With honour, as in war; since that to both
It stands in like request?

*Coriolanus.* Why force you this?

*Volumnia.* Because that now it lies you on to speak
To the people; not by your own instruction,
Nor by the matter which your heart prompts you to,

But with such words that are but roted in
Your tongue, though but bastards, and syllables
Of no allowance, to your bosom's truth.
Now, this no more dishonours you at all,
Than to take in a town with gentle words,
Which else would put you to your fortune, and
The hazard of much blood.—
I would dissemble with my nature, where
My fortunes, and my friends, at stake, requir'd,
I should do so in honour: I am in this,
Your wife, your son, these senators, the nobles;
And you will rather show our general lowts
How you can frown, than spend a fawn upon them,
For the inheritance of their loves, and safeguard
Of what that want might ruin.

* * * * *

*Volumnia.* I pr'ythee now, my son,
Go to them, with this bonnet in thy hand;
And thus far having stretch'd it (here be with them),
Thy knee bussing the stones (for in such business
Action is eloquence, and the eyes of the ignorant
More learned than the ears), waving thy head,
Which often, thus, correcting thy stout heart,
Now humble, as the ripest mulberry
That will not hold the handling: Or, say to them,
Thou art their soldier, and being bred in broils,
Hast not the soft way, which, thou dost confess,
Were fit for thee to use, as they to claim,
In asking their good loves; but thou wilt frame
Thyself, forsooth, hereafter theirs, so far
As thou hast power, and person.

*Menenius.* This but done,
Even as she speaks, why, all their hearts were yours:

For they have pardons, being ask'd, as free
As words to little purpose.
*Volumnia.* Pr'ythee now,
Go, and be rul'd: although, I know, thou hadst rather
Follow thine enemy in a fiery gulf,
Than flatter him in a bower. Here is Cominius.

* * * * *

*Volumnia.* I pr'ythee now, sweet son; as thou hast said,
My praises made thee first a soldier, so,
To have my praise for this, perform a part
Thou hast not done before.

## Act IV. Scene II.

*Volumnia.* Ay, fool; is that a shame?—Note but this fool.—
Was not a man my father? Hadst thou foxship
To banish him that struck more blows for Rome,
Than thou hast spoken words?
*Sicinius.* O blessed heavens!
*Volumnia.* More noble blows, than ever thou wise words;
And for Rome's good.—I'll tell thee what:—Yet go:—
Nay, but thou shalt stay too:—I would my son
Were in Arabia, and thy tribe before him,
His good sword in his hand.
*Sicinius.* What then?

* * * * *

*Volumnia.* I would be had! 'Twas you incens'd the rabble:
Cats, that can judge as fitly of his worth,
As I can of those mysteries which heaven

Will not have earth to know.
*Brutus.* Pray, let us go.
*Volumnia.* Now, pray, sir, get you gone:
You have done a brave deed. Ere you go, hear this:
As far as doth the Capitol exceed
The meanest house in Rome: so far, my son
(This lady's husband here, this, do you see),
Whom you have banish'd, does exceed you all.
*Brutus.* Well, well, we'll leave you.
*Volumnia.* Take my prayers with you.—
I would the gods had nothing else to do,
But to confirm my curses! Could I meet them
But once a day, it would unclog my heart
Of what lies heavy to 't.
*Menenius.* You have told them home,
And, by my troth, you have cause. You'll sup with me?
*Volumnia.* Anger's my meat; I sup upon myself,
And so shall starve with feeding.—Come, let 's go:
Leave this faint puling, and lament as I do,
In anger, Juno-like. Come, come, come.

## Act V. Scene III.

*Volumnia.* * * * Thou know'st, great son,
The end of war's uncertain; but this certain,
That, if thou conquer Rome, the benefit
Which thou shalt thereby reap, is such a name,
Whose repetition will be dogg'd with curses:
Whose chronicle thus writ,—The man was noble,
But with his last attempt he wip'd it out;
Destroy'd his country; and his name remains
To the ensuing age, abhorr'd. Speak to me, son:

Thou hast affected the fine strains of honour,
To imitate the graces of the gods;
To tear with thunder the wide cheeks o' the air,
And yet to charge thy sulphur with a bolt
That should but rive an oak. Why dost not speak ?
Think'st thou it honourable for a noble man
Still to remember wrongs ?—Daughter, speak you :
He cares not for your weeping.—Speak thou, boy :
Perhaps, thy childishness will move him more
Than can our reasons.—There is no man in the world
More bound to his mother: yet here he lets me prate
Like one i' the stocks. Thou hast never in thy life
Show'd thy dear mother any courtesy;
When she (poor hen !) fond of no second brood,
Has cluck'd thee to the wars, and safely home,
Loaden with honour. Say, my request 's unjust,
And spurn me back : But, if it be not so,
Thou art not honest; and the gods will plague thee,
That thou restrain'st from me the duty, which
To a mother's part belongs.—He turns away :
Down, ladies; let us shame him with our knees.
To his surname Coriolanus 'longs more pride,
Than pity to our prayers. Down; an end :
This is the last;—So we will home to Rome,
And die among our neighbours.—Nay, behold us:
This boy, that cannot tell what he would have,
But kneels, and holds up hands, for fellowship,
Does reason our petition with more strength
Than thou hast to deny 't.—Come, let us go:
This fellow had a Volcian to his mother;
His wife is in Corioli, and his child
Like him by chance :—Yet give us our despatch;
I am hush'd until our city be afire,

And then I'll speak a little.

*Coriolanus.* O mother, mother!

[*Holding Volumnia by the hands, silent.*

What have you done? Behold, the heavens do ope,
The gods look down, and this unnatural scene
They laugh at. O my mother, mother! O!
You have won a happy victory to Rome:
But, for your son,—believe it, O, believe it,
Most dangerously you have with him prevail'd,
If not most mortal to him. But, let it come:—
Aufidius, though I cannot make true wars,
I'll frame convenient peace. Now, good Aufidius,
Were you in my stead, say, would you have heard
A mother less? or granted less, Aufidius?

*Aufidius.* I was mov'd withal.

* * * * *

*Coriolanus.* Ay, by and by;
But we will drink together; and you shall bear
A better witness back than words, which we,
On like conditions, will have counterseal'd.
Come, enter with us. Ladies, you deserve
To have a temple built you: all the swords
In Italy, and her confederate arms,
Could not have made this peace.

## Scene IV.

*Enter the* Ladies, *accompanied by* Senators, Patricians *and* People

1*st. Senator.* Behold our patroness, the life of Rome:
Call all your tribes together, praise the gods,
And make triumphant fires; strew flowers before them:

Unshout the noise that banish'd Marcius,
Repeal him with the welcome of his mother;
Cry,—Welcome, ladies, welcome!—
*All.* Welcome, ladies!
Welcome!

## Scene V.

*1st. Lord.* Bear from hence his body,
And mourn you for him: let him be regarded
As the most noble corse, that ever herald
Did follow to his urn.
*2nd. Lord.* His own impatience
Takes from Aufidius a great part of blame.
Let's make the best of it.
*Aufidius.* My rage is gone,
And I am struck with sorrow.—Take him up:
Help, three o' the chiefest officers; I'll be one.—
Beat thou the drum that it speak mournfully:
Trail your steel pikes.—Though in this city he
Hath widow'd and unchilded many a one,
Which to this hour bewail the injury,
Yet he shall have a noble memory.—
Assist. [*A dead march sounded.*

# KING HENRY VIII.

## Act II. Scene II.

*Norfolk.*

HOW holily he works in all his business !
And with what zeal ! For, now he has crack'd the league
Between us and the emperor, the queen's great nephew,
He dives into the king's soul ; and there scatters
Dangers, doubts, wringing of the conscience,
Fears, and despairs, and all these for his marriage :
And, out of all these to restore the king,
He counsels a divorce ; a loss of her,
That, like a jewel, has hung twenty years
About his neck, yet never lost her lustre ;
Of her, that loves him with that excellence
That angels love good men with ; even of her
That, when the greatest stroke of fortune falls,
Will bless the king : And is not this course pious ?

### Scene III.

*Anne Bullen.* Not for that neither;—Here's the pang that pinches:
His highness having liv'd so long with her: and she
So good a lady, that no tongue could ever
Pronounce dishonour of her,—by my life,
She never knew harm-doing;—O now, after
So many courses of the sun enthron'd,
Still growing in a majesty and pomp,—the which
To leave is a thousand-fold more bitter, than
'Tis sweet at first to acquire! it is a pity
Would move a monster.

### Scene IV.

*Queen Katharine.* Sir, I desire you, do me right and justice;
And to bestow your pity on me: for
I am a most poor woman, and a stranger,
Born out of your dominions; having here
No judge indifferent, nor no more assurance
Of equal friendship and proceeding. Alas, sir,
In what have I offended you? what cause
Hath my behaviour given to your displeasure,
That thus you should proceed to put me off,
And take your good grace from me? Heaven witness,
I have been to you a true and humble wife,
At all times to your will conformable:
Ever in fear to kindle your dislike,
Yea, subject to your countenance; glad, or sorry,
As I saw it inclin'd. When was the hour,

I ever contradicted your desire,
Or made it not mine too? Or which of your friends
Have I not strove to love, although I knew
He were mine enemy? what friend of mine
That had to him deriv'd your anger, did I
Continue in my liking? nay, gave notice
He was from thence discharg'd? Sir, call to mind
That I have been your wife, in this obedience,
Upwards of twenty years, and have been blest
With many children by you: If, in the course
And process of this time, you can report,
And prove it too, against mine honour aught,
My bond to wedlock, or my love and duty,
Against your sacred person, in God's name,
Turn me away; and let the foul'st contempt
Shut door upon me, and so give me up
To the sharpest kind of justice. Please you, sir,
The king, your father, was reputed for
A prince most prudent, of an excellent
And unmatch'd wit and judgment: Ferdinand,
My father, king of Spain, was reckon'd one
The wisest prince, that there had reign'd by many
A year before: It is not to be question'd
That they had gather'd a wise council to them
Of every realm, that did debate this business,
Who deem'd our marriage lawful: wherefore I humbly
Beseech you, sir, to spare me, till I may
Be by my friends in Spain advis'd; whose counsel
I will implore: if not; i' the name of God,
Your pleasure be fulfill'd!

* * * * *

*Queen Katharine.* Lord Cardinal,—
To you I speak.

*Wolsey.* Your pleasure, madam?

*Queen Katharine.* Sir,
I am about to weep; but, thinking that
We are a queen (or long have dream'd so), certain
The daughter of a king, my drops of tears
I'll turn to sparks of fire.

*Wolsey.* Be patient yet.

*Q. Katharine.* I will, when you are humble; nay, before,
Or God will punish me. I do believe,
Induc'd by potent circumstances, that
You are mine enemy; and make my challenge,
You shall not be my judge: for it is you
Have blown this coal betwixt my lord and me,—
Which God's dew quench!—Therefore, I say again,
I utterly abhor, yea, from my soul,
Refuse you for my judge; whom, yet once more,
I hold my most malicious foe, and think not
At all a friend to truth.

* * * * *

*Q. Katharine.* My lord! my lord
I am a simple woman, much too weak
To oppose your cunning. You are meek, and humble mouth'd;
You sign your place and calling, in full seeming,
With meekness and humility; but your heart
Is cramm'd with arrogancy, spleen, and pride.
You have, by fortune, and his highness' favours,
Gone slightly o'er low steps; and now are mounted
Where powers are your retainers: and your wards,
Domesticks to you, serve your will, as 't please
Yourself pronounce their office. I must tell you,
You tender more your person's honour, than
Your high profession spiritual: That again

I do refuse you for my judge; and here,
Before you all, appeal unto the pope,
To bring my whole cause 'fore his holiness,
And to be judg'd by him.

* * * * *

*K. Henry.* Go thy ways, Kate:
That man i' the world, who shall report he has
A better wife, let him in nought be trusted,
For speaking false in that; Thou art, alone,
(If thy rare qualities, sweet gentleness,
Thy meekness saint-like, wife-like government,—
Obeying in commanding,—and thy parts
Sovereign and pious else, could speak thee out),
The queen of earthly queens:—She is noble born;
And, like her true nobility, she has
Carried herself towards me.

* * * * *

*K. Henry.* I then mov'd you,
My lord of Canterbury; and got your leave
To make this present summons:—Unsolicited
I left no reverend person in this court;
But by particular consent proceeded,
Under your hands and seals. Therefore, go on:
For no dislike i' the world against the person
Of the good queen, but the sharp thorny points
Of my alleged reasons, drive this forward:
Prove but our marriage lawful, by my life,
And kingly dignity, we are contented
To wear our mortal state to come, with her,
Katharine our queen, before the primest creature
That's paragon'd o' the world.

ACT III. SCENE I.

*Wolsey.* Tanta est ergà te mentis integritas,
Regina serenissima,—

*Q. Katharine.* O, good my lord, no Latin;
I am not such a truant since my coming,
As not to know the language I have liv'd in:
A strange tongue makes my cause more strange, suspicious;
Pray, speak in English: here are some will thank you,
If you speak truth, for their poor mistress' sake;
Believe me, she has had much wrong: Lord cardinal,
The willing'st sin I ever yet committed,
May be absolv'd in English.

* * * * *

*Q. Katharine.* Ye tell me what ye wish for both, my ruin:
Is this your Christian counsel? out upon ye!
Heaven is above all yet; there sits a judge,
That no king can corrupt.

* * * * *

*Q. Katharine.* Have I liv'd thus long—(let me speak myself,
Since virtue finds no friends),—a wife, a true one?
A woman (I dare say, without vain-glory),
Never yet branded with suspicion?
Have I with all my full affections
Still met the king? lov'd him next heaven? obey'd him?
Been, out of fondness, superstitious to him?
Almost forgot my prayers to content him?
And am I thus rewarded? 'tis not well, lords.
Bring me a constant woman to her husband,
One that ne'er dream'd a joy beyond his pleasure;

And to that woman, when she has done most,
Yet will I add an honour,—a great patience.

*Wolsey.* Madam, you wander from the good we aim at.

*Q. Katharine.* My lord, I dare not make myself so guilty,
To give up willingly that noble title
Your master wed me to: nothing but death
Shall e'er divorce my dignities.

*Wolsey.* 'Pray, hear me.

*Q. Katharine.* 'Would I had never trod this English earth,
Or felt the flatteries that grow upon it!
Ye have angels' faces, but heaven knows your hearts.
What will become of me now, wretched lady?
I am the most unhappy woman living.—
Alas! poor wenches, where are now your fortunes?
[*To her women.*
Shipwreck'd upon a kingdom, where no pity,
No friends, no hope; no kindred weep for me,
Almost, no grave allow'd me:—Like the lily,
That once was mistress of the field, and flourish'd,
I'll hang my head, and perish.

## Act IV. Scene II.

*Griffith,* How does your grace?

*Katharine.* O Griffith, sick to death:
My legs, like loaden branches, bow to the earth,
Willing to leave their burden: Reach a chair;—
So,—now, methinks, I feel a little ease.
Didst thou not tell me, Griffith, as thou led'st me,
That the great child of honour, Cardinal Wolsey,
Was dead?

*Griffith.* Yes, madam; but, I think, your grace,
Out of the pain you suffer'd, gave no ear to't.

*Katharine.* Pr'ythee, good Griffith, tell me how he died:
If well, he stepp'd before me, happily,
For my example.

*Griffith.* Well, the voice goes, madam:
For after the stout Earl Northumberland
Arrested him at York, and brought him forward
(As a man sorely tainted) to his answer,
He fell sick suddenly, and grew so ill,
He could not sit his mule.

*Katharine.* Alas! poor man!

*Griffith.* At last, with easy roads, he came to Leicester,
Lodg'd in the Abbey; where the reverend abbot,
With all his convent, honourably receiv'd him;
To whom he gave these words,—O father abbot,
An old man, broken with the storms of state,
Is come to lay his weary bones among ye;
Give him a little earth for charity!
So went to bed: where eagerly his sickness
Pursu'd him still; and, three nights after this,
About the hour of eight (which he himself
Foretold, should be his last), full of repentance,
Continual meditations, tears, and sorrows,
He gave his honours to the world again,
His blessed part to heaven, and slept in peace.

*Katharine.* So may he rest; his faults lie gently on him!
Yet thus far, Griffith, give me leave to speak him,
And yet with charity,—He was a man
Of an unbounded stomach, ever ranking
Himself with princes; one, that by suggestion
Ty'd all the kingdom: simony was fair play;
His own opinion was his law: I' the presence

He would say untruths; and be ever double,
Both in his words and meaning: He was never,
But where he meant to ruin, pitiful:
His promises were, as he then was, mighty;
But his performance, as he is now, nothing.
Of his own body he was ill, and gave
The clergy ill example.

*Griffith.* Noble madam,
Men's evil manners live in brass; their virtues
We write in water. May it please your highness
To hear me speak his good now?

*Katharine.* Yes, good Griffith;
I were malicious else.

*Griffith.* This cardinal,
Though from an humble stock, undoubtedly
Was fashion'd to much honour from his cradle.
He was a scholar, and a ripe, and good one;
Exceeding wise, fair spoken, and persuading:
Lofty, and sour, to them that lov'd him not;
But, to those men that sought him, sweet as summer.
And though he were unsatisfied in getting
(Which was a sin), yet in bestowing, madam,
He was most princely: Ever witness for him
Those twins of learning, that he rais'd in you,
Ipswich, and Oxford! one of which fell with him,
Unwilling to outlive the good that did it;
The other, though unfinish'd, yet so famous,
So excellent in art, and still so rising,
That Christendom shall ever speak his virtue.
His overthrow heap'd happiness upon him;
For then, and not till then, he felt himself,
And found the blessedness of being little:
And, to add greater honours to his age

Than man could give him, he died, fearing God.

*Katharine.* After my death I wish no other herald,
No other speaker of my living actions,
To keep mine honour from corruption,
But such an honest chronicler as Griffith.
Whom I most hated living, thou hast made me,
With thy religious truth, and modesty,
Now in his ashes honour: Peace be with him!—
Patience, be near me still; and set me lower:
I have not long to trouble thee.—Good Griffith,
Cause the musicians play me that sad note
I nam'd my knell, whilst I sit meditating
On that celestial harmony I go to.

*Griffith.* She is asleep: Good wench, let's sit down quiet,
For fear we wake her;—Softly, gentle Patience.

[*The Vision takes place.*

*Katharine.* Spirits of peace, where are ye? Are ye all gone?
And leave me here in wretchedness behind ye?

*Griffith.* Madam, we are here.

*Katharine.* It is not you I call for:
Saw ye none enter, since I slept?

*Griffith.* None, madam.

*Katharine.* No? Saw you not, even now, a blessed troop
Invite me to a banquet; whose bright faces
Cast thousand beams upon me, like the sun?
They promis'd me eternal happiness;
And brought me garlands, Griffith, which I feel
I am not worthy yet to wear: I shall,
Assuredly.

*Griffith.* I am most joyful, madam, such good dreams

Possess your fancy.

*Katharine.* Bid the musick leave,
They are harsh and heavy to me.

*Patience.* Do you note,
How much her grace is alter'd on the sudden?
How long her face is drawn? How pale she looks,
And of an earthly cold? Mark you her eyes?

*Griffith.* She is going, wench; pray, pray.

*Patience.* Heaven comfort her!

* * * * *

*Re-enter* GRIFFITH *with* CAPUCIUS.

*Katharine.* If my sight fail not,
You should be lord ambassador from the emperor,
My royal nephew, and your name Capucius.

*Capucius.* Madam, the same, your servant.

*Katharine.* O my lord,
The times, and titles, now are alter'd strangely
With me, since first you knew me. But, I pray you,
What is your pleasure with me?

*Capucius.* Noble lady,
First, mine own service to your grace; the next,
The king's request that I would visit you;
Who grieves much for your weakness, and by me
Sends you his princely commendations,
And heartily entreats you take good comfort.

*Katharine.* O my good lord, that comfort comes too late;
'Tis like a pardon after execution:
That gentle physick, given in time, had cur'd me;
But now I am past all comforts here, but prayers.
How does his highness?

*Capucius.* Madam, in good health.

*Katharine.* So may he ever do ! and ever flourish,
When I shall dwell with worms, and my poor name
Banish'd the kingdom !—Patience, is that letter
I caus'd you write, yet sent away ?

*Patience.* No, madam.

*Katharine.* Sir, I most humbly pray you to deliver
This to my lord the king.

*Capucius.* Most willing, madam.

*Katharine.* In which I have commended to his goodness
The model of our chaste loves, his young daughter :—
The dews of heaven fall thick in blessings on her !—
Beseeching him, to give her virtuous breeding
(She is young, and of a noble modest nature;
I hope, she will deserve well) ; and a little
To love her for her mother's sake, that lov'd him,
Heaven knows how dearly. My next poor petition
Is that his noble grace would have some pity
Upon my wretched women, that so long
Have follow'd both my fortunes faithfully :
Of which there is not one, I dare avow
(And now I should not lie), but will deserve,
For virtue, and true beauty of the soul,
For honesty, and decent carriage,
A right good husband, let him be a noble ;
And, sure, those men are happy that shall have them.
The last is, for my men : they are the poorest,
But poverty could never draw them from me ;—
That they may have their wages duly paid them,
And something over to remember me by ;
If heaven had pleas'd to have given me longer life,
And able means, we had not parted thus.
These are the whole contents ;—And, good my lord,
By that you love the dearest in this world,

As you wish christian peace to souls departed,
Stand these poor people's friend, and urge the king
To do me this last right.
*Capucius.* By heaven, I will;
Or let me lose the fashion of a man!
*Katharine.* I thank you, honest lord. Remember me
In all humility unto his highness;
Say, his long trouble now is passing
Out of this world: tell him, in death I bless'd him,
For so I will.—Mine eyes grow dim.—Farewell,
My lord.—Griffith, farewell.—Nay, Patience,
You must not leave me yet. I must to bed;
Call in more women.—When I am dead, good wench,
Let me be us'd with honour; strew me over
With maiden flowers, that all the world may know
I was a chaste wife to my grave: embalm me,
Then lay me forth: although unqueen'd, yet like
A queen, and daughter to a king, inter me.
I can no more.——

## FIRST PART OF KING HENRY IV.

### ACT II. SCENE III.

*Lady Percy.*

O MY good lord, why are you thus alone?
For what offence have I, this fortnight, been
A banish'd woman from my Harry's bed?
Tell me, sweet lord, what is't that takes from thee
Thy stomach, pleasure, and thy golden sleep?
Why dost thou bend thine eyes upon the earth;
And start so often when thou sit'st alone?
Why hast thou lost the fresh blood in thy cheeks;
And given my treasures, and my rights of thee,
To thick-ey'd musing, and curs'd melancholy?
In thy faint slumbers, I by thee have watch'd,
And heard thee murmur tales of iron wars:
Speak terms of manage to thy bounding steed;
Cry, Courage!—to the field! And thou hast talk'd
Of sallies, and retires; of trenches, tents,
Of palisadoes, frontiers, parapets;
Of basilisks, of cannon, culverin;
Of prisoners' ransom, and of soldiers slain,

And all the 'currents of a heady fight.
Thy spirit within thee hath been so at war,
And thus hath so bestirr'd thee in thy sleep,
That beads of sweat have stood upon thy brow,
Like bubbles in a late disturbed stream:
And in thy face strange motions have appear'd,
Such as we see when men restrain their breath
On some great sudden haste. O, what portents are these?
Some heavy business hath my lord in hand,
And I must know it, else he loves me not.

*Hotspur.* What, ho! is Gilliams with the packet gone?

*Enter* Servant.

*Servant.* He is, my lord, an hour ago.

*Hotspur.* Hath Butler brought those horses from the sheriff?

*Servant.* One horse, my lord, he brought even now.

*Hotspur.* What horse? a roan, a crop-ear, is it not?

*Servant.* It is, my lord.

*Hotspur.* That roan shall be my throne.
Well, I will back him straight: O *espérance!*—
Bid Butler lead him forth into the park. [*Exit Servant.*

*Lady.* But hear you, my lord.

*Hotspur.* What say'st thou, my lady?

*Lady.* What is it carries you away?

*Hotspur.* My horse,
My love, my horse.

*Lady.* Out, you mad-headed ape!
A weasel hath not such a deal of spleen,
As you are toss'd with. In faith,
I'll know your business, Harry, that I will.
I fear, my brother Mortimer doth stir
About his title; and hath sent for you,

To line his enterprise: But if you go—
*Hotspur.* So far afoot, I shall be weary, love.
*Lady.* Come, come, you paraquito, answer me
Directly to this question that I ask.
In faith, I'll break thy little finger, Harry,
An if thou wilt not tell me all things true.
*Hotspur.* Away,
Away, you trifler!—Love?—I love thee not,
I care not for thee, Kate: this is no world,
To play with mammets, and to tilt with lips:
We must have bloody noses, and crack'd crowns,
And pass them current too.—Gods me, my horse!—
What say'st thou, Kate? what wouldst thou have with me?
*Lady.* Do you not love me? do you not indeed?
Well, do not then; for since you love me not,
I will not love myself. Do you not love me?
Nay, tell me, if you speak in jest, or no.
*Hotspur.* Come, wilt thou see me ride?
And when I am o' horse-back, I will swear
I love thee infinitely. But hark you, Kate;
I must not have you henceforth question me
Whither I go, nor reason whereabout:
Whither I must, I must; and, to conclude,
This evening must I leave you, gentle Kate.
I know you wise; but yet no further wise,
Than Harry Percy's wife: constant you are;
But yet a woman: and for secrecy,
No lady closer; for I well believe,
Thou wilt not utter what thou dost not know;
And so far will I trust thee, gentle Kate!
*Lady.* How! so far?
*Hotspur.* Not an inch further. But hark you, Kate?
Whither I go, thither shall you go too;

To-day will I set forth, to-morrow you.—
Will this content you, Kate?

*Lady.* It must, of force.

[*Exeunt.*

## Act III. Scene I.

*Mortimer.* I understand thy looks: that pretty Welsh
Which thou pourest down from these swelling heavens,
I am too perfect in; and, but for shame,
In such a parley would I answer thee. [*Lady M. speaks.*
I understand thy kisses, and thou mine,
And that 's a feeling disputation:
But I will never be a truant, love,
Till I have learn'd thy language; for thy tongue
Makes Welsh as sweet as ditties highly penn'd,
Sung by a fair queen in a summer's bower,
With ravishing division, to her lute.

*Glendower.* Nay, if you melt, then will she run mad.

[*Lady M. speaks again.*

*Mortimer.* O, I am ignorance itself in this.

*Glendower.* She bids you on the wanton rushes lay you down,
And rest your gentle head upon her lap,
And she will sing the song that pleaseth you,
And on your eyelids crown the god of sleep,
Charming your blood with pleasing heaviness;
Making such difference 'twixt wake and sleep,
As is the difference betwixt day and night,
The hour before the heavenly-harness'd team
Begins his golden progress in the east.

*Mortimer.* With all my heart I'll sit, and hear her sing:

By that time will our book, I think, be drawn.
*Glendower.* Do so ;
And those musicians that shall play to you,
Hang in the air a thousand leagues from hence ;
And straight they shall be here : sit, and attend.
*Hotspur.* Come, Kate, thou art perfect in lying down :
Come, quick, quick ; that I may lay my head in thy lap.
*Lady P.* Go, ye giddy goose.

## SECOND PART OF KING HENRY IV.

### ACT II. SCENE. III.

*Northumberland.*

I PRAY thee, loving wife, and gentle daughter,
Give even way unto my rough affairs;
Put not you on the visage of the times,
And be, like them, to Percy troublesome.

*Lady N.* I have given over, I will speak no more:
Do what you will; your wisdom be your guide.

*Northumberland.* Alas, sweet wife, my honour is at pawn;
And, but my going, nothing can redeem it.

*Lady Percy.* O, yet, for God's sake, go not to these wars!
The time was, father, that you broke your word,
When you were more endear'd to it than now;
When your own Percy, when my heart's dear Harry,
Threw many a northward look, to see his father
Bring up his powers: but he did long in vain.
Who then persuaded you to stay at home?
There were two honours lost; yours, and your son's.
For yours,—may heavenly glory brighten it!

For his,—it stuck upon him, as the sun
In the grey vault of heaven: and, by his light,
Did all the chivalry of England move
To do brave acts; he was, indeed, the glass
Wherein the noble youth did dress themselves.
He had no legs, that practis'd not his gait:
And speaking thick, which nature made his blemish,
Became the accents of the valiant;
For those that could speak low, and tardily,
Would turn their own perfection to abuse,
To seem like him: So that, in speech, in gait,
In diet, in affections of delight,
In military rules, humours of blood,
He was the mark and glass, copy and book,
That fashion'd others. And him,—O wondrous him!
O miracle of men!—him did you leave
(Second to none, unseconded by you),
To look upon the hideous god of war
In disadvantage; to abide a field,
Where nothing but the sound of Hotspur's name
Did seem defensible:—so you left him:
Never, O never, do his ghost the wrong,
To hold your honour more precise and nice
With others, than with him; let them alone;
The marshal, and the archbishop, are strong:
Had my sweet Harry had but half their numbers,
To-day might I, hanging on Hotspur's neck,
Have talk'd of Monmouth's grave.

* * * * *

*Lady Northumberland.* O, fly to Scotland,
Till that the nobles, and the armed commons,
Have of their puissance made a little taste.

*Lady Percy.* If they get ground and vantage of the king,

Then join you with them, like a rib of steel,
To make strength stronger; but, for all our loves,
First let them try themselves: So did your son;
He was so suffer'd; so came I a widow;
And never shall have length of life enough,
To rain upon remembrance with mine eyes,
That it may grow and sprout as high as heaven,
For recordation to my noble husband.

*Northumberland.* Come, come, go in with me: 'tis with my mind
As with the tide swell'd up unto its height,
That makes a still-stand, running neither way.
Fain would I go to meet the archbishop,
But many thousand reasons hold me back:—
I will resolve for Scotland; there am I,
Till time and vantage crave my company.

## FIRST PART OF KING HENRY VI.

### Act I. Scene II.

*Bastard.*

WHERE 's the prince Dauphin? I have news for him.

*Charles.* Bastard of Orleans, thrice welcome to us.

*Bastard.* Methinks, your looks are sad, your cheer appall'd;
Hath the late overthrow wrought this offence?
Be not dismay'd, for succour is at hand:
A holy maid hither with me I bring
Which, by a vision sent to her from heaven,
Ordained is to raise this tedious siege,
And drive the English forth the bounds of France.
The spirit of deep prophecy she hath,
Exceeding the nine sibyls of old Rome;
What 's past, and what 's to come, she can descry.
Speak, shall I call her in? Believe my words,
For they are certain and unfallible.

*Charles.* Go, call her in: But, first to try her skill
Reignier, stand thou as Dauphin in my place:

Question her proudly, let thy looks be stern :—
By this means shall we sound what skill she hath.

*Enter* LA PUCELLE *and others.*

*Reignier.* Fair maid, is 't thou wilt do these wond'rous feats?

*Pucelle.* Reignier, is 't thou that thinkest to beguile me?—
Where is the Dauphin ?—come, come from behind ;
I know thee well, though never seen before.
Be not amaz'd, there 's nothing hid from me :
In private will I talk with thee apart :—
Stand back, you lords, and give us leave a while.

*Reignier.* She takes upon her bravely at first dash.

*Pucelle.* Dauphin, I am by birth a shepherd's daughter,
My wit untrain'd in any kind of art.
Heaven and our Lady gracious, hath it pleas'd
To shine on my contemptible estate :
Lo, whilst I waited on my tender lambs,
And to sun's parching heat display'd my cheeks,
God's mother deigned to appear to me ;
And, in a vision full of majesty,
Will'd me to leave my base vocation,
And free my country from calamity :
Her aid she promis'd, and assur'd success :
In complete glory she reveal'd herself ;
And, whereas I was black and swart before,
With those clear rays which she infus'd on me,
That beauty am I bless'd with, which you see.
Ask me what question thou canst possible,
And I will answer unpremeditated :
My courage try by combat, if thou dar'st,
And thou shalt find that I exceed my sex,

Resolve on this : Thou shalt be fortunate,
If thou receive me for thy warlike mate.

* * * * *

*Pucelle.* Assign'd am I to be the English scourge.
This night the siege assuredly I'll raise :
Expect Saint Martin's summer, halcyon days,
Since I have entered into these wars.
Glory is like a circle in the water,
Which never ceaseth to enlarge itself,
Till, by broad spreading, it disperse to nought
With Henry's death, the English circle ends ;
Dispersed are the glories it included.
Now am I like that proud insulting ship,
Which Cæsar and his fortune bore at once.
*Charles.* Was Mahomet inspired with a dove ?
Thou with an eagle art inspired then.
Helen, the mother of great Constantine,
Nor yet Saint Philip's daughters, were like thee.
Bright star of Venus, fall'n down on the earth,
How may I reverently worship thee enough ?
*Alençon.* Leave off delays, and let us raise the siege.
*Reignier.* Woman, do what thou canst to save our honours ;
Drive them from Orleans, and be immortaliz'd.
*Charles.* Presently we'll try :—Come, let's away about it :
No prophet will I trust, if she prove false.

## Scene VI.

*Pucelle.* Advance our waving colours on the walls ;
Rescu'd is Orleans from the English wolves :—
Thus Joan la Pucelle hath perform'd her word.
*Charles.* Divinest creature, bright Astrea's daughter,

How shall I honour thee for this success?
Thy promises are like Adonis' gardens,
That one day bloom'd, and fruitful were the next.—
France, triumph in thy glorious prophetess?—
Recover'd is the town of Orleans:
More blessed hap did ne'er befall our state.
*Reignier.* Why ring not out the bells throughout the town?
Dauphin, command the citizens make bonfires,
And feast and banquet in the open streets,
To celebrate the joy that God hath given us.
*Alençon.* All France will be replete with mirth and joy,
When they shall hear how we have play'd the men.
*Charles.* 'Tis Joan, not we, by whom the day is won;
For which, I will divide my crown with her:
And all the priests and friars in my realm
Shall, in procession, sing her endless praise.
A statelier pyramis to her I'll rear,
Than Rhodope's, of Memphis, ever was:
In memory of her, when she is dead,
Her ashes, in an urn more precious
Than the rich-jewel'd coffer of Darius,
Transported shall be at high festivals
Before the kings and queens of France.
No longer on Saint Dennis will we cry,
But Joan la Pucelle shall be France's saint.
Come in; and let us banquet royally,
After this golden day of victory.

# THIRD PART OF KING HENRY VI.

## Act III. Scene II.

*King Edward.*

BROTHER of Gloster, at St. Albans' field
This lady's husband, Sir John Grey, was slain,
His lands then seiz'd on by the conqueror:
Her suit is now, to repossess those lands;
Which we in justice cannot well deny,
Because in quarrel of the house of York
The worthy gentleman did lose his life.

*Gloster.* Your highness shall do well, to grant her suit;
It were dishonour, to deny it her.

*K. Edw.* It were no less; but yet I'll make a pause.

*Gloster* (*aside to Clarence*). Yea! is it so?
I see, the lady hath a thing to grant,
Before the king will grant her humble suit.

*K. Edw.* Widow, we will consider of your suit;
And come some other time, to know our mind.

*Lady Grey.* Right gracious lord, I cannot brook delay:
May it please your highness to resolve me now;
And what your pleasure is, shall satisfy me.

* * * * *

*K. Edw.* How many children hast thou, widow? tell me.

*Lady Grey.* Three, my most gracious lord.

*K. Edw.* 'Twere pity, they should lose their father's land.

*Lady Grey.* Be pitiful, dread lord, and grant it then.

*K. Edw.* Now tell me, madam, do you love your children?

*Lady Grey.* Ay, full as dearly as I love myself.

*K. Edw.* And would you not do much, to do them good?

*Lady Grey.* To do them good, I would sustain some harm.

*K. Edw.* Then get your husband's lands, to do them good.

*Lady Grey.* Therefore come I unto your majesty.

*K. Edw.* I'll tell you how these lands are to be got.

*Lady Grey.* So shall you bind me to your highness' service.

*K. Edw.* What service wilt thou do me, if I give them?

*Lady Grey.* What you command, that rests in me to do.

*K. Edw.* But you will take exceptions to my boon.

*Lady Grey.* No, gracious lord, except I cannot do it.

*K. Edw.* Ay, but thou canst do what I mean to ask.

*Lady Grey.* Why, then I will do what your grace commands.

* * * * *

*Lady Grey.* Why stops my lord? shall I not hear my task?

*K. Edw.* An easy task; 'tis but to love a king.

*Lady Grey.* That's soon performed, because I am a subject.

*K. Edw.* Why then, thy husband's lands I freely give thee.

*Lady Grey.* I take my leave with many thousand thanks.

*K. Edw.* But stay thee, 'tis the fruits of love I mean.

*Lady Grey.* The fruits of love I mean, my loving liege.

*K. Edw.* Ay, but I fear me, in another sense.
What love, think'st thou, I sue so much to get?

*Lady Grey.* My love till death, my humble thanks, my prayers;
That love, which virtue begs, and virtue grants.

*K. Edw.* No, by my troth, I do not mean such love.

*Lady Grey.* Why, then you mean not as I thought you did.

*K. Edw.* But now you partly may perceive my mind.

*Lady Grey.* My mind will never grant what I perceive
Your highness aims at, if I aim aright.

*K. Edw.* To tell thee plain, I am to lie with thee.

*Lady Grey.* To tell you plain, I had rather lie in prison.

*K. Edw.* Why, then thou shalt not have thy husband's lands.

*Lady Grey.* Why, then mine honesty shall be my dower;
For by that loss I will not purchase them.

*K. Edw.* Therein thou wrong'st thy children mightily.

*Lady Grey.* Herein your highness wrongs both them and me.
But, mighty lord, this merry inclination
Accords not with the sadness of my suit;
Please you dismiss me, either with ay, or no.

*K. Edw.* Ay; if thou wilt say ay, to my request:
No; if thou dost say no, to my demand.

*Lady Grey.* Then, no, my lord. My suit is at an end.

*K. Edw.* (*aside*). Her looks do argue her replete with modesty;
Her words do show her wit incomparable;
All her perfections challenge sovereignty:
One way, or other, she is for a king;
And she shall be my love, or else my queen.—

Say, that King Edward take thee for his queen?

*Lady Grey.* 'Tis better said than done, my gracious lord:

I am a subject fit to jest withal,
But far unfit to be a sovereign.

*K. Edw.* Sweet widow, by my state I swear to thee,
I speak no more than what my soul intends;
And that is, to enjoy thee for my love.

*Lady Grey.* And that is more than I will yield unto:
I know I am too mean to be your queen:
And yet too good to be your concubine.

*K. Edw.* You cavil, widow; I did mean, my queen.

*Lady Grey.* 'Twill grieve your grace, my sons should call you—father.

*K. Edw.* No more, than when thy daughters call thee mother.

Thou art a widow, and thou hast some children;
And, by God's mother, I, being but a bachelor,
Have other some: why, 'tis a happy thing
To be the father unto many sons.
Answer no more, for thou shalt be my queen.

## Act IV. Scene I.

*Gloster.* Now tell me, brother Clarence, what think you
Of this new marriage with the Lady Grey?
Hath not our brother made a worthy choice?

*Clarence.* Alas, you know, 'tis far from hence to France;
How could he stay till Warwick made return?

*Somerset.* My lords, forbear this talk; here comes the king.

*Gloster.* And his well chosen bride.

*Clarence.* I mind to tell him plainly what I think.

*Enter the* KING *and* LADY GREY, *as* QUEEN ELIZABETH, *attended.*

*K. Edw.* Now, brother of Clarence, how like you our choice,
That you stand pensive as half malcontent?

*     *     *     *     *

*K. Edw.* Setting your scorns, and your mislike, aside,
Tell me some reason, why the Lady Grey
Should not become my wife, and England's queen:—
And you too, Somerset, and Montague,
Speak fully what you think.

*     *     *     *     *

*K. Edw.* Alas, poor Clarence! is it for a wife,
That thou art malcontent? I will provide thee.

*Clarence.* In choosing for yourself, you show'd your judgment;
Which being shallow, you shall give me leave
To play the broker in mine own behalf;
And to that end, I shortly mind to leave you.

*K. Edw.* Leave me, or tarry, Edward will be king,
And not be tied unto his brother's will.

*Q. Eliz.* My lords, before it pleased his majesty
To raise my state to title of a queen,
Do me but right, and you must all confess
That I was not ignoble of descent,
And meaner than myself have had like fortune.
But as this title honours me and mine,
So your dislikes, to whom I would be pleasing,
Do cloud my joys with danger and with sorrow.

*K. Edw.* My love, forbear to fawn upon their frowns:
What danger, or what sorrow can befall thee,
So long as Edward is thy constant friend,

And their true sovereign, whom they must obey?
Nay, whom they shall obey, and love thee too,
Unless they seek for hatred at my hands:
Which if they do, yet will I keep thee safe,
And they shall feel the vengeance of my wrath.

## ACT V. SCENE VII.

KING EDWARD *is discovered sitting on his throne.* QUEEN ELIZABETH *with the infant* PRINCE, CLARENCE, GLOSTER, HASTINGS *and others, near him.*

*K. Edw.* Once more we sit in England's royal throne,
Repurchas'd with the blood of enemies.
What valiant foemen, like to autumn's corn,
Have we mow'd down, in tops of all their pride?
Three dukes of Somerset, threefold renown'd
For hardy and undoubted champions:
Two Cliffords, as the father and the son,
And two Northumberlands; two braver men
Ne'er spurr'd their coursers at the trumpet's sound:
With them, the two brave bears, Warwick and Montague,
That in their chains fetter'd the kingly lion,
And made the forest tremble when they roar'd.
Thus have we swept suspicion from our seat,
And made our footstool of security.—
Come hither, Bess, and let me kiss my boy:—
Young Ned, for thee, thine uncles, and myself,
Have in our armours watch'd the winter's night;
Went all a foot in summer's scalding heat,
That thou might'st repossess the crown in peace;
And of our labours thou shalt reap the gain.

# KING RICHARD II.

## ACT III. SCENE IV.

*Queen.*

WHAT sport shall we devise here in this garden,
To drive away the heavy thought of care?
*Lady.* Madam, we 'll play at bowls.
*Queen.* 'T will make me think,
The world is full of rubs, and that my fortune
Runs 'gainst the bias.
*Lady.* Madam, we will dance.
*Queen.* My legs can keep no measure in delight,
When my poor heart no measure keeps in grief;
Therefore, no dancing, girl; some other sport.
*Lady.* Madam, we 'll tell tales.
*Queen.* Of sorrow, or of joy?
*Lady.* Of either, madam.
*Queen.* Of neither, girl:
For if of joy, being altogether wanting,
It doth remember me the more of sorrow;
Or if of grief, being altogether had,
It adds more sorrow to my want of joy:

For what I have, I need not to repeat:
And what I want, it boots not to complain.
*Lady.* Madam, I 'll sing.
*Queen.* 'Tis well, that thou hast cause;
But thou should'st please me better, would'st thou weep.
*Lady.* I could weep, madam, would it do you good.
*Queen.* And I could weep, would weeping do me good,
And never borrow any tear of thee.
But stay, here come the gardeners:
Let 's step into the shadow of these trees.—
My wretchedness unto a row of pins,
They 'll talk of state; for every one doth so
Against a change: Woe is forerun with woe.
[*Queen and Ladies retire.*

* * * * *

*Gardener.* Depress'd he is already; and depos'd,
'Tis doubt, he will be: Letters came last night
To a dear friend of the good Duke of York's,
That tell black tidings.
*Queen.* O, I am press'd to death,
Through want of speaking!—Thou, old Adam's likeness,
[*Coming from her concealment.*
Set to dress this garden, how dares
Thy harsh-rude tongue sound this unpleasing news?
What Eve, what serpent hath suggested thee
To make a second fall of cursed man?
Why dost thou say, King Richard is depos'd?
Dar'st thou, thou little better thing than earth,
Divine his downfall? Say, where, when, and how,
Cam'st thou by these ill tidings? speak, thou wretch.
*Gardener.* Pardon me, madam: little joy have I,
To breathe this news; yet, what I say is true.
King Richard, he is in the mighty hold

Of Bolingbroke: their fortunes both are weigh'd:
In your lord's scale is nothing but himself,
And some few vanities that make him light;
But in the balance of great Bolingbroke,
Besides himself, are all the English peers,
And with that odds he weighs King Richard down.
Post you to London, and you'll find it so;
I speak no more than every one doth know.

*Queen.* Nimble mischance, that art so light of foot,
Doth not thy embassage belong to me,
And am I last that knows it? O, thou think'st
To serve me last, that I may longest keep
Thy sorrow in my breast.—Come, ladies, go,
To meet at London London's king in woe.—
What, was I born to this! that my sad look
Should grace the triumph of great Bolingbroke?—
Gardener, for telling me this news of woe,
I would, the plants thou graft'st, may never grow.
[*Exeunt Queen and Ladies.*

*Gardener.* Poor queen! so that thy state might be no worse,
I would, my skill were subject to thy curse.—
Here did she drop a tear; here, in this place,
I'll set a bank of rue, sour herb of grace:
Rue, even for ruth, here shortly shall be seen,
In the remembrance of a weeping queen. [*Exeunt.*

## ACT V. SCENE I.

*Queen.* This way the king will come; this is the way
To Julius Cæsar's ill-erected tower,
To whose flint bosom my condemned lord

Is doom'd a prisoner, by proud Bolingbroke:
Here let us rest, if this rebellious earth
Have any resting for her true king's queen.

*Enter* KING RICHARD *and* GUARDS.

But soft, but see, or rather do not see,
My fair rose wither: Yet look up; behold;
That you in pity may dissolve to dew,
And wash him fresh again with true-love tears.—
Ah, thou, the model where old Troy did stand;
Thou map of honour; thou King Richard's tomb,
And not King Richard; thou most beauteous inn,
Why should hard-favour'd grief be lodg'd in thee,
When triumph is become an alehouse guest?
*K. Rich.* Join not with grief, fair woman, do not so,
To make my end too sudden: learn, good soul,
To think our former state a happy dream;
From which awak'd, the truth of what we are
Shows us but this; I am sworn brother, sweet,
To grim necessity; and he and I
Will keep a league till death. Hie thee to France,
And cloister thee in some religious house:
Our holy lives must win a new world's crown,
Which our profane hours here have stricken down.
*Queen.* What, is my Richard both in shape and mind
Transform'd and weakened? Hath Bolingbroke
Depos'd thine intellect? hath he been in thy heart?
The lion, dying, thrusteth forth his paw,
And wounds the earth, if nothing else, with rage
To be o'erpower'd; and wilt thou, pupil-like,
Take thy correction mildly? kiss the rod,
And fawn on rage with base humility,
Which art a lion, and a king of beasts?

*K. Rich.* A king of beasts, indeed; if aught but beasts,
I had been still a happy king of men.
Good sometime queen, prepare thee hence for France:
Think, I am dead; and that even here thou tak'st,
As from my death-bed, my last living leave.
In winter's tedious nights, sit by the fire
With good old folks, and let them tell thee tales
Of woful ages, long ago betid:
And, ere thou bid good night, to quit their grief,
Tell thou the lamentable fall of me,
And send the hearers weeping to their beds.
For why, the senseless brands will sympathize
The heavy accent of thy moving tongue,
And, in compassion, weep the fire out:
And some will mourn in ashes, some coal-black,
For the deposing of a rightful king.

* * * * *

*Northumberland.* My guilt be on my head, and there an end.
Take leave, and part; for you must part forthwith.
*K. Rich.* Doubly divorc'd?—Bad men, ye violate
A twofold marriage; 'twixt my crown and me;
And then, betwixt me and my married wife.—
Let me unkiss the oath 'twixt thee and me;
And yet not so, for with a kiss 'twas made.—
Part us, Northumberland: I towards the north,
Where shivering cold and sickness pines the clime;
My wife to France; from whence, set forth in pomp,
She came adorned hither like sweet May,
Sent back like Hallowmas, or short'st of day.
*Queen.* And must we be divided? must we part?
*K. Rich.* Ay, hand from hand, my love, and heart from heart.

*Queen.* Banish us both, and send the king with me.
*Northumberland.* That were some love, but little policy.
*Queen.* Then whither he goes, thither let me go?
*K. Rich.* So two, together weeping, make one woe.
Weep thou for me in France, I for thee here;
Better far off, than—near, be ne'er the near.
Go, count thy way with sighs; I, mine with groans.
*Queen.* So longest way shall have the longest moans.
*K. Rich.* Twice for one step I'll groan, the way being short,
And piece the way out with a heavy heart.
Come, come, in wooing sorrow let's be brief,
Since, wedding it, there is such length in grief.
One kiss shall stop our mouths, and dumbly part:
Thus give I mine, and thus I take thy heart. [*They kiss.*
*Queen.* Give me mine own again; 'twere no good part,
To take on me to keep, and kill thy heart. [*Kiss again.*
So now I have mine own again, begone,
That I may strive to kill it with a groan.
*K. Rich.* We make woe wanton with this fond delay:
Once more, adieu; the rest let sorrow say.

## Scene II.

*Duchess.* My lord, you told me, you would tell the rest,
When weeping made you break the story off
Of our two cousins coming into London.
*York.* Where did I leave?
*Duchess.* At that sad stop, my lord,
Where rude misgovern'd hands, from windows' tops,
Threw dust and rubbish on King Richard's head.
*York.* Then, as I said, the duke, great Bolingbroke,—

Mounted upon a hot and fiery steed,
Which his aspiring rider seem'd to know,
With slow, but stately pace, kept on his course,
While all tongues cried—God save thee, Bolingbroke!
You would have thought the very windows spake,
So many greedy looks of young and old
Through casements darted their desiring eyes
Upon his visage; and that all the walls,
With painted imag'ry, had said at once,—
Jesu preserve thee! welcome, Bolingbroke!
Whilst he, from one side to the other turning,
Bare-headed, lower than his proud steed's neck,
Bespake them thus,—I thank you, countrymen:
And thus still doing, thus he pass'd along.

*Duchess.* Alas, poor Richard! where rides he the while?

*York.* As in a theatre, the eyes of men,
After a well grac'd actor leaves the stage,
Are idly bent on him that enters next,
Thinking his prattle to be tedious:
Even so, or with much more contempt, men's eyes
Did scowl on Richard; no man cried, God save him;
No joyful tongue gave him his welcome home:
But dust was thrown upon his sacred head;
Which with such gentle sorrow he shook off,—
His face still combating with tears and smiles,
The badges of his grief and patience,—
That had not God, for some strong purpose, steel'd
The hearts of men, they must perforce have melted,
And barbarism itself have pitied him.
But heaven hath a hand in these events;
To whose high will we bound our calm contents.
To Bolingbroke are we sworn subjects now,
Whose state and honour I for aye allow.

## PRINCE OF TYRE.

### Act I. Scene I.

*Pericles.*

SEE, where she comes, apparell'd like the spring,
Graces her subjects, and her thoughts the king
Of every virtue gives renown to men !
Her face, the book of praises, where is read
Nothing but curious pleasures, as from thence
Sorrow were ever ras'd, and testy wrath
Could never be her mild companion.
Ye gods that made me man, and sway in love,
That have inflam'd desire in my breast,
To taste the fruit of yon celestial tree,
Or die in the adventure, be my helps,
As I am son and servant to your will,
To compass such a boundless happiness !

### Act III. Scene II.

*Cerimon.* She is alive ; behold
Her eyelids, cases to those heavenly jewels

Which Pericles hath lost,
Begin to part their fringes of bright gold ;
The diamonds of a most praised water
Appear, to make the world twice rich. O live,
And make us weep to hear your fate, fair creature,
Rare as you seem to be !

## ACT IV. SCENE I.

*Enter* MARINA, *with a basket of flowers.*

*Marina.* No, no, I will rob Tellus of her weed,
To strew thy green with flowers : the yellows, blues,
The purple violets, and marigolds,
Shall, as a chaplet, hang upon thy grave,
While summer days do last. Ah me ! poor maid,
Born in a tempest, when my mother died,
This world to me is like a lasting storm,
Whirring me from my friends.

* * * * *

*Marina.* Why should she have me killed ?
Now, as I can remember, by my troth,
I never did her hurt in all my life ;
I never spake bad word, nor did ill turn
To any living creature : believe me, la,
I never kill'd a mouse, nor hurt a fly :
I trod upon a worm against my will,
But I wept for it. How have I offended,
Wherein my death might yield her profit, or
My life imply her danger ?

ACT V. SCENE I.

*Marina.* I am a maid,
My lord, that ne'er before invited eyes,
But have been gaz'd on, comet-like: she speaks,
My lord, that, may be, hath endur'd a grief
Might equal yours, if both were justly weigh'd.
Though wayward fortune did malign my state,
My derivation was from ancestors
Who stood equivalent with mighty kings:
But time hath rooted out my parentage,
And to the world and awkward casualties
Bound me in servitude.—I will desist;
But there is something glows upon my cheek,
And whispers in mine ear, Go not till he speak.

* * * * *

*Pericles.* I am great with woe, and shall deliver weeping.
My dearest wife was like this maid, and such a one
My daughter might have been: my queen's square brows;
Her stature to an inch; as wand-like straight;
As silver-voic'd; her eyes as jewel-like,
And cas'd as richly: in pace another Juno;
Who starves the ears she feeds, and makes them hungry,
The more she gives them speech.—Where do you live?

* * * * *

*Pericles.* Pr'ythee speak;
Falseness cannot come from thee, for thou look'st
Modest as justice, and thou seem'st a palace
For the crown'd truth to dwell in: I'll believe thee,
And make my senses credit thy relation.
To points that seem impossible; for thou look'st
Like one I lov'd indeed. What were thy friends?

Didst thou not say, when I did push thee back
(Which was when I perceiv'd thee), that thou cam'st
From good descending?

* * * * *

*Marina.* My name, sir, is Marina.
*Pericles.* O, I am mock'd,
And thou by some incensed god sent hither
To make the world laugh at me.
*Marina.* Patience, good sir,
Or here I'll cease.
*Pericles.* Nay, I'll be patient;
Thou little know'st how thou dost startle me,
To call thyself Marina.
*Marina.* The name Marina
Was given me by one that had some power;
My father, and a king.
*Pericles.* How! a king's daughter?
And call'd Marina?
*Marina.* You said you would believe me;
But, not to be a troubler of your peace,
I will end here.
*Pericles.* But are you flesh and blood?
Have you a working pulse? and are no fairy?
No motion? Well; speak on. Where were you born?
And wherefore call'd Marina?
*Marina.* Call'd Marina,
For I was born at sea.
*Pericles.* At sea? thy mother?
*Marina.* My mother was the daughter of a king;
Who died the very minute I was born,
As my good nurse Lychorida hath oft
Deliver'd weeping.

* * * * *

*Pericles.* O Helicanus, strike me, honour'd sir;
Give me a gash, put me to present pain;
Lest this great sea of joys rushing upon me,
O'erbear the shores of my mortality,
And drown me with their sweetness. O, come hither,
Thou that beget'st him that did thee beget;
Thou that wast born at sea, buried at Tharsus,
And found at sea again! O Helicanus,
Down on thy knees, thank the holy gods, as loud
As thunder threatens us; This is Marina.—
What was thy mother's name? tell me but that,
For truth can never be confirm'd enough,
Though doubts did ever sleep.

* * * * *

*Pericles.* I embrace you, sir.
Give me my robes; I am wild in my beholding.
O heavens bless my girl! But hark, what musick?—
Tell Helicanus, my Marina, tell him
O'er point by point, for yet he seems to doubt,
How sure you are my daughter.—But what musick?
*Helicanus.* My lord, I hear none.
*Pericles.* None?
The musick of the spheres: list, my Marina.
*Lysimachus.* It is not good to cross him; give him way.
*Pericles.* Rarest sounds!
Do ye not hear?
*Lysimachus.* Musick? My lord, I hear—
*Pericles.* Most heavenly musick:
It nips me unto list'ning, and thick slumber
Hangs on mine eyelids; let me rest. [*He sleeps.*

## Scene III.

*Pericles.* This, this; no more, you gods! your present kindness
Makes my past miseries sport: You shall do well,
That on the touching of her lips I may
Melt, and no more be seen. O come, be buried
A second time within these arms.

*Marina.* My heart
Leaps to be gone into my mother's bosom.
[*Kneels to Thaisa.*

*Pericles.* Look, who kneels here! Flesh of thy flesh, Thaisa;
Thy burden at the sea, and call'd Marina,
For she was yielded there.

*Thaisa.* Bless'd and mine own!

*Helicanus.* Hail, madam, and my queen!

# TITUS ANDRONICUS.

## Act I. Scene II.

*Tamora.*

STAY, Roman brethren;—Gracious conqueror,
Victorious Titus, rue the tears I shed,
A mother's tears in passion for her son:
And, if thy sons were ever dear to thee,
O, think my son to be as dear to me.
Sufficeth not, that we are brought to Rome,
To beautify thy triumphs, and return,
Captive to thee, and to thy Roman yoke;
But must my sons be slaughter'd in the streets,
For valiant doings in their country's cause?
O! if to fight for king and commonweal
Were piety in thine, it is in these.
Andronicus, stain not thy tomb with blood:
Wilt thou draw near the nature of the gods?
Draw near them then in being merciful:
Sweet mercy is nobility's true badge;
Thrice-noble Titus, spare my first-born son.

# THE TEMPEST.

## Act I. Scene II.

*Miranda.*

IF by your art, my dearest father, you have
Put the wild waters in this roar, allay them :
The sky, it seems, would pour down stinking pitch,
But that the sea, mounting to the welkin's cheek,
Dashes the fire out. O, I have suffer'd
With those that I saw suffer ! a brave vessel,
Who had no doubt some noble creatures in her,
Dash'd all to pieces. O, the cry did knock
Against my very heart ! Poor souls ! they perish'd.
Had I been any god of power, I would
Have sunk the sea within the earth, or e'er
It should the good ship so have swallowed, and
The freighting souls within her.

* * * * *

*Miranda.* Alack ! what trouble
Was I then to you !

*Prospero.* O ! a cherubim
Thou wast, that did preserve me ! Thou didst smile,
Infused with a fortitude from heaven,

When I have deck'd the sea with drops full salt;
Under my burden groan'd; which rais'd in me
A stubborn resolution, to bear up
Against what should ensue.

* * * * *

*Miranda.* There's nothing ill can dwell in such a temple:
If the ill spirit have so fair an house,
Good things will strive to dwell with 't.

## Act III. Scene I.

*Ferdinand.* Admir'd Miranda!
Indeed, the top of admiration; worth
What 's dearest to the world! Full many a lady
I have ey'd with best regard; and many a time
The harmony of their tongues hath into bondage
Brought my too diligent ear: for several virtues
Have I lik'd several women; never any
With so full soul, but some defect in her
Did quarrel with the noblest grace she ow'd,
And put it to the foil: But you, O you,
So perfect, and so peerless, are created
Of every creature's best.

*Miranda.* I do not know
One of my sex; no woman's face remember,
Save, from my glass, mine own; nor have I seen
More that I may call men, than you, good friend,
And my dear father: how features are abroad,
I am skill-less of; but, by my modesty,
(The jewel in my dower,) I would not wish
Any companion in the world but you;
Nor can imagination form a shape,

Besides yourself, to like of: but I prattle
Something too wildly, and my father's precepts
Therein forget.

*Ferdinand.* I am, in my condition,
A prince, Miranda; I do think, a king;
(I would, not so!)

* * * * *

Hear my soul speak;—
The very instant that I saw you, did
My heart fly to your service; there resides,
To make me slave to it; and, for your sake,
Am I this patient log-man.

*Miranda.* Do you love me?

*Ferdinand.* O heaven, O earth, bear witness to this sound,
And crown what I profess with kind event,
If I speak true; if hollowly, invert
What best is boded me to mischief! I,
Beyond all limit of what else i' the world,
Do love, prize, honour you.

*Miranda.* I am a fool,
To weep at what I am glad of.[12]

*Ferdinand.* Wherefore weep you?

*Miranda.* At mine unworthiness, that dare not offer
What I desire to give; and much less take,
What I shall die to want: But this is trifling;
And all the more it seeks to hide itself,
The bigger bulk it shows. Hence, bashful cunning!
And prompt me, plain and holy innocence!
I am your wife, if you will marry me;
If not, I'll die your maid: to be your fellow
You may deny me; but I'll be your servant,
Whether you will or no.

*Ferdinand.* My mistress, dearest,

And I thus humble ever.

*Miranda.* My husband then?

*Ferdinand.* Ay, with a heart as willing
As bondage e'er of freedom : here's my hand.

*Miranda.* And mine, with my heart in't : And now farewell,
Till half an hour hence.

## Act V. Scene I.

*Ferdinand.* Sir, she's mortal;
But, by immortal Providence, she's mine;
I chose her, when I could not ask my father
For his advice; nor thought I had one : she
Is daughter to this famous duke of Milan,
Of whom so often I have heard renown,
But never saw before; of whom I have
Received a second life, and second father
This lady makes him to me.

## TWO GENTLEMEN OF VERONA.

### ACT II. SCENE VII.

*Lucetta.*

BETTER forbear, till Proteus make return.
*Julia.* O, know'st thou not, his looks are my soul's food?
Pity the dearth that I have pined in,
By longing for that food so long a time.
Didst thou but know the inly touch of love,
Thou would'st as soon go kindle fire with snow,
As seek to quench the fire of love with words.
*Lucetta.* I do not seek to quench your love's hot fire;
But qualify the fire's extreme rage,
Lest it should burn above the bounds of reason.
*Julia.* The more thou dam'st it up, the more it burns;[13]
The current, that with gentle murmur glides,
Thou know'st, being stopp'd, impatiently doth rage;
But, when his fair course is not hindered,
He makes sweet musick with th' enamel'd stones,
Giving a gentle kiss to every sedge
He overtaketh in his pilgrimage;
And so by many winding nooks he strays,

With willing sport to the wild ocean.
Then let me go, and hinder not my course:
I'll be as patient as a gentle stream,
And make a pastime of each weary step,
Till the last step have brought me to my love;
And there I'll rest, as, after much turmoil,
A blessed soul doth in Elysium.

* * * * *

*Julia.* That is the least, Lucetta, of my fear:
A thousand oaths, an ocean of his tears,
And instances of infinite of love,
Warrant me welcome to my Proteus.

*Lucetta.* All these are servants to deceitful men.

*Julia.* Base men, that use them to so base effect!
But truer stars did govern Proteus' birth:
His words are bonds, his oaths are oracles;
His love sincere, his thoughts immaculate;
His tears, pure messengers sent from his heart;
His heart as far from fraud, as heaven from earth.

*Lucetta.* Pray heaven, he prove so, when you come to him!

*Julia.* Now, as thou lov'st me, do him not that wrong,
To bear a hard opinion of his truth;
Only deserve my love, by loving him;
And presently go with me to my chamber,
To take a note of what I stand in need of,
To furnish me upon my longing journey.
All that is mine I leave at thy dispose,
My goods, my lands, my reputation;
Only, in lieu thereof despatch me hence:
Come, answer not, but to it presently;
I am impatient of my tarriance.

## Act III. Scene I.

*Valentine.* And why not death, rather than living torment?
To die, is to be banish'd from myself;
And Silvia is myself: banish'd from her,
Is self from self: a deadly banishment!
What light is light, if Silvia be not seen?
What joy is joy, if Silvia be not by?
Unless it be to think that she is by,
And feed upon the shadow of perfection,
Except I be by Silvia in the night,
There is no musick in the nightingale;
Unless I look on Silvia in the day,
There is no day for me to look upon:
She is my essence; and I leave to be,
If I be not by her fair influence
Foster'd, illumin'd, cherish'd, kept alive.
I fly not death, to fly his deadly doom;
Tarry I here, I but attend on death;
But, fly I hence, I fly away from life.

## Act IV. Scene II.

*Proteus.* Already have I been false to Valentine,
And now I must be as unjust to Thurio.
Under the colour of commending him,
I have access my own love to prefer;
But Silvia is too fair, too true, too holy,
To be corrupted with my worthless gifts.
When I protest true loyalty to her,

She twits me with my falsehood to my friend ;
When to her beauty I commend my vows,
She bids me think, how I have been forsworn
In breaking faith with Julia whom I lov'd :
And, notwithstanding all her sudden quips,
The least whereof would quell a lover's hope,
Yet, spaniel-like, the more she spurns my love,
The more it grows and fawneth on her still.
But here comes Thurio; now must we to her window,
And give some evening musick to her ear.

* * * * *

*Silvia.* You have your wish; my will is even this,—
That presently you hie you home to bed.
Thou subtle, perjur'd, false, disloyal man!
Think'st thou, I am so shallow, so conceitless,
To be seduced by thy flattery,
That hast deceiv'd so many with thy vows?
Return, return, and make thy love amends.
For me,—by this pale queen of night I swear,
I am so far from granting thy request,
That I despise thee for thy wrongful suit;
And by and by intend to chide myself,
Even for this time I spend in talking to thee.

## Scene III.

*Silvia.* O Eglamour, thou art a gentleman,
(Think not, I flatter, for I swear, I do not),
Valiant, wise, remorseful, well accomplish'd.
Thou art not ignorant, what dear good-will
I bear unto the banish'd Valentine;
Nor how my father would enforce me marry
Vain Thurio, whom my very soul abhorr'd.

Thyself hast lov'd ; and I have heard thee say,
No grief did ever come so near thy heart,
As when thy lady and thy true love died,
Upon whose grave thou vow'dst pure chastity.
Sir Eglamour, I would to Valentine,
To Mantua, where, I hear, he makes abode ;
And, for the ways are dangerous to pass,
I do desire thy worthy company,
Upon whose faith and honour I repose.
Urge not my father's anger, Eglamour,
But think upon my grief, a lady's grief ;
And on the justice of my flying hence,
To keep me from a most unholy match,
Which heaven and fortune still reward with plagues.
I do desire thee, even from a heart
As full of sorrows as the sea of sands,
To bear me company, and go with me :
If not, to hide what I have said to thee,
That I may venture to depart alone.

### Scene IV.

*Julia.* How many women would do such a message?
Alas, poor Proteus ! thou hast entertained
A fox, to be the shepherd of thy lambs :
Alas, poor fool ! why do I pity him
That with his very heart despiseth me ?
Because he loves her, he despiseth me ;
Because I love him, I must pity him.
This ring I gave him, when he parted from me,
To bind him to remember my good-will :
And now am I (unhappy messenger !)
To plead for that, which I would not obtain ;
To carry that which I would have refus'd ;

To praise his faith which I would have disprais'd.
I am my master's true confirmed love;
But cannot be true servant to my master,
Unless I prove false traitor to myself.
Yet I will woo for him: but yet so coldly,
As, heaven, it knows, I would not have him speed.

* * * * *

*Julia.* She hath been fairer, madam, than she is:
When she did think my master lov'd her well,
She, in my judgment, was as fair as you;
But since she did neglect her looking-glass,
And threw her sun-expelling mask away,
The air hath starv'd the roses in her cheeks,
And pinch'd the lily-tincture of her face,
That now she is become as black as I.

* * * * *

*Silvia.* She is beholden to thee, gentle youth!—
Alas, poor lady! desolate and left!—
I weep myself, to think upon thy words.
Here, youth, there is my purse; I give thee this
For thy sweet mistress' sake, because thou lov'st her.
Farewell.

## Act V. Scene IV.

*Valentine.* How use doth breed a habit in a man!
This shadowy desert, unfrequented woods,
I better brook than flourishing peopled towns:
Here can I sit alone, unseen of any,
And, to the nightingale's complaining notes,
Tune my distresses, and record my woes.
O thou that dost inhabit in my breast,[14]
Leave not the mansion so long tenantless;

Lest, growing ruinous, the building fall,
And leave no memory of what it was!
Repair me with thy presence, Silvia;
Thou gentle nymph, cherish thy forlorn swain!—
What halloing, and what stir, is this to-day?
These are my mates, that make their wills their law,
Have some unhappy passenger in chase:
They love me well; yet I have much to do
To keep them from uncivil outrages.
Withdraw thee, Valentine; who 's this comes here?
[*Steps aside.*

* * * * *

*Silvia.* Had I been seized by a hungry lion,
I would have been a breakfast to the beast,
Rather than have false Proteus rescue me.
O, heaven be judge, how I love Valentine,
Whose life 's as tender to me as my soul;
And full as much (for more there cannot be)
I do detest false perjur'd Proteus:
Therefore be gone, solicit me no more.

*Proteus.* What dangerous action, stood it next to death,
Would I not undergo for one calm look?
O, 'tis the curse in love, and still approv'd,
When women cannot love where they 're belov'd.

*Silvia.* When Proteus cannot love where he 's belov'd.
Read over Julia's heart, thy first best love,
For whose dear sake thou didst then rend thy faith
Into a thousand oaths; and all those oaths
Descended into perjury, to love me.
Thou hast no faith left now, unless thou hadst two,
And that 's far worse than none; better have none
Than plural faith, which is too much by one:
Thou counterfeit to thy true friend!

# MEASURE FOR MEASURE.

## Act II. Scene II.

*Isabella.*

I HAVE a brother is condemn'd to die:
I do beseech you, let it be his fault,
And not my brother.[15]
*Angelo.* Condemn the fault, and not the actor of it?
Why, every fault 's condemn'd ere it be done.
Mine were the very cipher of a function,
To fine the fault, whose fine stands in record,
And let go by the actor.

* * * * *

*Isabella.* Too late? why, no; I, that do speak a word,
May call it back again. Well, believe this,
No ceremony that to great ones 'longs,
Not the king's crown, nor the deputed sword,
The marshal's truncheon, nor the judge's robe,
Become them with one half so good a grace
As mercy does. If he had been as you,
And you as he, you would have slipt like him;

But he, like you, would not have been so stern.
*Angelo.* Pray you, be gone.
*Isabella.* I would to heaven I had your potency,
And you were Isabel! should it then be thus?
No; I would tell what 'twere to be a judge,
And what a prisoner.
*Angelo.* Your brother is a forfeit of the law,
And you but waste your words.
*Isabella.* Alas, alas!
Why, all the souls that were, were forfeit once;
And He that might the vantage best have took,
Found out the remedy. How would you be,
If He, which is the top of judgment, should
But judge you as you are? O! think on that;
And mercy then will breathe within your lips,
Like man new made.[16]

* * * * *

*Isabella.* To-morrow? O, that's sudden! Spare him, spare him!—
He's not prepar'd for death. Even for our kitchens
We kill the fowl of season: shall we serve heaven
With less respect than we do minister
To our gross selves? Good, good my lord, bethink you:
Who is it that hath died for this offence?
There's many have committed it.

* * * * *

*Isabella.* So you must be the first that gives this sentence,
And he that suffers. O! it is excellent
To have a giant's strength; but it is tyrannous
To use it like a giant.
*Lucio.* That's well said.
*Isabella.* Could great men thunder

As Jove himself does, Jove would ne'er be quiet;
For every pelting, petty officer,
Would use his heaven for thunder,—Merciful heaven!
Nothing but thunder.
Thou rather with thy sharp and sulphurous bolt
Split'st the unwedgeable and gnarled oak,
Than the soft myrtle: but man, proud man!
Drest in a little brief authority,—
Most ignorant of what he 's most assur'd,
His glassy essence,—like an angry ape,
Plays such fantastick tricks before high heaven,
As make the angels weep; who, with our spleens,
Would all themselves laugh mortal.

* * * * *

*Isabella.* We cannot weigh our brother with ourself:
Great men may jest with saints; 'tis wit in them,
But, in the less, foul profanation.

* * * * *

*Isabella.* That in the captain 's but a choleric word,
Which in the soldier is flat blasphemy.

*Angelo.* Why do you put these sayings upon me?

*Isabella.* Because authority, though it err like others,
Hath yet a kind of medicine in itself,
That skins the vice o' the top; Go to your bosom;
Knock there, and ask your heart what it doth know
That 's like my brother's fault: if it confess
A natural guiltiness such as is his,
Let it not sound a thought upon your tongue
Against my brother's life.

*Angelo.* She speaks, and 'tis
Such sense, that my sense breeds with it.
Fare you well.

*Isabella.* Gentle, my lord, turn back.

*Angelo.* I will bethink me: come again to-morrow.

*Isabella.* Hark how I'll bribe you: good my lord, turn back.

*Angelo.* How! bribe me!

*Isabella.* Ay, with such gifts, that heaven shall share with you.

* * * * *

*Isabella.* Not with fond shekels of the tested gold,
Or stones, whose rates are either rich or poor
As fancy values them; but with true prayers,
That shall be up at heaven, and enter there
Ere sun-rise,—prayers from preservèd souls,
From fasting maids, whose minds are dedicate
To nothing temporal.

*Angelo.* Well; come to me to-morrow.

* * * * *

*Angelo.* From thee; even from thy virtue!—
What 's this, what 's this? Is this her fault or mine?
The tempter or the tempted, who sins most, ha?
Not she; nor doth she tempt: but it is I,
That lying by the violet in the sun,
Do, as the carrion does, not as the flower,
Corrupt with virtuous season. Can it be,
That modesty may more betray our sense
Than woman's lightness? Having waste ground enough,
Shall we desire to raze the sanctuary,
And pitch our evils there? O, fie!
What dost thou? or what art thou, Angelo?
O, let her brother live!
Thieves for their robbery have authority,
When judges steal themselves. What! do I love her,
That I desire to hear her speak again,
And feast upon her eyes? What is 't I dream on?

O cunning enemy, that, to catch a saint,
With saints dost bait thy hook! Most dangerous
Is that temptation, that doth goad us on
To sin in loving virtue.
This virtuous maid
Subdues me quite:—ever, till now,
When men were fond, I smil'd, and wonder'd how.

## Scene IV.

*Isabella.* O, pardon me, my lord; it oft falls out,
To have what we would have, we speak not what we mean:
I something do excuse the thing I hate,
For his advantage that I dearly love.

* * * * *

*Angelo.* Nay, women are frail too.
*Isabella.* Ay, as the glasses where they view themselves;
Which are as easy broke as they make forms.
Women!—Help heaven! men their creation mar
In profiting by them. Nay, call us ten times frail;
For we are soft as our complexions are,
And credulous to false prints.

## Act III. Scene I.

*Isabella.* O! I do fear thee, Claudio; and I quake,
Lest thou a feverous life shouldst entertain,
And six or seven winters more respect,
Than a perpetual honour. Dar'st thou die?
The sense of death is most in apprehension;
And the poor beetle, that we tread upon,

In corporal sufferance finds a pang as great
As when a giant dies.
*Claudio.* Why give you me this shame?
Think you I can a resolution fetch
From flowery tenderness? If I must die,
I will encounter darkness as a bride,
And hug it in mine arms.
*Isabella.* There spake my brother: there my father's grave
Did utter forth a voice! Yes, thou must die:
Thou art too noble to conserve a life
In base appliances. This outward-sainted deputy—
Whose settled visage and deliberate word
Nips youth i' the head, and follies doth enmew
As falcon doth the fowl—is yet a devil;
His filth within being cast, he would appear
A pond as deep as hell.
*Claudio.* The princely Angelo?
*Isabella.* O, 'tis the cunning livery of hell,
The damned'st body to invest and cover
In priestly guards! Dost thou think, Claudio,—
If I would yield him my virginity,
Thou mightst be freed.

## ACT V. SCENE I.

*Duke.* Nay, it is ten times strange.
*Isabella.* O prince, I conjure thee, as thou believ'st
There is another comfort than this world,
That thou neglect me not, with that opinion
That I am touch'd with madness! Make not impossible
That which but seems unlike. 'Tis not impossible,

But one, the wicked'st caitiff on the ground,
May seem as shy, as grave, as just, as absolute
As Angelo; even so may Angelo,
In all his dressings, characts, titles, forms,
Be an arch-villain: believe it, royal prince:
If he be less, he 's nothing; but he 's more,
Had I more name for badness.

*Duke.* By mine honesty,
If she be mad,—as I believe no other,—
Her madness hath the oddest frame of sense,
Such a dependency of thing on thing,
As e'er I heard in madness.

*Isabella.* O gracious duke,
Harp not on that; nor do not banish reason
For inequality; but let your reason serve
To make the truth appear where it seems hid,
And hide the false seems true.

* * * * *

*Mariana.* O my good lord! Sweet Isabel, take my part:
Lend me your knees, and, all my life to come,
I'll lend you all my life to do you service.

*Duke.* Against all sense you do importune her:
Should she kneel down in mercy of this fact,
Her brother's ghost his paved bed would break,
And take her hence in horror.

*Mariana.* Isabel,
Sweet Isabel, do yet but kneel by me:
Hold up your hands, say nothing,—I'll speak all.
They say best men are moulded out of faults;
And, for the most, become much more the better
For being a little bad: so may my husband.
O, Isabel! will you not lend a knee?

*Duke.* He dies for Claudio's death.

*Isabella.* Most bounteous sir,
Look, if it please you, on this man condemn'd,
As if my brother liv'd, I partly think,
A due sincerity govern'd his deeds,
Till he did look on me : since it is so,
Let him not die. My brother had but justice,
In that he did the thing for which he died :
For Angelo,
His act did not o'ertake his bad intent;
And must be buried but as an intent
That perish'd by the way : thoughts are no subjects ;
Intents but merely thoughts.

# TWELFTH NIGHT; OR, WHAT YOU WILL.[17]

## Act I. Scene V.

*Viola (disguised as a page).*

TIS beauty truly blent, whose red and white
Nature's own sweet and cunning hand laid on:
Lady, you are the cruel'st she alive,
If you will lead these graces to the grave,
And leave the world no copy.

* * * * *

*Viola.* I see you what you are: you are too proud;
But, if you were the devil, you are fair.
My lord and master loves you; O, such love
Could be but recompens'd, though you were crown'd
The nonpareil of beauty!

* * * * *

*Olivia.* What is your parentage?
"Above my fortunes, yet my state is well:
I am a gentleman."—I'll be sworn thou art,
Thy tongue, thy face, thy limbs, actions, and spirit,
Do give thee five-fold blazon;—Not too fast:—soft! soft!

Unless the master were the man.—How now?
Even so quickly may one catch the plague?
Methinks, I feel this youth's perfections,
With an invisible and subtle stealth,
To creep in at mine eyes. Well, let it be.—
What, ho, Malvolio!—

*Re-enter* MALVOLIO.

*Malvolio.* Here, madam, at your service.
*Olivia.* Run after that same peevish messenger,
The county's man: he left this ring behind him,
Would I, or not; tell him, I'll none of it.
Desire him not to flatter with his lord,
Nor hold him up with hopes! I am not for him:
If that the youth will come this way to-morrow,
I'll give him reasons for 't. Hie thee, Malvolio.
*Malvolio.* Madam, I will.
*Olivia.* I do I know not what: and fear to find
Mine eye too great a flatterer for my mind.[18]
Fate, show thy force: ourselves we do not owe;
What is decreed, must be; and be this so!

## ACT II. SCENE I.

*Sebastian.* A lady, sir, though it was said she much resembled me, was yet of many accounted beautiful: but, though I could not, with such estimable wonder, overfar believe that, yet thus far I will boldly publish her, she bore a mind that envy could not but call fair: she is drowned already, sir, with salt water, though I seem to drown her remembrance again with more.

## Scene II.

*Viola.* I left no ring with her: What means this lady?
Fortune forbid my outside have not charm'd her!
She made good view of me; indeed so much,
That, sure, methought her eyes had lost her tongue,
For she did speak in starts distractedly.
She loves me, sure; the cunning of her passion
Invites me in this churlish messenger.
None of my lord's ring! why, he sent her none.
I am the man;—If it be so, (as 'tis),
Poor lady, she were better love a dream.
Disguise, I see, thou art a wickedness,
Wherein the pregnant enemy does much.
How easy is it for the proper-false
In women's waxen hearts to set their forms!
Alas, our frailty is the cause, not we;
For, such as we are made of, such we be.
How will this fadge? My master loves her dearly;
And I, poor monster, fond as much on him;
And she, mistaken, seems to dote on me:
What will become of this! As I am man,
My state is desperate for my master's love;
As I am woman, now alas the day!
What thriftless sighs shall poor Olivia breathe?
O time, thou must untangle this, not I;
It is too hard a knot for me to untie.

## Scene IV.

*Duke.* Too old, by heaven; Let still the woman take
An elder than herself; so wears she to him,
So sways she level in her husband's heart.

For, boy, however we do praise ourselves,
Our fancies are more giddy and unfirm,
More longing, wavering, sooner lost and worn,
Than women's are.

*Viola.* I think it well, my lord.

*Duke.* Then let thy love be younger than thyself
Or thy affection cannot hold the bent:
For women are as roses; whose fair flower,
Being once display'd, doth fall that very hour.

*Viola.* And so they are: alas, that they are so;
To die, even when they to perfection grow!

* * * * *

*Duke.* Once more, Cesario,
Get thee to yon' same sovereign cruelty:
Tell her, my love, more noble than the world,
Prizes not quantity of dirty lands;
The parts that fortune hath bestow'd upon her,
Tell her, I hold as giddily as fortune;
But 'tis that miracle, and queen of gems,
That nature pranks her in, attracts my soul.

*Viola.* But, if she cannot love you, sir?

*Duke.* I cannot be so answer'd.

*Viola.* 'Sooth, but you must.
Say, that some lady, as, perhaps, there is,
Hath for your love as great a pang of heart
As you have for Olivia: you cannot love her;
You tell her so; Must she not then be answer'd?

*Duke.* There is no woman's sides
Can bide the beating of so strong a passion
As love doth give my heart: no woman's heart
So big, to hold so much; they lack retention.
Alas, their love may be call'd appetite,—
No motion of the liver, but the palate,—

That suffer surfeit, cloyment, and revolt;
But mine is all as hungry as the sea,
And can digest as much: make no compare
Between that love a woman can bear me,
And that I owe Olivia.

*Viola.* Ay, but I know,—

*Duke.* What dost thou know?

*Viola.* Too well what love women to men may owe:
In faith, they are as true of heart as we.
My father had a daughter lov'd a man,
As it might be, perhaps, were I a woman,
I should your lordship.

*Duke.* And what 's her history?

*Viola.* A blank, my lord: She never told her love,[19]
But let concealment, like a worm i' the bud,
Feed on her damask cheek: she pin'd in thought;
And, with a green and yellow melancholy,
She sat like patience on a monument,
Smiling at grief. Was not this love, indeed?
We men may say more, swear more: but, indeed,
Our shows are more than will; for still we prove
Much in our vows, but little in our love.

*Duke.* But died thy sister of her love, my boy?

*Viola.* I am all the daughters of my father's house,
And all the brothers too;—and yet I know not:—
Sir, shall I to this lady?

*Duke.* Ay, that 's the theme.
To her in haste; give her this jewel; say,
My love can give no place, bide no denay.

## Act III. Scene I.

*Olivia.* O, by your leave, I pray you;
I bade you never speak again of him:
But, would you undertake another suit,
I had rather hear you to solicit that,
Than musick from the spheres.
*Viola.* Dear lady,—
*Olivia.* Give me leave, 'beseech you: I did send,
After the last enchantment you did here,
A ring in chase of you; so did I abuse
Myself, my servant, and, I fear me, you:
Under your hard construction must I sit,
To force that on you, in a shameful cunning,
Which you knew none of yours: What might you think?
Have you not set mine honour at the stake,
And baited it with all the unmuzzled thoughts
That tyrannous heart can think? To one of your receiving
Enough is shown; a cyprus, not a bosom,
Hides my heart: So let me hear you speak.
*Viola.* I pity you.
*Olivia.* That's a degree to love.

* * * * *

*Olivia.* O, what a deal of scorn looks beautiful
In the contempt and anger of his lip!
A murd'rous guilt shows not itself more soon
Than love that would seem hid: love's night is noon.
Cesario, by the roses of the spring,
By maidhood, honour, truth, and every thing,
I love thee so, that, maugre all thy pride,
Nor wit, nor reason, can my passion hide.
Do not extort thy reasons from this clause,

For, that I woo, thou therefore hast no cause :
But, rather, reason thus with reason fetter :
Love sought is good, but given unsought, is better.

### Scene IV.

*Antonio.* Will you deny me now?
Is 't possible, that my deserts to you
Can lack persuasion? Do not tempt my misery,
Lest that it make me so unsound a man,
As to upbraid you with those kindnesses
That I have done for you.
*Viola.* I know of none;
Nor know I you by voice, or any feature :
I hate ingratitude more in a man,
Than lying, vainness, babbling, drunkenness,
Or any taint of vice, whose strong corruption
Inhabits our frail blood.

* * * * *

*Viola.* He nam'd Sebastian; I my brother know
Yet living in my glass; even such, and so,
In favour was my brother; and he went
Still in this fashion, colour, ornament,
For him I imitate: O, if it prove,
Tempests are kind, and salt waves fresh in love.

### Act IV. Scene III.

*Olivia.* Blame not this haste of mine : If you mean well,[20]
Now go with me, and with this holy man,
In the chantry by: there, before him,
And underneath that consecrated roof,

Plight me the full assurance of your faith ;
That my most jealous and too doubtful soul
May live at peace : He shall conceal it,
Whiles you are willing it shall come to note ;
What time we will our celebration keep
According to my birth.—What do you say?

Act V. Scene I.

*Viola.* And all those sayings will I over-swear ;
And all those swearings keep as true in soul,
As doth that orbed continent the fire
That severs day from night.

# MERRY WIVES OF WINDSOR.

## Act III. Scene IV.

*Fenton.*

NO, heaven so speed me in my time to come!
Albeit, I will confess, thy father's wealth
Was the first motive that I woo'd thee, Anne:
Yet, wooing thee, I found thee of more value
Than stamps in gold, or sums in sealed bags;
And 'tis the very riches of thyself
That now I aim at.

## Act V. Scene V.

*Mrs. Quickly.* About, about;
Search Windsor Castle, elves, within and out:
Strew good luck, ouphes, on every sacred room;
That it may stand till the perpetual doom,
In state as wholesome, as in state 'tis fit;
Worthy the owner, and the owner it.
The several chairs of order look you scour

With juice of balm, and every precious flower:
Each fair instalment, coat, and several crest,
With loyal blazon, evermore be blest!
And nightly, meadow-fairies, look you sing,
Like to the Garter's compass, in a ring:
The expressure that it bears, green let it be,
More fertile-fresh than all the field to see;
And, *Hony soit qui mal y pense*, write,
In emerald tufts, flowers purple, blue, and white;
Like sapphire, pearl, and rich embroidery,
Buckled below fair knighthood's bending knee:—
Fairies use flowers for their charactery.
Away; disperse: But, till 'tis one o'clock,
Our dance of custom, round about the oak
Of Herne the hunter, let us not forget.

# MUCH ADO ABOUT NOTHING.

## Act I. Scene I.

*Claudio.*

O MY lord,
When you went onward on this ended action,
I look'd upon her with a soldier's eye,
That lik'd, but had a rougher task in hand
Than to drive liking to the name of love:
But now I am return'd, and that war-thoughts
Have left their places vacant, in their rooms
Come thronging soft and delicate desires,
All prompting me how fair young Hero is,
Saying, I lik'd her ere I went to wars.
*Don Pedro.* Thou wilt be like a lover presently,
And tire the hearer with a book of words.
If thou dost love fair Hero, cherish it;
And I will break with her, and with her father,
And thou shalt have her. Was't not to this end
That thou began'st to twist so fine a story?
*Claudio.* How sweetly do you minister to love,
That know love's grief by his complexion!
But lest my liking might too sudden seem,
I would have salv'd it with a longer treatise.

*Don Pedro.* What need the bridge much broader than the flood?
The fairest grant is the necessity.
Look, what will serve is fit: 'tis once, thou lovest;
And I will fit thee with the remedy.
I know we shall have revelling to-night;
I will assume thy part in some disguise,
And tell fair Hero I am Claudio;
And in her bosom I'll unclasp my heart,
And take her hearing prisoner with the force
And strong encounter of my amorous tale;
Then, after, to her father will I break;
And the conclusion is, she shall be thine:
In practice let us put it presently.

## Act III. Scene I.

*Hero.* For look where Beatrice, like a lapwing, runs [21]
Close by the ground, to hear our conference.

* * * * *

*Hero.* O God of love! I know he doth deserve
As much as may be yielded to a man:
But nature never fram'd a woman's heart
Of prouder stuff than that of Beatrice;
Disdain and scorn ride sparkling in her eyes,
Misprising what they look on; and her wit
Values itself so highly, that to her
All matter else seems weak: she cannot love,
Nor take no shape nor project of affection,
She is so self-endear'd.
*Ursula.* Sure, I think so;
And therefore certainly it were not good

She knew his love, lest she make sport of it.
*Hero.* Why, you speak truth. I never yet saw man,
How wise, how noble, young, how rarely featur'd,
But she would spell him backward: if fair fac'd,
She 'd swear the gentleman should be her sister;
If black, why, nature, drawing of an antick,
Made a foul blot; if tall, a lance ill-headed;
If low, an agate very vilely cut;
If speaking, why, a vane blown with all winds;
If silent, why a block moved with none.
So turns she every man the wrong side out;
And never gives to truth and virtue that
Which simpleness and merit purchaseth.

* * * * *

BEATRICE *advances.*

*Beatrice.* What fire is in mine ears? Can this be true?
Stand I condemn'd for pride and scorn so much?
Contempt, farewell! and maiden pride, adieu!
No glory lives behind the back of such.
And, Benedick, love on, I will requite thee:
Taming my wild heart to thy loving hand.[22]
If thou dost love, my kindness shall incite thee
To bind our loves up in a holy band:
For others say thou dost deserve; and I
Believe it better than reportingly.

ACT IV. SCENE I.

*Beatrice.* O, on my soul, my cousin is belied!

* * * * *

*Friar.* Hear me a little;

For I have only been silent so long,
And given way unto this course of fortune,
By noting of the lady : I have mark'd
A thousand blushing apparitions start
Into her face ; a thousand innocent shames
In angel whiteness bear away those blushes ;
And in her eye there hath appear'd a fire,
To burn the errors that these princes hold
Against her maiden truth. Call me a fool ;
Trust not my reading nor my observation,
Which with experimental seal doth warrant
The tenour of my book ; trust not my age,
My reverence, calling, nor divinity,
If this sweet lady lie not guiltless here
Under some biting error.

* * * * *

*Friar.* Marry, this, well carried, shall on her behalf
Change slander to remorse ; that is some good :
But not for that dream I on this strange course,
But on this travail look for greater birth.
She dying, as it must be so maintain'd,
Upon the instant that she was accus'd,
Shall be lamented, pitied, and excused
Of every hearer : for it so falls out,
That what we have we prize not to the worth
Whiles we enjoy it ; but being lack'd and lost,
Why, then we rack the value, then we find
The virtue that possession would not show us
Whiles it was ours.—So will it fare with Claudio :
When he shall hear she died upon his words,
The idea of her life shall sweetly creep
Into his study of imagination ;
And every lovely organ of her life

Shall come apparell'd in more precious habit,
More moving delicate, and full of life,
Into the eye and prospect of his soul,
Than when she liv'd indeed :—then shall he mourn,
And wish he had not so accused her ;
No, though he thought his accusation true.
Let this be so, and doubt not but success
Will fashion the event in better shape
Than I can lay it down in likelihood.
But if all aim but this be levell'd false,
The supposition of the lady's death
Will quench the wonder of her infamy :
And if it sort not well, you may conceal her
(As best befits her wounded reputation)
In some reclusive and religious life,
Out of all eyes, tongues, minds, and injuries.

* * * * *

*Benedick.* Lady Beatrice, have you wept all this while?

*Beatrice.* Yea, and I will weep a while longer.

*Benedick.* I will not desire that.

*Beatrice.* You have no reason, I do it freely.

*Benedick.* Surely, I do believe your fair cousin is wronged.

*Beatrice.* Ah! how much might the man deserve of me that would right her.

*Benedick.* Is there any way to show such friendship?

*Beatrice.* A very even way, but no such friend.

*Benedick.* May a man do it?

*Beatrice.* It is a man's office, but not yours.

*Benedick.* I do love nothing in the world so well as you; is not that strange?

*Beatrice.* As strange as the thing I know not. It were as possible for me to say I loved nothing so well as you :

but believe me not; and yet I lie not; I confess nothing; nor I deny nothing.—I am sorry for my cousin.

*Benedick.* By my sword, Beatrice, thou lovest me.

*Beatrice.* Do not swear by it, and eat it.

*Benedick.* I will swear by it that you love me; and I will make him eat it that says I love not you.

*Beatrice.* Will you not eat your word?

*Benedick.* With no sauce that can be devised to it: I protest, I love thee.

*Beatrice.* Why then, God forgive me!

*Benedick.* What offence, sweet Beatrice?

*Beatrice.* You have staid me in a happy hour, I was about to protest I loved you.[23]

*Benedick.* And do it with all thy heart.

*Beatrice.* I love you with so much of my heart that none is left to protest.

*Benedick.* Come, bid me do any thing for thee.

*Beatrice.* Kill Claudio.

*Benedick.* Ha! not for the wide world.

*Beatrice.* You kill me to deny it. Farewell.

*Benedick.* Tarry, sweet Beatrice.

*Beatrice.* I am gone, though I am here: there is no love in you.—Nay, I pray you, let me go.

*Benedick.* Beatrice,—

*Beatrice.* In faith, I will go.

*Benedick.* We'll be friends first.

*Beatrice.* You dare easier be friends with me, than fight with mine enemy.

*Benedick.* Is Claudio thine enemy?

*Beatrice.* Is he not approved in the height a villain, that hath slandered, scorned, dishonoured my kinswoman?—O, that I were a man!—What! bear her in hand until they come to take hands, and then, with public accusation, uncovered slander, unmitigated rancour.—O God, that I were a man! I would eat his heart in the market-place.

*Benedick.* Hear me, Beatrice;—

*Beatrice.* Talk with a man out of a window!—a proper saying!

*Benedick.* Nay, but Beatrice,—

*Beatrice.* Sweet Hero!—she is wronged, she is slandered, she is undone.

*Benedick.* Beat—

*Beatrice.* Princes and counties! Surely, a princely testimony, a goodly count-confect; a sweet gallant, surely! O that I were a man for his sake! or that I had any friend would be a man for my sake! But manhood is melted into courtesies, valour into compliment, and men are only turned into tongue, and trim ones too: he is now as valiant as Hercules, that only tells a lie, and swears it.—I cannot be a man with wishing, therefore I will die a woman with grieving.

*Benedick.* Tarry, good Beatrice. By this hand, I love thee.

*Beatrice.* Use it for my love some other way than swearing by it.

*Benedick.* Think you in your soul the Count Claudio hath wronged Hero?

*Beatrice.* Yea, as sure as I have a thought or a soul.

*Benedick.* Enough! I am engaged; I will challenge him. I will kiss your hand, and so leave you. By this hand, Claudio shall render me a dear account. As you hear of me, so think of me. Go, comfort your cousin. I must say she is dead: and so, farewell.

## ACT V. SCENE II.

LEONATO'S *Garden.*

*Enter* URSULA.

*Ursula.* Madam, you must come to your uncle; yonder 's old coil at home; it is proved, my lady Hero hath been falsely accused, the Prince and Claudio mightily abus'd; and Don John is the author of all, who is fled and gone. Will you come presently?

*Beatrice.* Will you go hear this news, signior?

*Benedick.* I will live in thy heart, die in thy lap, and be buried in thy eyes; and, moreover, I will go with thee to thy uncle's.

# MIDSUMMER NIGHT'S DREAM.

## Act II. Scene II.

*Oberon.*

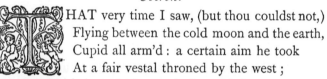

THAT very time I saw, (but thou couldst not,)
Flying between the cold moon and the earth,
Cupid all arm'd: a certain aim he took
At a fair vestal throned by the west;
And loos'd his love-shaft smartly from his bow,
As it should pierce a hundred thousand hearts;
But I might see young Cupid's fiery shaft
Quench'd in the chaste beams of the wat'ry moon;
And the imperial vot'ress passed on
In maiden meditation, fancy-free.
Yet mark'd I where the bolt of Cupid fell:
It fell upon a little western flower,
Before milk-white, now purple with love's wound,
And maidens call it, love-in-idleness.
Fetch me that flower; the herb I show'd thee once;
The juice of it on sleeping eye-lids laid,
Will make or man or woman madly dote
Upon the next wild creature that it sees.
Fetch me this herb; and be thou here again

Ere the Leviathan can swim a league.

*Puck.* I'll put a girdle round about the earth
In forty minutes.

*Oberon.* Having once this juice,
I'll watch Titania when she is asleep,
And drop the liquor of it in her eyes.
The next thing then she waking looks upon,
(Be it on lion, bear, or wolf, or bull,
On meddling monkey, or on busy ape,)
She shall pursue it with the soul of love:
And ere I take this charm off from her sight,
(As I can take it, with another herb,)
I'll make her render up her page to me.
But who comes here? I am invisible;
And I will overhear their conference.

*Enter* DEMETRIUS, HELENA *following him.*

*Demetrius.* I love thee not, therefore pursue me not.
Where is Lysander, and fair Hermia?
The one I'll slay, the other slayeth me.
Thou told'st me they were stolen into this wood,
And here am I, and wood within this wood,
Because I cannot meet with Hermia.
Hence! get thee gone, and follow me no more.

*Helena.* You draw me, you hard-hearted adamant;
But yet you draw not iron, for my heart
Is true as steel: leave you your power to draw,
And I shall have no power to follow you.

*Demetrius.* Do I entice you? Do I speak you fair?
Or, rather, do I not in plainest truth
Tell you—I do not nor cannot love you?

*Helena.* And even for that do I love you the more.
I am your spaniel; and, Demetrius,

The more you beat me, I will fawn on you:
Use me but as your spaniel, spurn me, strike me,
Neglect me, lose me; only give me leave,
Unworthy as I am, to follow you.
What worser place can I beg in your love,
(And yet a place of high respect with me,)
Than to be used as you use your dog?

*Demetrius.* Tempt not too much the hatred of my spirit;
For I am sick when I do look on thee.

*Helena.* And I am sick when I look not on you.

*Demetrius.* You do impeach your modesty too much
To leave the city, and commit yourself
Into the hands of one that loves you not;
To trust the opportunity of night,
And the ill counsel of a desert place,
With the rich worth of your virginity.

*Helena.* Your virtue is my privilege for that.
It is not night, when I do see your face,
Therefore I think I am not in the night;
Nor doth this wood lack worlds of company,
For you, in my respect, are all the world:
Then how can it be said I am alone,
When all the world is here to look on me?

*Demetrius.* I'll run from thee, and hide me in the brakes,
And leave thee to the mercy of wild beasts.

*Helena.* The wildest hath not such a heart as you.
Run when you will, the story shall be chang'd,—
Apollo flies, and Daphne holds the chase;
The dove pursues the griffin; the mild hind
Makes speed to catch the tiger:—bootless speed!
When cowardice pursues, and valour flies.

*Demetrius.* I will not stay thy questions; let me go:
Or, if thou follow me, do not believe

But I shall do thee mischief in the wood.

*Helena.* Ay, in the temple, in the town, the field,
You do me mischief. Fye, Demetrius!
Your wrongs do set a scandal on my sex:
We cannot fight for love, as men may do;
We should be woo'd, and were not made to woo.
I'll follow thee, and make a heaven of hell,
To die upon the hand I love so well.

[*Exeunt Demetrius and Helena.*

*Oberon.* Fare thee well, nymph: ere he do leave this grove,
Thou shalt fly him, and he shall seek thy love.—

*Re-enter* PUCK.

Hast thou the flower there? Welcome, wanderer.

*Puck.* Ay, there it is.

*Oberon.* I pray thee, give it me.
I know a bank whereon the wild thyme blows,
Where ox-lips and the nodding violet grows;
Quite over-canopied with luscious woodbine,
With sweet musk-roses, and with eglantine;
There sleeps Titania, some time of the night,
Lull'd in these flowers with dances and delight;
And there the snake throws her enamel'd skin,
Weed wide enough to wrap a fairy in:
And with the juice of this I'll streak her eyes,
And make her full of hateful fantasies.
Take thou some of it, and seek through this grove:
A sweet Athenian lady is in love
With a disdainful youth: anoint his eyes;
But do it, when the next thing he espies
May be the lady. Thou shalt know the man
By the Athenian garments he hath on.

Effect it with some care, that he may prove
More fond on her, than she upon her love :
And look thou meet me ere the first cock crow.
*Puck.* Fear not, my lord, your servant shall do so.

### Scene III.

*Titania.* Come, now a roundel, and a fairy song ;
Then, for the third part of a minute, hence ;
Some, to kill cankers in the musk-rose buds ;
Some, war with rear-mice for their leathern wings,
To make my small elves coats ; and some, keep back
The clamorous owl, that nightly hoots, and wonders
At our quaint spirits. Sing me now asleep ;
Then to your offices, and let me rest.

*Enter* Oberon.

*Oberon.* What thou seest when thou dost wake,
[*Squeezes the flower on Titania's eye-lids.*
Do it for thy true love take ;
Love, and languish for his sake :
Be it ounce, or cat, or bear,
Pard, or boar with bristled hair,
In thy eye that shall appear
When thou wak'st, it is thy dear.
Wake when some vile thing is near.

### Act III. Scene I.

*Titania.* Out of this wood do not desire to go ;
Thou shalt remain here, whether thou wilt or no.
I am a spirit of no common rate ;
The summer still doth tend upon my state ;

And I do love thee: therefore go with me;
I'll give thee fairies to attend on thee;
And they shall fetch thee jewels from the deep,
And sing, while thou on pressed flowers dost sleep:
And I will purge thy mortal grossness so,
That thou shalt like an airy spirit go.—
Peas blossom! Cobweb! Moth! and Mustard-seed!

*Enter four Fairies.*

1*st. Fairy.* Ready.
2*nd. Fairy.* And I.
3*rd. Fairy.* And I.
4*th. Fairy.* Where shall we go?
*Titania.* Be kind and courteous to this gentleman:
Hop in his walks, and gambol in his eyes;
Feed him with apricots, and dewberries,
With purple grapes, green figs, and mulberries;
The honey bags steal from the humble-bees,
And for night-tapers crop their waxen thighs,
And light them at the fiery glow-worm's eyes,
To have my love to bed, and to arise;
And pluck the wings from painted butterflies,
To fan the moon-beams from his sleeping eyes:
Nod to him, elves, and do him courtesies.

## Scene II.

*Helena.* O spite! O hell! I see you all are bent
To set against me, for your merriment.
If you were civil, and knew courtesy,
You would not do me thus much injury.
Can you not hate me, as I know you do,

But you must join in souls to mock me too?
If you were men, as men you are in show,
You would not use a gentle lady so;
To vow, and swear, and superpraise my parts,
When I am sure you hate me with your hearts.
You both are rivals, and love Hermia;
And now both rivals, to mock Helena:
A trim exploit, a manly enterprise,
To conjure tears up in a poor maid's eyes
With your derision! None of noble sort
Would so offend a virgin, and extort
A poor soul's patience, all to make you sport.

* * * * *

*Enter* HERMIA.

*Hermia.* Dark night, that from the eye his function takes,
The ear more quick of apprehension makes;
Wherein it doth impair the seeing sense,
It pays the hearing double recompense.—
Thou art not by mine eye, Lysander, found;
Mine ear, I thank it, brought me to thy sound.
But why unkindly didst thou leave me so?

* * * * *

*Helena.* Lo, she is one of this confederacy!
Now I perceive they have conjoin'd, all three,
To fashion this false sport in spite of me.
Injurious Hermia! most ungrateful maid!
Have you conspir'd, have you with these contriv'd
To bait me with this foul derision?
In all the counsel that we two have shar'd,
The sisters' vows, the hours that we have spent,
When we have chid the hasty-footed time
For parting us,—O! and is all forgot?

All school-days' friendship, childhood innocence?
We, Hermia, like two artificial gods,
Have with our neelds created both one flower,
Both on one sampler, sitting on one cushion,
Both warbling of one song, both in one key;
As if our hands, our sides, voices, and minds,
Had been incorporate. So we grew up together,
Like to a double cherry, seeming parted;
But yet a union in partition,
Two lovely berries moulded on one stem;
So, with two seeming bodies, but one heart;
Two of the first, like coats in heraldry,
Due but to one, and crowned with one crest.
And will you rent our ancient love asunder,
To join with men in scorning your poor friend?
It is not friendly, 'tis not maidenly:
Our sex, as well as I, may chide you for it,
Though I alone do feel the injury.

*　　*　　*　　*　　*

*Enter* HELENA.

*Helena.* O weary night! O long and tedious night!
Abate thy hours: shine, comforts, from the east,
That I may back to Athens, by day-light,
From these that my poor company detest:—
And sleep, that sometimes shuts up sorrow's eye,
Steal me a while from mine own company.

*　　*　　*　　*　　*

*Hermia.* Never so weary, never so in woe;
Bedabbled with the dew, and torn with briers;
I can no further crawl, no further go;
My legs can keep no pace with my desires

Here will I rest me, till the break of day,
Heavens shield Lysander, if they mean a fray !

### Act IV. Scene I.

Oberon *advances.*

*Oberon.* Welcome, good Robin. Seest thou this sweet sight ?
Her dotage now I do begin to pity ;
For, meeting her of late behind the wood,
Seeking sweet savours for this hateful fool,
I did upbraid her, and fall out with her ;
For she his hairy temples then had rounded
With coronet of fresh and fragrant flowers ;
And that same dew, which sometime on the buds
Was wont to swell, like round and orient pearls,
Stood now within the pretty flow'rets' eyes,
Like tears, that did their own disgrace bewail.
When I had at my pleasure taunted her,
And she in mild terms begg'd my patience,
I then did ask of her her changeling child ;
Which straight she gave me, and her fairies sent,
To bear him to my bower in fairyland.
And now I have the boy, I will undo
This hateful imperfection in her eyes.
And, gentle Puck, take this transformed scalp
From off the head of this Athenian swain ;
That he, awaking when the other do,
May all to Athens back again repair,
And think no more of this night's accidents,
But as the fierce vexation of a dream.
But first I will release the fairy queen.

* * * * *

*Oberon.* Sound, musick. Come, my queen, take hands with me,
And rock the ground whereon these sleepers be.
Now thou and I are new in amity,
And will to-morrow midnight solemnly
Dance in Duke Theseus' house triumphantly,
And bless it to all fair prosperity.
There shall the pairs of faithful lovers be
Wedded, with Theseus, all in jollity.

*Puck.* Fairy king, attend and mark :
I do hear the morning lark.

*Oberon.* Then, my queen, in silence sad,
Trip we after the night's shade :
We the globe can compass soon,
Swifter than the wandering moon.

*Titania.* Come, my lord ; and in our flight,
Tell me how it came this night,
That I sleeeping here was found
With these mortals on the ground.

[*Horns sound.*

*Enter* THESEUS, HIPPOLYTA, EGEUS, *and train.*

*Theseus.* Go, one of you, find out the forester ;
For now our observation is perform'd ;
And since we have the vaward of the day,
My love shall hear the musick of my hounds :—
Uncouple in the western valley ; go :
Despatch, I say, and find the forester.—
We will, fair queen, up to the mountain's top,

And mark the musical confusion
Of hounds and echo in conjunction.

*Hippolyta.* I was with Hercules and Cadmus once,
When in a wood of Crete they bay'd the bear
With hounds of Sparta; never did I hear
Such gallant chiding, for, besides the groves,
The skies, the fountains, every region near
Seem'd all one mutual cry: I never heard
So musical a discord, such sweet thunder.

*Theseus.* My hounds are bred out of the Spartan kind,
So flew'd, so sanded; and their heads are hung
With ears that sweep away the morning dew;
Crook-knee'd, and dew-lapp'd like Thessalian bulls;
Slow in pursuit, but match'd in mouth like bells,
Each under each. A cry more tuneable
Was never holla'd to, nor cheer'd with horn,
In Crete, in Sparta, nor in Thessaly;
Judge, when you hear.—But, soft! what nymphs are these?

*Egeus.* My lord, this is my daughter here asleep;
And this, Lysander; this Demetrius is;
This Helena, old Nedar's Helena:
I wonder of their being here together.

*Theseus.* No doubt they rose up early to observe
The right of May, and, hearing our intent,
Came here in grace of our solemnity.—
But speak, Egeus; is not this the day
That Hermia should give answer of her choice?

*Egeus.* It is, my lord.

*Theseus.* Go bid the huntsmen wake them with their horns.

[*Horns sound. Demetrius, Lysander, Hermia and Helena start up.*

*Theseus.* Good morrow, friends. St. Valentine is past:
Begin these wood-birds but to couple now?

*Lysander.* Pardon, my lord.

[*He and the rest kneel to Theseus.*

*Theseus.* I pray you all, stand up.
I know you are two rival enemies;
How comes this gentle concord in the world,
That hatred is so far from jealousy,
To sleep by hate, and fear no enmity?

*Lysander.* My lord, I shall reply amazedly,
Half sleep, half waking; but as yet, I swear,
I cannot truly say how I came here;
But, as I think (for truly would I speak,—
And now I do bethink me, so it is),
I came with Hermia hither: our intent
Was to be gone from Athens, where we might be
Without the peril of the Athenian law.—

*Egeus.* Enough, enough, my lord; you have enough:
I beg the law, the law, upon his head.—
They would have stolen away; they would, Demetrius,
Thereby to have defeated you and me,
You of your wife, and me, of my consent;
Of my consent that she should be your wife.

*Demetrius.* My lord, fair Helen told me of their stealth,
Of this their purpose hither to this wood;
And I in fury hither follow'd them,
Fair Helena in fancy following me.
But, my good lord, I wot not of what power,
(But by some power it is,) my love to Hermia,
Melted as doth the snow, seems to be now
As the remembrance of an idle gawd
Which in my childhood I did dote upon;
And all the faith, the virtue of my heart,
The object, and the pleasure of mine eye,
Is only Helena. To her, my lord,

Was I betroth'd ere I saw Hermia;
But, like in sickness, did I loathe this food;
But, as in health, come to my natural taste,
Now do I wish it, love it, long for it,
And will for evermore be true to it.

*Theseus.* Fair lovers, you are fortunately met:
Of this discourse we more will hear anon.—
Egeus, I will overbear your will;
For in the temple, by and by, with us,
These couples shall eternally be knit.
And, for the morning now is something worn,
Our purpos'd hunting shall be set aside.
Away, with us, to Athens: three and three,
We'll hold a feast in great solemnity.—
Come, Hippolyta.

* * * * *

### Act V. Scene I.

*Hippolyta.* 'Tis strange, my Theseus, that these lovers speak of.

*Theseus.* More strange than true. I never may believe
These antique fables, nor these fairy toys.
Lovers and madmen have such seething brains,
Such shaping fantasies, that apprehend
More than cool reason ever comprehends.
The lunatick, the lover, and the poet,
Are of imagination all compact:—
One sees more devils than vast hell can hold,—
That is, the madman; the lover, all as frantick,
Sees Helen's beauty in a brow of Egypt;
The poet's eye, in a fine frenzy rolling,

Doth glance from heaven to earth, from earth to heaven;
And, as imagination bodies forth
The forms of things unknown, the poet's pen
Turns them to shapes, and gives to airy nothing
A local habitation and a name.
Such tricks hath strong imagination,
That, if it would but apprehend some joy,
It comprehends some bringer of that joy;
Or in the night, imagining some fear,
How easy is a bush suppos'd a bear!

*Hippolyta.* But all the story of the night told over,
And all their minds transfigur'd so together,
More witnesseth than fancy's images,
And grows to something of great constancy;
But, howsoever, strange and admirable.

# LOVE'S LABOUR'S LOST.

## Act IV. Scene III.

*Biron.*

O'TIS more than need !—
Have at you then, affection's men at arms !
Consider what you first did swear unto ;
To fast, to study, and to see no woman ;
Flat treason 'gainst the kingly state of youth.
Say, can you fast ? your stomachs are too young ;
And abstinence engenders maladies ;
And where that you have vow'd to study, lords,
In that each of you hath forsworn his book ;
Can you still dream, and pore, and thereon look ?
For when would you, my lord, or you, or you,
Have found the ground of study's excellence,
Without the beauty of a woman's face ?
From women's eyes this doctrine I derive,—
They are the ground, the books, the Academes
From whence doth spring the true Promethean fire.
Why, universal plodding prisons up
The nimble spirits in the arteries,
As motion, and long-during action, tires

The sinewy vigour of the traveller.
Now, for not looking on a woman's face,
You have in that forsworn the use of eyes,
And study too, the causer of your vow:
For where is any author in the world,
Teaches such beauty as a woman's eye?
Learning is but an adjunct to ourself,
And where we are, our learning likewise is.
Then, when ourselves we see in ladies' eyes,
Do we not likewise see our learning there?
O, we have made a vow to study, lords,
And in that vow we have forsworn our books;
For when would you, my liege, or you, or you,
In leaden contemplation, have found out
Such fiery numbers, as the prompting eyes
Of beauteous tutors have enrich'd you with?
Other slow arts entirely keep the brain;
And, therefore, finding barren practisers,
Scarce show a harvest of their heavy toil:
But love, first learned in a lady's eyes
Lives not alone immured in the brain;
But, with the motion of the elements,
Courses as swift as thought in every power,
And gives to every power a double power,
Above their functions and their offices.
It adds a precious seeing to the eye;
A lover's eyes will gaze an eagle blind,
A lover's ear will hear the lowest sound,
When the suspicious head of theft is stopp'd;
Love's feeling is more soft, and sensible,
Than are the tender horns of cockled snails:
Love's tongue proves dainty Bacchus gross in taste:
For valour is not Love a Hercules,

Still climbing trees in the Hesperides?
Subtle as sphinx; as sweet and musical
As bright Apollo's lute, strung with his hair;
And, when Love speaks, the voice of all the gods
Makes heaven drowsy with the harmony.
Never durst poet touch a pen to write,
Until his ink were temper'd with Love's sighs:
O, then his lines would ravish savage ears,
And plant in tyrants mild humility.
From women's eyes this doctrine I derive:
They sparkle still the right Promethean fire;
They are the books, the arts, the Academes,
That show, contain, and nourish all the world,
Else none at all in aught proves excellent.
Then, fools you were these women to forswear;
Or, keeping what is sworn, you will prove fools.
For wisdom's sake, a word that all men love;
Or for love's sake, a word that loves all men;
Or for men's sake, the authors of these women;
Or women's sake, by whom we men are men;
Let us once lose our oaths, to find ourselves,
Or else we lose ourselves to keep our oaths.
It is religion to be thus forsworn;
For charity itself fulfils the law,—
And who can sever love from charity?

## Act V. Scene II.

*King.* Now, at the latest minute of the hour,
Grant us your loves.
*Princess.* A time, methinks, too short
To make a world-without-end bargain in.

No, no, my lord, your grace is perjur'd much,
Full of dear guiltiness; and therefore this,—
If for my love (as there is no such cause)
You will do aught, this shall you do for me:
Your oath I will not trust; but go with speed
To some forlorn and naked hermitage,
Remote from all the pleasures of the world;
There stay, until the twelve celestial signs
Have brought about their annual reckoning.
If this austere insociable life
Change not your offer made in heat of blood;
If frosts, and fasts, hard lodging, and thin weeds,
Nip not the gaudy blossoms of your love,
But that it bear this trial, and last love;
Then, at the expiration of the year,
Come challenge me, challenge me by these deserts,
And, by this virgin palm, now kissing thine,
I will be thine; and, till that instant, shut
My woeful self up in a mourning house,
Raining the tears of lamentation
For the remembrance of my father's death.
If this thou do deny, let our hands part;
Neither intitled in the other's heart.

*King.* If this, or more than this, I would deny,
To flatter up these powers of mine with rest,
The sudden hand of death close up mine eye!
Hence ever then my heart is in thy breast.

*  *  *  *  *

*Rosalind.* Oft have I heard of you, my lord Biron,
Before I saw you; and the world's large tongue
Proclaims you for a man replete with mocks,
Full of comparisons and wounding flouts,
Which you on all estates will execute,

That lie within the mercy of your wit.
To weed this wormwood from your fruitful brain,
And, therewithal, to win me, if you please
(Without the which I am not to be won),
You shall this twelvemonth term from day to day
Visit the speechless sick, and still converse
With groaning wretches; and your task shall be,
With all the fierce endeavour of your wit
To enforce the pained impotent to smile.

*Biron.* To move wild laughter in the throat of death!
It cannot be; it is impossible:
Mirth cannot move a soul in agony.

*Rosalind.* Why, that 's the way to choke a gibing spirit,
Whose influence is begot of that loose grace
Which shallow laughing hearers give to fools:
A jest's prosperity lies in the ear
Of him that hears it, never in the tongue
Of him that makes it: then, if sickly ears,
Deaf'd with the clamours of their own dear groans,
Will hear your idle scorns, continue then,
And I will have you, and that fault withal;
But, if they will not, throw away that spirit,
And I shall find you empty of that fault,
Right joyful of your reformation.

*Biron.* A twelvemonth! well, befall what will befall,
I'll jest a twelvemonth in a hospital.[24]

*Princess.* Ay, sweet my lord; and so I take my leave.
[*To the King.*

# MERCHANT OF VENICE.

## Act II. Scene IV.

*Enter* Launcelot *with a letter.*

*Lorenzo.*

I KNOW the hand: in faith, 'tis a fair hand;
And whiter than the paper it writ on,
Is the fair hand that writ.

* * * *

*Gratiano.* Was not that letter from fair Jessica?

*Lorenzo.* I must needs tell thee all: She hath directed,
How I shall take her from her father's house;
What gold, and jewels, she is furnish'd with;
What page's suit she hath in readiness.
If e'er the Jew her father come to heaven,
It will be for his gentle daughter's sake:
And never dare misfortune cross her foot,
Unless she do it under this excuse,—
That she is issue to a faithless Jew.
Come, go with me; peruse this, as thou goest:
Fair Jessica shall be my torch-bearer.

## Scene VI.

*Jessica.* What, must I hold a candle to my shames?
They in themselves, good sooth, are too, too light.
Why, 'tis an office of discovery, love;
And I should be obscur'd.

* * * * *

*Gratiano.* Now, by my hood, a Gentile, and no Jew.
*Lorenzo.* Beshrew me, but I love her heartily:
For she is wise, if I can judge of her;
And fair she is, if that mine eyes be true;
And true she is, as she hath proved herself;
And therefore, like herself, wise, fair, and true,
Shall she be placed in my constant soul.

*Enter* Jessica, *below.*

What, art thou come?—On, gentlemen, away;
Our masquing mates by this time for us stay.

## Act III. Scene II.

*Belmont. A Room in* Portia's *House.*

*Portia.* I pray you, tarry; pause a day or two,
Before you hazard; for, in choosing wrong,
I lose your company; therefore, forbear a while:
There 's something tells me (but it is not love),
I would not lose you; and you know yourself,
Hate counsels not in such a quality:
But lest you should not understand me well
(And yet a maiden hath no tongue but thought)

I would detain you here some month or two,
Before you venture for me. I could teach you,
How to choose right, but then I am forsworn;
So will I never be: so may you miss me;
But if you do, you 'll make me wish a sin,
That I had been forsworn. Beshrew your eyes,
They have o'erlook'd me, and divided me;
One half of me is yours, the other half yours,—
Mine own, I would say; but if mine, then yours,
And so all yours: O! these naughty times
Put bars between the owners and their rights;
And so, though yours, not yours.—Prove it so,
Let fortune go to hell for it,—not I.
I speak too long; but 'tis to peize the time;
To eke it, and to draw it out in length,
To stay you from election.

* * * * *

*Portia.* Away then: I am lock'd in one of them;
If you do love me, you will find me out.—
Nerissa, and the rest, stand all aloof.—
Let musick sound, while he doth make his choice;
Then, if he lose, he makes a swan-like end,
Fading in musick: that the comparison
May stand more proper, my eye shall be the stream,
And wat'ry death-bed for him: He may win;
And what is musick then? then musick is
Even as the flourish when true subjects bow
To a new-crowned monarch: such it is,
As are those dulcet sounds in break of day,
That creep into the dreaming bridegroom's ear,
And summon him to marriage. Now he goes,
With no less presence, but with much more love,
Than young Alcides, when he did redeem

The virgin tribute paid by howling Troy
To the sea-monster: I stand for sacrifice,
The rest aloof are the Dardanian wives,
With bleared visages, come forth to view
The issue of the exploit. Go, Hercules!
Live thou, I live:—With much much more dismay
I view the fight, than thou that mak'st the fray.

* * * * *

*Portia.* How all the other passions fleet to air,
As doubtful thoughts, and rash-embrac'd despair,
And shudd'ring fear and green-ey'd jealousy.
O love, be moderate, allay thy ecstasy,
In measure rain thy joy, scant this excess;
I feel too much thy blessing, make it less,
For fear I surfeit!

*Bassanio.* What find I here?

[*Opening the leaden casket.*

Fair Portia's counterfeit? What demi-god
Hath come so near creation? Move these eyes?
Or whether, riding on the balls of mine,
Seem they in motion? Here are sever'd lips,
Parted with sugar breath; so sweet a bar
Should sunder such sweet friends: Here in her hairs
The painter plays the spider; and hath woven
A golden mesh to entrap the hearts of men,
Faster than gnats in cobwebs: But her eyes,—
How could he see to do them? having made one,
Methinks it should have power to steal both his,
And leave itself unfurnished: Yet look, how far
The substance of my praise doth wrong this shadow
In underprizing it, so far this shadow
Doth limp behind the substance.—Here's the scroll,
The continent and summary of my fortune.

"You that choose not by the view,
Chance as fair, and choose as true!
Since this fortune falls to you,
Be content, and seek no new.
If you be well pleas'd with this,
And hold your fortune for your bliss,
Turn you where your lady is,
And claim her with a loving kiss."

A gentle scroll:—Fair lady, by your leave; [*Kissing her.*
I come by note, to give, and to receive.
Like one of two contending in a prize,
That thinks he hath done well in people's eyes,
Hearing applause, and universal shout,
Giddy in spirit, still gazing, in a doubt
Whether those peals of praise be his or no;
So, thrice fair lady, stand I, even so;
As doubtful whether what I see be true,
Until confirm'd, sign'd, ratified by you.

* * * * *

*Portia.* You see me, lord Bassanio, where I stand,
Such as I am: though, for myself alone,
I would not be ambitious in my wish,
To wish myself much better; yet, for you,
I would be trebled twenty times myself;
A thousand times more fair, ten thousand times more rich;
That only to stand high on your account,
I might in virtues, beauties, livings, friends,
Exceed account: but the full sum of me
Is sum of something; which, to term in gross,
Is an unlesson'd girl, unschool'd, unpractis'd:
Happy in this, she is not yet so old
But she may learn; happier than this,
She is not bred so dull but she can learn;

Happiest of all, is, that her gentle spirit
Commits itself to yours to be directed,
As from her lord, her governor, her king.
Myself, and what is mine, to you, and yours
Is now converted: but now I was the lord
Of this fair mansion, master of my servants,
Queen o'er myself; and even now, but now,
This house, these servants, and this same myself,
Are yours, my lord; I give them with this ring;
Which when you part from, lose, or give away,
Let it presage the ruin of your love,
And be my vantage to exclaim on you.

*Bassanio.* Madam, you have bereft me of all words,
Only my blood speaks to you in my veins:
And there is such confusion in my powers,
As, after some oration fairly spoke
By a beloved prince, there doth appear
Among the buzzing pleased multitude:
Where every something, being blent together,
Turns to a wild of nothing, save of joy,
Express'd, and not express'd: But when this ring
Parts from this finger, then parts life from hence;
O, then be bold to say, Bassanio's dead.

* * * * *

*Portia.* There are some shrewd contents in yon' same paper,
That steal the colour from Bassanio's cheek:
Some dear friend dead; else nothing in the world
Could turn so much the constitution
Of any constant man. What, worse and worse?—
With leave, Bassanio; I am half yourself,
And I must freely have the half of any thing
That this same paper brings you.

* * * * *

*Portia.* Is it your dear friend, that is thus in trouble?
*Bassanio.* The dearest friend to me, the kindest man,
The best condition'd and unwearied spirit
In doing courtesies; and one in whom
The ancient Roman honour more appears,
Than any that draws breath in Italy.
*Portia.* What sum owes he the Jew?
*Bassanio.* For me, three thousand ducats.
*Portia.* What, no more?
Pay him six thousand, and deface the bond;
Double six thousand, and then treble that,
Before a friend of this description
Shall lose a hair through Bassanio's fault.
First, go with me to church, and call me wife:
And then away to Venice to your friend;
For never shall you lie by Portia's side
With an unquiet soul. You shall have gold
To pay the petty debt twenty times over;
When it is paid, bring your true friend along:
My maid Nerissa and myself, mean time,
Will live as maids and widows. Come, away;
For you shall hence upon your wedding-day:
Bid your friends welcome, show a merry cheer;
Since you are dear bought, I will love you dear.—
But let me hear the letter of your friend.

*Bassanio* (*reads*). "Sweet Bassanio, my ships have all miscarried, my creditors grow cruel, my estate is very low, my bond to the Jew is forfeit; and since, in paying it, it is impossible I should live, all debts are cleared between you and I, if I might but see you at my death: notwithstanding, use your pleasure: if your love do not persuade you to come, let not my letter."

*Portia.* O love, despatch all business, and be gone.
*Bassanio.* Since I have your good leave to go away,
I will make haste: but, till I come again,
No bed shall e'er be guilty of my stay,
Nor rest be interposer 'twixt us twain. [*Exeunt.*

ACT IV. SCENE I.—*A Court of Justice.*

*Portia.* Then must the Jew be merciful.
*Shylock.* On what compulsion must I? tell me that.
*Portia.* The quality of mercy is not strain'd;
It droppeth, as the gentle rain from heaven
Upon the place beneath: it is twice bless'd;
It blesseth him that gives, and him that takes:
'Tis mightiest in the mightiest; it becomes
The throned monarch better than his crown:
His sceptre shows the force of temporal power,
The attribute to awe and majesty,
Wherein doth sit the dread and fear of kings;
But mercy is above this sceptred sway,
It is enthroned in the hearts of kings,
It is an attribute to God himself;
And earthly power doth then show likest God's,
When mercy seasons justice. Therefore, Jew,
Though justice be thy plea, consider this,—
That in the course of justice, none of us
Should see salvation: we do pray for mercy,
And that same prayer doth teach us all to render
The deeds of mercy. I have spoke thus much,
To mitigate the justice of thy plea;
Which if thou follow, this strict court of Venice
Must needs give sentence 'gainst the merchant there.

*    *    *    *    *

*Portia.* Why, this bond is forfeit;
And lawfully by this the Jew may claim
A pound of flesh, to be by him cut off
Nearest the merchant's heart:—Be merciful;
Take thrice thy money; bid me tear the bond.

*    *    *    *    *

*Portia.* Tarry a little:—there is something else.—
This bond doth give thee here no jot of blood;
The words expressly are, a pound of flesh:
Take then thy bond; take thou thy pound of flesh;
But, in the cutting it, if thou dost shed
One drop of Christian blood, thy lands and goods
Are, by the laws of Venice, confiscate
Unto the state of Venice.

*    *    *    *    *

*Portia.* Therefore prepare thee to cut off the flesh,
Shed thou no blood; nor cut thou less, nor more,
But just a pound of flesh: if thou tak'st more,
Or less, than just a pound,—be it but so much
As makes it light, or heavy, in the substance,
Or the division of the twentieth part
Of one poor scruple; nay, if the scale do turn
But in the estimation of a hair,—
Thou diest, and all thy goods are confiscate.

*    *    *    *    *

*Portia.* He is well paid that is well satisfied;
And I, delivering you, am satisfied,
And therein doth account myself well paid;
My mind was never yet more mercenary.
I pray you know me, when we meet again;
I wish you well, and so I take my leave.

ACT V. SCENE I.

*Lorenzo.* The moon shines bright :—In such a night as this,
When the sweet wind did gently kiss the trees,
And they did make no noise ; in such a night,
Troilus, methinks, mounted the Trojan walls,
And sigh'd his soul toward the Grecian tents,
Where Cressid lay that night.
*Jessica.* In such a night
Did Thisbe fearfully o'ertrip the dew ;
And saw the lion's shadow ere himself,
And ran dismay'd away.
*Lorenzo.* In such a night,
Stood Dido, with a willow in her hand
Upon the wild sea-banks, and wav'd her love
To come again to Carthage.
*Jessica.* In such a night,
Medea gather'd the enchanted herbs
That did renew old Æson.
*Lorenzo.* In such a night,
Did Jessica steal from the wealthy Jew ;
And with an unthrift love did run from Venice,
As far as Belmont.
*Jessica.* In such a night,
Did young Lorenzo swear he loved her well ;
Stealing her soul with many vows of faith,
And ne'er a true one.
*Lorenzo.* In such a night,
Did pretty Jessica, like a little shrew,
Slander her love, and he forgave it her.

*Jessica.* I would out-night you, did nobody come;
But, hark, I hear the footing of a man.

* * * * *

*Lorenzo.* How sweet the moonlight sleeps upon this bank!
Here will we sit, and let the sounds of musick
Creep in our ears; soft stillness, and the night,
Become the touches of sweet harmony.
Sit, Jessica: Look, how the floor of heaven
Is thick inlaid with patines of bright gold;
There 's not the smallest orb, which thou behold'st,
But in his motion like an angel sings,
Still quiring to the young-ey'd cherubins;
Such harmony is in immortal souls;
But, whilst this muddy vesture of decay
Doth grossly close us in, we cannot hear it.—

*Enter* Musicians.

Come, ho, and wake Diana with a hymn:
With sweetest touches pierce your mistress' ear,
And draw her home with musick.
*Jessica.* I am never merry when I hear sweet musick.
*Lorenzo.* The reason is, your spirits are attentive;
For do but note a wild and wanton herd,
Or race of youthful and unhandled colts,
Fetching mad bounds, bellowing, and neighing loud,
Which is the hot condition of their blood;
If they but hear perchance a trumpet sound,
Or any air of musick touch their ears,
You shall perceive them make a mutual stand,
Their savage eyes turn'd to a modest gaze,
By the sweet power of musick: Therefore, the poet

Did feign that Orpheus drew trees, stones, and floods;
Since nought so stockish, hard, and full of rage,
But musick for a time doth change his nature:
The man that hath no musick in himself,
Nor is not mov'd by concord of sweet sounds,
Is fit for treasons, stratagems, and spoils;
The motions of his spirit are dull as night,
And his affections dark as Erebus:
Let no such man be trusted.—Mark the musick.

*Enter* PORTIA *and* NERISSA *at a distance.*

*Portia.* That light we see, is burning in my hall.
How far that little candle throws his beams!
So shines a good deed in a naughty world.

*Nerissa.* When the moon shone, we did not see the candle.

*Portia.* So doth the greater glory dim the less:
A substitute shines brightly as a king
Until a king be by; and then his state
Empties itself, as doth an inland brook
Into the main of waters. Musick! hark!

*Nerissa.* It is your musick, madam, of the house.

*Portia.* Nothing is good, I see, without respect;
Methinks, it sounds much sweeter than by day.

*Nerissa.* Silence bestows that virtue on it, madam.

*Portia.* The crow doth sing as sweetly as the lark
When neither is attended; and, I think,
The nightingale, if she should sing by day,
When every goose is cackling, would be thought
No better a musician than the wren.
How many things by season season'd are
To their right praise, and true perfection!—

Peace, hoa! the moon sleeps with Endymion,
And would not be awak'd.

*Lorenzo.* That is the voice,
Or I am much deceiv'd, of Portia.

*Portia.* He knows me, as the blind man knows the cuckoo,
By the bad voice.

*Lorenzo.* Dear lady, welcome home.

*Portia.* We have been praying for our husbands' welfare,
Which speed, we hope, the better for our words.
Are they return'd?

*Lorenzo.* Madam, they are not yet;
But there is come a messenger before,
To signify their coming.

*Portia.* Go in, Nerissa,
Give order to my servants, that they take
No note at all of our being absent hence;—
Nor you, Lorenzo;—Jessica, nor you.

*Lorenzo.* Your husband is at hand, I hear his trumpet;
We are no tell-tales, madam; fear you not.

*Portia.* This night, methinks, is but the daylight sick,
It looks a little paler; 'tis a day
Such as the day is when the sun is hid.

# OTHELLO, THE MOOR OF VENICE.

## Act I. Scene III.

*Othello.*

MOST potent, grave, and reverend signiors,
My very noble and approv'd good masters,—
That I have ta'en away this old man's daughter,
It is most true ; true, I have married her ;
The very head and front of my offending
Hath this extent, no more. Rude am I in my speech,
And little bless'd with the set phrase of peace ;
For since these arms of mine had seven years' pith,
Till now, some nine moons wasted, they have us'd
Their dearest action in the tented field ;
And little of this great world can I speak,
More than pertains to feats of broil and battle ;
And therefore little shall I grace my cause,
In speaking for myself. Yet, by your gracious patience,
I will a round unvarnish'd tale deliver
Of my whole course of love ; what drugs, what charms,
What conjuration, and what mighty magic,—
For such proceeding I am charg'd withal,—
I won his daughter with.

*Brabantio.* A maiden never bold;
Of spirit so still and quiet, that her motion
Blush'd at herself; and she,—in spite of nature,
Of years, of country, credit, everything,—
To fall in love with what she fear'd to look on!
It is a judgment maim'd and most imperfect,
That will confess perfection so could err
Against all rules of nature; and must be driven
To find out practices of cunning hell,
Why this should be. I therefore vouch again,
That with some mixtures powerful o'er the blood,
Or with some dram conjur'd to this effect,
He wrought upon her.

*Duke.* To vouch this, is no proof,
Without more certain and more overt test,
Than these thin habits and poor likelihoods
Of modern seeming do prefer against him.

*1st Senator.* But, Othello, speak:—
Did you, by indirect and forced courses,
Subdue and poison this young maid's affections?
Or came it by request, and such fair question
As soul to soul affordeth.

*Othello.* I do beseech you,
Send for the lady to the Sagittary,
And let her speak of me before her father:
If you do find me foul in her report,
The trust, the office, I do hold of you,
Not only take away, but let your sentence
Even fall upon my life.

*Duke.* Fetch Desdemona hither.

*Othello.* Ancient, conduct them; you best know the place.—
And, till she come, as truly as to heaven

I do confess the vices of my blood,
So justly to your grave ears I'll present
How I did thrive in this fair lady's love,
And she in mine.

*Duke.* Say it, Othello.

*Othello.* Her father lov'd me ; oft invited me ;
Still question'd me the story of my life,
From year to year ; the battles, sieges, fortunes,
That I have pass'd.
I ran it through, even from my boyish days,
To the very moment that he bade me tell it :
Wherein I spoke of most disastrous chances,
Of moving accidents by flood and field ;
Of hair-breadth 'scapes i' the imminent deadly breach ;
Of being taken by the insolent foe,
And sold to slavery ; of my redemption thence,
And portance in my travel's history :
Wherein of antres vast, and deserts idle,
Rough quarries, rocks, and hills whose heads touch heaven,
It was my hint to speak ; such was the process ;
And of the cannibals that each other eat,
The Anthropophagi, and men whose heads
Do grow beneath their shoulders. These things to hear,
Would Desdemona seriously incline :
But still the house affairs would draw her thence ;
Which ever as she could with haste despatch,
She 'd come again, and with a greedy ear
Devour up my discourse :—which I observing,
Took once a pliant hour ; and found good means
To draw from her a prayer of earnest heart,
That I would all my pilgrimage dilate,
Whereof by parcels she had something heard
But not intentively : I did consent ;

And often did beguile her of her tears,
When I did speak of some distressful stroke
That my youth suffer'd. My story being done,
She gave me for my pains a world of sighs;
She swore,—in faith, 'twas strange, 'twas passing strange;
'Twas pitiful, 'twas wondrous pitiful:
She wish'd she had not heard it; yet she wish'd
That heaven had made her such a man: she thank'd me,
And bade me, if I had a friend that lov'd her,
I should but teach him how to tell my story,
And that would woo her. Upon this hint I spake;
She lov'd me for the dangers I had pass'd;
And I lov'd her that she did pity them.
This only is the witchcraft I have used:—
Here comes the lady, let her witness it.

*Enter* DESDEMONA, IAGO, *and* Attendants.

*Duke.* I think this tale would win my daughter too.—
Good Brabantio,
Take up this mangled matter at the best;
Men do their broken weapons rather use,
Than their bare hands.

*Brabantio.* I pray you, hear her speak;
If she confess that she was half the wooer,
Destruction on my head, if my bad blame
Light on the man!—Come hither, gentle mistress:
Do you perceive in all this noble company,
Where most you owe obedience?

*Desdemona.* My noble father,
I do perceive here a divided duty:
To you, I am bound for life and education;
My life and education both do learn me
How to respect you; you are the lord of duty,—

I am hitherto your daughter: but here 's my husband;
And so much duty as my mother show'd
To you, preferring you before her father,
So much I challenge, that I may profess
Due to the Moor my lord.

*Brabantio.* God be with you!—I have done.—
Please it your grace, on to the state affairs;
I had rather to adopt a child than get it.—
Come hither, Moor:
I here do give thee that with all my heart,
Which, but thou hast already, with all my heart
I would keep from thee.—For your sake, jewel,
I am glad at soul I have no other child,
For thy escape would teach me tyranny,
To hang clogs on them.—I have done, my lord.

* * * * *

*Desdemona.* That I did love the Moor to live with him,
My downright violence and storm of fortunes
May trumpet to the world; my heart 's subdu'd
Even to the very quality of my lord:
I saw Othello's visage in his mind;
And to his honours, and his valiant parts,
Did I my soul and fortunes consecrate,
So that, dear lords, if I be left behind,
A moth of peace, and he go to the war,
The rites for which I love him are bereft me,
And I a heavy interim shall support
By his dear absence. Let me go with him.

*Othello.* Your voices, lords:—'beseech you, let her will
Have a free way.

## ACT II. SCENE I.

*Montano.* But, good lieutenant, is your general wiv'd?
*Cassio.* Most fortunately; he hath achiev'd a maid
That paragons description and wild fame;
One that excels the quirks of blazoning pens,
And in th' essential vesture of creation,
Does bear all excellency.—How now! who has put in?
*2nd Gentleman.* 'Tis one Iago, ancient to the general.
*Cassio.* He has had most favourable and happy speed:
Tempests themselves, high seas, and howling winds,
The gutter'd rocks, and congregated sands,—
Traitors ensteep'd to clog the guiltless keel,—
As having sense of beauty, do omit
Their mortal natures, letting go safely by
The divine Desdemona.
*Montano.* What is she?
*Cassio.* She that I spake of, our great captain's captain,
Left in the conduct of the bold Iago;
Whose footing here anticipates our thoughts,
A se'nnight's speed.—Great Jove, Othello guard,
And swell his sail with thine own powerful breath,
That he may bless this bay with his tall ship,
Make love's quick pants in Desdemona's arms,
Give renew'd fire to our extincted spirits,
And bring all Cyprus comfort!—O, behold,
The riches of the ship is come on shore!
Ye men of Cyprus, let her have your knees.—
Hail to thee, lady! and the grace of heaven,
Before, behind thee, and on every hand,
Enwheel thee round!

* * * * *

*Othello.* O my fair warrior!
*Desdemona.* My dear Othello!
*Othello.* It gives me wonder great as my content,
To see you here before me. O my soul's joy!
If after every tempest comes such calms,
May the winds blow till they have waken'd death!
And let the labouring bark climb hills of seas,
Olympus-high, and duck again as low
As hell's from heaven! If it were now to die,
'Twere now to be most happy; for, I fear,
My soul hath her content so absolute,
That not another comfort like to this
Succeeds in unknown fate.
*Desdemona.* The heavens forbid
But that our loves and comforts should increase,
Even as our days do grow!
*Othello.* Amen to that, sweet powers!—
I cannot speak enough of this content;
It stops me here; it is too much of joy:
And this and this, [*Kissing her*] the greatest discords be,
That e'er our hearts shall make!
*Iago* (*aside*). O, you are well tun'd now!
But I'll set down the pegs that make this music,
As honest as I am.
*Othello.* Come, let us to the castle.—
News, friends; our wars are done, the Turks are drown'd.
How does my old acquaintance of this isle?
Honey, you shall be well desired in Cyprus;
I have found great love amongst them. O my sweet,
I prattle out of fashion, and I dote
In mine own comforts.—I pr'ythee, good Iago,
Go to the bay, and disembark my coffers:

Bring thou the master to the citadel;
He is a good one, and his worthiness
Does challenge much respect.—Come, Desdemona,
Once more well met at Cyprus.

## Act III. Scene III.

*Desdemona.* Be thou assur'd, good Cassio, I will do
All my abilities in thy behalf.
*Emilia.* Good madam, do; I warrant it grieves my husband,
As if the case were his.
*Desdemona.* O, that's an honest fellow.—Do not doubt, Cassio,
But I will have my lord and you again
As friendly as you were.
*Cassio.* Bounteous madam,
Whatever shall become of Michael Cassio,
He's never anything but your true servant.
*Desdemona.* O sir, I thank you. You do love my lord:
You have known him long; and be you well assur'd,
He shall in strangeness stand no farther off
That in a politic distance.
*Cassio.* Ay, but, lady,
That policy may either last so long,
Or feed upon such nice and waterish diet,
Or breed itself so out of circumstance,
That, I being absent, and my place supplied,
My general will forget my love and service.
*Desdemona.* Do not doubt that; before Emilia here,
I give thee warrant of thy place: assure thee,
If I do vow a friendship, I'll perform it
To the last article: my lord shall never rest;

I'll watch him tame, and talk him out of patience;
His bed shall seem a school, his board a shrift;
I'll intermingle every thing he does
With Cassio's suit: therefore be merry, Cassio;
For thy solicitor shall rather die,
Than give thy cause away.

*Emilia.* Madam, here comes my lord.

*Cassio.* Madam, I'll take my leave.

*Desdemona.* Why, stay, and hear me speak.

*Cassio.* Madam, not now: I am very ill at ease,
Unfit for mine own purpose.

*Desdemona.* Well, do your discretion.

*Iago.* Ha! I like not that.

*Othello.* What dost thou say?

*Iago.* Nothing, my lord: or if—I know not what.

*Othello.* Was not that Cassio parted from my wife?

*Iago.* Cassio, my lord? No, sure, I cannot think it,
That he would steal away so guilty-like,
Seeing you coming.

*Othello.* I do believe 'twas he.

*Desdemona.* How now, my lord!
I have been talking with a suitor here,
A man that languishes in your displeasure.

*Othello.* Who is 't you mean?

*Desdemona.* Why, your lieutenant, Cassio. Good my lord,
If I have any grace or power to move you,
His present reconciliation take;
For if he be not one that truly loves you,
That errs in ignorance, and not in cunning,
I have no judgment in an honest face:
I pr'ythee, call him back.

*Othello.* Went he hence now?

*Desdemona.* Ay, sooth; so humbled,
That he hath left part of his grief with me,
I suffer with him. Good love, call him back.

*Othello.* Not now, sweet Desdemona; some other time.

*Desdemona.* But shall 't be shortly?

*Othello.* The sooner, sweet, for you.

*Desdemona.* Shall 't be to-night at supper?

*Othello.* No, not to-night.

*Desdemona.* To-morrow dinner, then?

*Othello.* I shall not dine at home;
I meet the captains at the citadel.

*Desdemona.* Why then, to-morrow night; or Tuesday morn;
On Tuesday noon, or night; on Wednesday morn:—
I pr'ythee, name the time; but let it not
Exceed three days: in faith, he 's penitent;
And yet his trespass, in our common reason,
(Save that, they say, the wars must make examples
Out of their best,) is not almost a fault
To incur a private check. When shall he come?
Tell me, Othello: I wonder in my soul,
What you could ask me that I should deny,
Or stand so mammering on. What! Michael Cassio,
That came a wooing with you; and so many a time,
When I have spoke of you dispraisingly,
Hath ta'en your part; to have so much to do
To bring him in! Trust me, I could do much,—

*Othello.* Pr'ythee, no more: let him come when he will;
I will deny thee nothing.

*Desdemona.* Why, this is not a boon;
'Tis as I should entreat you wear your gloves,
Or feed on nourishing dishes, or keep you warm,
Or sue to you to do a peculiar profit

To your own person: nay, when I have a suit
Wherein I mean to touch your love indeed,
It shall be full of poise and difficulty,
And fearful to be granted.

*Othello.* I will deny thee nothing:
Whereon, I do beseech thee, grant me this,
To leave me but a little to myself.

*Desdemona.* Shall I deny you? no: farewell, my lord.

*Othello.* Farewell, my Desdemona: I'll come to thee straight.

*Desdemona.* Emilia, come.—Be it as your fancies teach you;
Whate'er you be, I am obedient.

*Othello.* Excellent wretch! Perdition catch my soul,
But I do love thee! and when I love thee not,
Chaos is come again.

*Iago.* My noble lord,—

* * * * *

*Othello.* If she be false, O, then heaven mocks itself!—
I'll not believe it.

*Desdemona.* How now, my dear Othello?
Your dinner and the generous islanders,
By you invited, do attend your presence.

*Othello.* I am to blame.

*Desdemona.* Why is your speech so faint? are you not well?

*Othello.* I have a pain upon my forehead here.

*Desdemona.* Faith, that's with watching: 'twill away again:
Let me but bind it hard, within this hour
It will be well.

*Othello.* Your napkin is too little;
Let it alone. Come, I'll go in with you.

*Desdemona.* I am very sorry that you are not well.

*Emilia.* I am glad I have found this napkin:
This was her first remembrance from the Moor:
My wayward husband hath a hundred times
Woo'd me to steal it; but she so loves the token,—
For he conjur'd her she should ever keep it,—
That she reserves it evermore about her,
To kiss, and talk too. I 'll have the work ta'en out,
And give 't Iago: what he will do with it,
Heaven knows, not I;
I nothing, but to please his fantasy.

*Iago.* How now! what do you here alone?

*Emilia.* Do not you chide; I have a thing for you.

*Iago.* A thing for me!—it is a common thing—

*Emilia.* Ha?

*Iago.* To have a foolish wife.

*Emilia.* O, is that all? What will you give me now
For that same handkerchief?

*Iago.* What handkerchief?

*Emilia.* What handkerchief!
Why, that the Moor first gave to Desdemona:
That which so often you did bid me steal.

*Iago.* Hast stolen it from her?

*Emilia.* No, 'faith; she let it drop by negligence;
And, to th' advantage, I, being here, took 't up.
Look, here it is.

*Iago.* A good wench; give it me.

*Emilia.* What will you do with 't, that you have been so earnest
To have me fetch it?

*Iago.* Why, what 's that to you?

*Emilia.* If it be not for some purpose of import,
Give 't me again: poor lady, she 'll run mad

When she shall lack it.

*Iago.* Be not acknown on 't; I have use for it.
Go, leave me.—
I will in Cassio's lodging lose this napkin,
And let him find it. Trifles, light as air,
Are to the jealous confirmations strong
As proofs of holy writ. This may do something.
The Moor already changes with my poison :—
Dangerous conceits are, in their natures, poisons,
Which at the first are scarce found to distaste;
But, with a little act upon the blood,
Burn like the mines of sulphur.—I did say so :—
Look, where he comes! Not poppy, nor mandragora,
Nor all the drowsy syrups of the world,
Shall ever medicine thee to that sweet sleep
Which thou ow'dst yesterday.

*Othello.* Ha! ha! false to me?

*Iago.* Why, how now, general! no more of that.

*Othello.* Avaunt! be gone! thou hast set me on the rack :—
I swear, 'tis better to be much abus'd,
Than but to know 't a little.

*Iago.* How now, my lord?

*Othello.* What sense had I of her stolen hours of lust?
I saw 't not, thought it not, it harm'd me not;
I slept the next night well, was free and merry;
I found not Cassio's kisses on her lips:
He that is robb'd, not wanting what is stolen,
Let him not know 't, and he 's not robb'd at all.

*Iago.* I am sorry to hear this.

*Othello.* I have been happy, if the general camp,
Pioneers and all, had tasted her sweet body,
So I had nothing known. O, now, for ever

Farewell the tranquil mind! farewell content!
Farewell the plumed troop, and the big wars,
That make ambition virtue! O, farewell!
Farewell the neighing steed, and the shrill trump,
The spirit-stirring drum, the ear-piercing fife,
The royal banner, and all quality,
Pride, pomp, and circumstance of glorious war!
And, O you mortal engines, whose rude throats
Th' immortal Jove's dread clamours counterfeit,
Farewell! Othello's occupation 's gone!

*Iago.* Is it possible, my lord?

*Othello.* Villain, be sure thou prove my love a whore,
Be sure of it; give me the ocular proof;
[*Seizing him by the throat.*
Or, by the worth of mine eternal soul,
Thou hadst been better had been born a dog,
Than answer my wak'd wrath.

*Iago.* Is 't come to this?

*Othello.* Make me to see 't; or, at the least, so prove it,
That the probation bear no hinge nor loop
To hang a doubt on; or woe upon thy life!

*Iago.* My noble lord,—

*Othello.* If thou dost slander her, and torture me,
Never pray more; abandon all remorse;
On horror's head horrors accumulate;
Do deeds to make heaven weep, all earth amaz'd;
For nothing canst thou to damnation add
Greater than that.

## Scene IV.

*Othello.* Well, my good lady.—[*Aside.*] O, hardness to dissemble!—
How do you, Desdemona?

*Desdemona.* Well, my good lord.

*Othello.* Give me your hand. This hand is moist, my lady.

*Desdemona.* It yet has felt no age, nor known no sorrow.

*Othello.* This argues fruitfulness, and liberal heart :—
Hot, hot, and moist : this hand of yours requires
A sequester from liberty, fasting and prayer,
Much castigation, exercise devout ;
For here's a young and sweating devil here,
That commonly rebels. 'Tis a good hand,
A frank one.

*Desdemona.* You may, indeed, say so ;
For 'twas that hand that gave away my heart.

*Othello.* A liberal hand : the hearts of old gave hands ;
But our new heraldry is—hands, not hearts.

*Desdemona.* I cannot speak of this. Come now, your promise.

*Othello.* What promise, chuck ?

*Desdemona.* I have sent to bid Cassio come speak with you.

*Othello.* I have a salt and sorry rheum offends me :
Lend me thy handkerchief.

*Desdemona.* Here, my lord.

*Othello.* That which I gave you.

*Desdemona.* I have it not about me.

*Othello.* Not ?

*Desdemona.* No, indeed, my lord.

*Othello.* That is a fault.
That handkerchief
Did an Egyptian to my mother give :
She was a charmer, and could almost read
The thoughts of people : she told her, while she kept it,

'Twould make her amiable, and subdue my father
Entirely to her love; but if she lost it,
Or made a gift of it, my father's eye
Should hold her loathed, and his spirits should hunt
After new fancies: she, dying, gave it me;
And bid me, when my fate would have me wive,
To give it her. I did so: and take heed on't;
Make it a darling like your precious eye,
To lose or give 't away were such perdition,
As nothing else could match.

*Desdemona.* Is 't possible?

*Othello.* 'Tis true; there 's magic in the web of it;
A sibyl, that had number'd in the world
The sun to course two hundred compasses
In her prophetic fury sew'd the work;
The worms were hallow'd that did breed the silk;
And it was dy'd in mummy, which the skilful
Conserv'd of maidens' hearts.

*Desdemona.* Indeed! is't true?

*Othello.* Most veritable; therefore look to 't well.

*Desdemona.* Then would to heaven that I had never seen it!

*Othello.* Ha! wherefore?

*Desdemona.* Why do you speak so startingly and rash?

*Othello.* Is 't lost? is 't gone? speak, is it out o' the way?

*Desdemona.* Heaven bless us!

*Othello.* Say you?

*Desdemona.* It is not lost; but what an if it were?

*Othello.* How?

*Desdemona.* I say, it is not lost.

*Othello.* Fetch 't, let me see 't.

*Desdemona.* Why, so I can, sir; but I will not now.
This is a trick, to put me from my suit:

Pray you, let Cassio be receiv'd again.

*Othello.* Fetch me the handkerchief: my mind misgives.

*Desdemona.* Come, come;
You 'll never meet a more sufficient man.

*Othello.* The handkerchief!

*Desdemona.* I pray, talk me of Cassio.

*Othello.* The handkerchief.

*Desdemona.* A man that, all his time,
Had founded his good fortunes on your love;
Shar'd dangers with you;—

*Othello.* The handkerchief!

*Desdemona.* In sooth, you are to blame.

*Othello.* Away. [*Exit.*

*Emilia.* Is not this man jealous?

*Desdemona.* I ne'er saw this before.
Sure, there 's some wonder in this handkerchief:
I am most unhappy in the loss of it.

*Emilia.* 'Tis not a year or two shows us a man:
They are all but stomachs, and we all but food;
They eat us hungerly, and when they are full
They belch us.—Look you,—Cassio, and my husband.

*Enter* IAGO *and* CASSIO.

*Iago.* There is no other way; 'tis she must do 't;
And, lo, the happiness! go, and importune her.

*Desdemona.* How now, good Cassio? what 's the news with you?

*Cassio.* Madam, my former suit; I do beseech you,
That by your virtuous means I may again
Exist, and be a member of his love,
Whom I, with all the duty of my heart,
Entirely honour: I would not be delay'd.
If my offence be of such mortal kind

That neither service past, nor present sorrows,
Nor purpos'd merit in futurity,
Can ransom me into his love again,
But to know so must be my benefit,
So shall I clothe me in a forc'd content
And shut myself up in some other course,
To fortune's alms.

*Desdemona.* Alas, gentle Cassio!
My advocation is not now in tune;
My lord is not my lord; nor should I know him
Were he in favour, as in humour alter'd.
So help me every spirit sanctified,
As I have spoken for you all my best,
And stood within the blank of his displeasure,
For my fell speech! You must a while be patient:
What I can do, I will; and more I will,
Than for myself I dare: let that suffice you.

*Iago.* Is my lord angry?

*Emilia.* He went hence but now,
And, certainly, in strange unquietness.

*Iago.* Can he be angry? I have seen the cannon
When it hath blown his ranks into the air;
And, like the devil, from his very arm
Puff'd his own brother;—and can he be angry?
Something of moment, then: I will go meet him:
There's matter in 't, indeed, if he be angry.

*Desdemona.* I pr'ythee, do so.—Something, sure, of state—
Either from Venice, or some unhatch'd practice
Made demonstrable here in Cyprus to him—
Hath puddled his clear spirit; and, in such cases,
Men's natures wrangle with inferior things,
Though great ones are their object. 'Tis even so;
For let our finger ache, and it indues

Our other healthful members e'en to that sense
Of pain : nay, we must think men are not gods;
Nor of them look for such observances
As fit the bridal.—Beshrew me much, Emilia,
I was (unhandsome warrior as I am)
Arraigning his unkindness with my soul;
But now I find, I had suborn'd the witness,
And he 's indicted falsely.

*Emilia.* Pray heaven, it be state affairs, as you think,
And no conception, nor no jealous toy,
Concerning you.

*Desdemona.* Alas the day! I never gave him cause.

*Emilia.* But jealous souls will not be answer'd so;
They are not ever jealous for the cause,
But jealous for they are jealous; 'tis a monster,
Begot upon itself, born on itself.

*Desdemona.* Heaven keep that monster from Othello's mind!

*Emilia.* Lady, amen.

*Desdemona.* I will go and seek him.—Cassio, walk hereabout;
If I do find him fit, I 'll move your suit,
And seek to effect it to my uppermost.

*Cassio.* I humbly thank your ladyship.

## Act IV. Scene I.

*Othello.* Excellent good.—[*A trumpet heard.*] What trumpet is that same?

*Iago.* Something from Venice, sure. 'Tis Lodovico,
Come from the duke : and, see, your wife is with him.

*Lodovico.* 'Save you, worthy general!

*Othello.* With all my heart, sir.

*Lodovico.* The duke and senators of Venice greet you.
[*Giving him a packet.*

*Othello.* I kiss the instrument of their pleasures.
[*Opens the packet and reads.*

*Desdemona.* And what 's the news, good cousin Lodovico?

*Iago.* I am very glad to see you, signior;
Welcome to Cyprus.

*Lodovico.* I thank you. How does lieutenant Cassio?

*Iago.* Lives, sir.

*Desdemona.* Cousin, there 's fallen between him and my lord
An unkind breach: but you shall make all well.

*Othello.* Are you sure of that?

*Desdemona.* My lord?

*Othello* (*reading*). "This fail you not to do, as you will"—

*Lodovico.* He did not call; he 's busy in the paper.
Is there division 'twixt my lord and Cassio?

*Desdemona.* A most unhappy one: I would do much
To atone them, for the love I bear to Cassio.

*Othello.* Fire and brimstone!

*Desdemona.* My lord?

*Othello.* Are you wise?

*Desdemona.* What, is he angry?

*Lodovico* May be, the letter mov'd him;
For, as I think, they do command him home,
Deputing Cassio in his government.

*Desdemona.* Trust me, I am glad on 't.

*Othello.* Indeed!

*Desdemona.* My lord?

*Othello.* I am glad to see you mad.

*Desdemona.* How, sweet Othello?

*Othello.* Devil! [*Striking her.*

*Desdemona.* I have not deserved this.

*Lodovico.* My lord, this would not be believ'd in Venice,
Though I should swear I saw it: 'tis very much:
Make her amends; she weeps.

*Othello.* O devil, devil!
If that the earth could teem with woman's tears,
Each drop she falls would prove a crocodile.—
Out of my sight!

*Desdemona.* I will not stay to offend you. [*Going.*

*Lodovico.* Truly, an obedient lady:—
I do beseech your lordship, call her back.

*Othello.* Mistress!

*Desdemona.* My lord?

*Othello.* What would you with her, sir?

*Lodovico.* Who, I, my lord?

*Othello.* Ay; you did wish that I would make her turn:
Sir, she can turn, and turn, and yet go on,
And turn again; and she can weep, sir, weep;
And she 's obedient, as you say,—obedient,—
Very obedient.—Proceed you in your tears.—
Concerning this, sir,—O well-painted passion!—
I am commanded home.—Get you away;
I'll send for you anon.—Sir, I obey the mandate,
And will return to Venice.—Hence, avaunt!
Cassio shall have my place. And, sir, to-night,
I do entreat that we may sup together:
You are welcome, sir, to Cyprus.—Goats and monkeys!

*Lodovico.* Is this the noble Moor whom our full senate
Call all-in-all sufficient? this the noble nature
Whom passion could not shake? whose solid virtue
The shot of accident, nor dart of chance,

Could neither graze nor pierce?

*Iago.* He is much chang'd.

*Lodovico.* Are his wits safe? is he not light of brain?

*Iago.* He 's that he is; I may not breathe my censure.
What he might be,—if, what he might, he is not,—
I would to heaven he were.

*Lodovico.* What, strike his wife!

*Iago.* 'Faith, that was not so well: yet would I knew
That stroke would prove the worst.

*Lodovico.* Is it his use?
Or did the letters work upon his blood,
And new-create this fault?

*Iago.* Alas, alas!
It is not honesty in me to speak
What I have seen and known. You shall observe him;
And his own courses will denote him so,
That I may save my speech: do but go after,
And mark how he continues.

*Lodovico.* I am sorry that I am deceiv'd in him.

## Scene II.

*Othello.* You have seen nothing then?

*Emilia.* Nor ever heard, nor ever did suspect.

*Othello.* Yes, you have seen Cassio and her together.

*Emilia.* But then I saw no harm; and then I heard
Each syllable that breath made up between them.

*Othello.* What, did they never whisper?

*Emilia.* Never, my lord.

*Othello.* Nor send you out o' the way?

*Emilia.* Never.

*Othello.* To fetch her fan, her gloves, her mask, nor nothing?

*Emilia.* Never, my lord.

*Othello.* That 's strange.

*Emilia.* I durst, my lord, to wager she is honest,
Lay down my soul at stake; if you think other,
Remove your thought; it doth abuse your bosom.
If any wretch hath put this in your head,
Let heaven requite it with the serpent's curse!
For, if she be not honest, chaste, and true,
There 's no man happy; the purest of their wives
Is foul as slander.

*Othello.* Bid her come hither:—go.—

SCENE III.

*Emilia.* How goes it now? he looks gentler than he did.

*Desdemona.* He says he will return incontinent;
He hath commanded me to go to bed,
And bade me to dismiss you.

*Emilia.* Dismiss me!

*Desdemona.* It was his bidding; therefore, good Emilia,
Give me my nightly wearing, and adieu;
We must not now displease him.

*Emilia.* I would you had never seen him!

*Desdemona.* So would not I; my love doth so approve him,
That even his stubbornness, his checks, and frowns,—
Pr'ythee, unpin me,—have grace and favour in them.

*Emilia.* I have laid those sheets you bade me on the bed.

*Desdemona.* All 's one—Good father! how foolish are our minds!—
If I do die before thee, pr'ythee, shroud me
In one of those same sheets.

*Emilia.* Come, come, you talk.

*Desdemona.* My mother had a maid call'd Barbara;
She was in love; and he she lov'd prov'd mad,
And did forsake her: she had a song of "willow";
An old thing 'twas, but it express'd her fortune,
And she died singing it: that song, to-night,
Will not go from my mind; I have much to do,
But to go hang my head all at one side,
And sing it like poor Barbara.—Pr'ythee, despatch.

*Emilia.* Shall I go fetch your night-gown?

*Desdemona.* No, unpin me here.—
This Lodovico is a proper man.

*Emilia.* A very handsome man.

*Desdemona.* And he speaks well.

*Emilia.* I know a lady in Venice who would have walked barefoot to Palestine for a touch of his nether lip.

*Desdemona.* The poor soul sat sighing by a sycamore
tree, [*Singing.*
Sing all a green willow;
Her hand on her bosom, her head on her knee,
Sing willow, willow, willow:
The fresh streams ran by her, and murmur'd her moans;
Sing willow, willow, willow:
Her salt tears fell from her, and soften'd the stones;—
Lay by these:—
Sing willow, willow, willow;
Pr'ythee, hie thee; he 'll come anon:—
Sing all a green willow must be my garland.
Let nobody blame him; his scorn I approve,—
Nay, that 's not next.—Hark! who is it that knocks?

*Emilia.* It is the wind.

*Desdemona.* I called my love false love; but what said
he then?

Sing willow, willow, willow ;
So, get thee gone : good night. Mine eyes do itch ;
Doth that bode weeping?

*Emilia.* 'Tis neither here nor there.

*Desdemona.* I have heard it said so.—O, these men, these men !—
Dost thou in conscience think,—tell me, Emilia,—
That there be women do abuse their husbands
In such gross kind?

*Emilia.* There be some such, no question.

*Desdemona.* Would'st thou do such a deed for all the world?

*Emilia.* Why, would not you?

*Desdemona.* No, by this heavenly light !

*Emilia.* Nor I neither by this heavenly light ;
I might do 't as well i' the dark.

*Desdemona.* Would'st thou do such a deed for all the world?

*Emilia.* The world is a huge thing : 'tis a great price
For a small vice.

*Desdemona.* Good troth, I think thou would'st not.

*Emilia.* By my troth, I think I should ; and undo 't when I had done. Marry, I would not do such a thing for a joint-ring, nor for measures of lawn, nor for gowns, petticoats, nor caps, nor any petty exhibition ; but, for the whole world,—Why, who would not make her husband a cuckold, to make him a monarch? I would venture purgatory for 't.

*Desdemona.* Beshrew me, if I would do such a wrong for the whole world. * * * * Good-night—good-night.—

## ACT V. SCENE II.[26]

*A bedchamber:* DESDEMONA *in bed asleep. A light burning.*

*Enter* OTHELLO.

*Othello.* It is the cause, it is the cause, my soul,—
Let me not name it to you, you chaste stars—
It is the cause.—Yet I 'll not shed her blood;
Nor scar that whiter skin of hers than snow,
And smooth as monumental alabaster.
[*Takes off his sword.*
Yet she must die, else she 'll betray more men.
Put out the light, and then—Put out the light!
If I quench thee, thou flaming minister,
I can again thy former light restore,
Should I repent me:—but once put out thine,
Thou cunning'st pattern of excelling nature,
I know not where is that Promethean heat,
That can thy light relume. When I have pluck'd thy rose,
I cannot give it vital growth again,
It needs must wither:—I'll smell it on the tree.—
[*Kissing her.*
O balmy breath, that dost almost persuade
Justice to break her sword!—One more, one more:—
Be thus when thou art dead, and I will kill thee,
And love thee after:—one more, and this the last;
So sweet was ne'er so fatal. I must weep,
But they are cruel tears: this sorrow 's heavenly;
It strikes, where it doth love.—She wakes.—
*Desdemona.* Who 's there? Othello?

*Othello.* Ay, Desdemona.

*Desdemona.* Will you come to bed, my lord?

*Othello.* Have you pray'd to-night, Desdemona?

*Desdemona.* Ay, my lord.

*Othello.* If you bethink yourself of any crime,
Unreconcil'd as yet to heaven and grace,
Solicit for it straight.

*Desdemona.* Alas, my lord, what may you mean by that?

*Othello.* Well, do it, and be brief; I will walk by:
I would not kill thy unprepared spirit;
No,—Heaven forefend!—I would not kill thy soul.

*Desdemona.* Talk you of killing?

*Othello.* Ay, I do.

*Desdemona.* Then heaven
Have mercy on me!

*Othello.* Amen, with all my heart!

*Desdemona.* If you say so, I hope you will not kill me.

*Othello.* Humph!

*Desdemona.* And yet I fear you; for you are fatal then,
When your eyes roll so! why should I fear I know not.
Since guiltiness I know not; but yet, I feel I fear.

*Othello.* Think on thy sins.

*Desdemona.* They are loves I bear to you.

*Othello.* Ay, and for that thou diest.

*Desdemona.* That death 's unnatural, that kills for loving.—
Alas, why gnaw you so your nether lip?
Some bloody passion shakes your very frame:
These are portents; but yet, I hope, I hope,
They do not point on me.

*Othello.* Peace, and be still!

*Desdemona.* I will so. What 's the matter?

*Othello.* That handkerchief, which I so lov'd, and gave thee,

Thou gav'st to Cassio.
*Desdemona.* No, by my life and soul!
Send for the man and ask him.
*Othello.* Sweet soul, take heed,
Take heed of perjury; thou 'rt on thy death-bed.
*Desdemona.* Ay, but not yet to die.
*Othello.* Yes, presently;
Therefore confess thee freely of thy sin;
For to deny each article with oath,
Cannot remove, nor choke, the strong conception
That I do groan withal. Thou art to die.
*Desdemona.* Then, Lord have mercy on me!
*Othello.* I say, amen.
*Desdemona.* And have you mercy too! I never did
Offend you in my life; never lov'd Cassio,
But with such general warranty of heaven
As I might love; I never gave him token.
*Othello.* By heaven, I saw my handkerchief in his hand.
O perjur'd woman! thou dost stone my heart,
And mak'st me call, what I intend to do,
A murder, which I thought a sacrifice:[27]
I saw the handkerchief.
*Desdemona.* He found it, then;
I never gave it him:—send for him hither,
And let him confess the truth.
*Othello.* He hath confess'd.
*Desdemona.* What, my lord?
*Othello.* That he hath—us'd thee.
*Desdemona.* How? unlawfully?
*Othello.* Ay.
*Desdemona.* He 'll not say so.
*Othello.* No, his mouth is stopp'd;
Honest Iago hath ta'en order for 't.

*Desdemona.* My fear interprets then.—What, is he dead?

*Othello.* Had all his hairs been lives, my great revenge
Had stomach for them all.

*Desdemona.* Alas! he is betray'd, and I undone.

*Othello.* Out, strumpet! Weep'st thou for him to my face?

*Desdemona.* O, banish me, my lord, but kill me not!

*Othello.* Down, strumpet!

*Desdemona.* Kill me to-morrow; let me live to-night!

*Othello.* Nay, if you strive,—

*Desdemona.* But half-an-hour!

*Othello.* Being done,
There is no pause.

*Desdemona.* But while I say one prayer!

[*He smothers her.*

*Othello.* It is too late.

*Emilia* (*within*). My lord, my lord! what, ho! my lord, my lord!

*Othello.* What noise is this?—Not dead? not yet quite dead?
I, that am cruel, am yet merciful;
I would not have thee linger in thy pain.—
So, so.

*Emilia* (*within*). What ho! my lord, my lord!

*Othello.* Who 's there?

*Emilia* (*within*). O, good my lord, I would speak a word with you!

*Othello.* Yes:—'tis Emilia:—by-and-by.—She 's dead.—
'Tis like she comes to speak of Cassio's death;
The noise was high.—Ha! no more moving?
Still as the grave.—Shall she come in? Were 't good?
I think she stirs again:—no.—What's best to do?
If she come in, she 'll sure speak to my wife:

My wife! my wife! what wife?—I have no wife.
O, insupportable! O heavy hour!
Methinks it should be now a huge eclipse
Of sun and moon, and that the affrighted globe
Should yawn at alteration.

*Emilia* (*within*). I do beseech you
That I may speak with you, O, good my lord!

*Othello.* I had forgot thee: O, come in, Emilia:—
Soft,—by-and-by:—let me the curtains draw.—
Where art thou? What 's the matter with thee now?
[*Unlocks the door.*

*Enter* EMILIA.

*Emilia.* O, good my lord, yonder 's foul murder done!

*Othello.* What, now?

*Emilia.* But now, my lord!

*Othello.* It is the very error of the moon;
She comes more near the earth than she was wont,
And makes men mad.

*Emilia.* Cassio, my lord, has kill'd a young Venetian,
Call'd Roderigo.

*Othello.* Roderigo kill'd!
And Cassio kill'd?

*Emilia.* No, Cassio is not kill'd.

*Othello.* Not Cassio kill'd! Then murder 's out of tune,
And sweet revenge grows harsh.

*Desdemona.* O, falsely, falsely murder'd!

*Emilia.* Alas! what cry is that?

*Othello.* That! what?

*Emilia.* Out, and alas! that was my lady's voice:—
Help! help, ho! help!—O lady, speak again!
Sweet Desdemona! O sweet mistress, speak!

*Desdemona.* A guiltless death I die.

*Emilia.* O, who hath done
This deed?

*Desdemona.* Nobody—I myself. Farewell:
Commend me to my kind lord: O, farewell! [*Dies.*

*Othello.* Why, how should she be murder'd?

*Emilia.* Alas, who knows?

*Othello.* You heard her say herself, it was not I.

*Emilia.* She said so; I must needs report the truth.

*Othello.* She's, like a liar, gone to burning hell:
'Twas I that kill'd her.

*Emilia.* O, the more angel she,
And you the blacker devil!

*Othello.* She turn'd to folly, and she was a whore.

*Emilia.* Thou dost belie her, and thou art a devil.

*Othello.* She was false as water.

*Emilia.* Thou art rash as fire, to say
That she was false: O, she was heavenly true!

*Othello.* Cassio did tup her; ask thy husband else.
O, that I were damn'd beneath all depth in hell,
But that I did proceed upon just grounds
To the extremity. Thy husband knew it all.

*Emilia.* My husband?

*Othello.* Thy husband.

*Emilia.* That she was false to wedlock?

*Othello.* Ay, with Cassio. Nay, had she been true,[28]
If heaven would make me such another world
Of one entire and perfect chrysolite,
I'd not have sold her for it.

*Emilia.* My husband?

*Othello.* Ay, 'twas he that told me first;
An honest man he is, and hates the slime
That sticks on filthy deeds.

*Emilia.* My husband?

*Othello.* What needs this iterance, woman? I say, thy husband.

*Emilia.* O mistress, villainy hath made mocks with love!—
My husband say that she was false?

*Othello.* He, woman;
I say, thy husband; dost understand the word?
My friend, thy husband, honest, honest Iago.

*Emilia.* If he say so, may his pernicious soul
Rot half a grain a day! he lies to the heart:
She was too fond of her most filthy bargain.

*Othello.* Ha!

*Emilia.* Do thy worst:
This deed of thine is no more worthy heaven,
Than thou wast worthy her.

*Othello.* Peace, you were best.

*Emilia.* Thou hast not half the power to do me harm,
As I have to be hurt. O gull! O dolt!
As ignorant as dirt! Thou hast done a deed,—
I care not for thy sword; I 'll make thee known,
Though I lost twenty lives:—Help! help! ho! help!
The Moor has kill'd my mistress! Murder! murder!

*Enter* MONTANO, GRATIANO, *and* IAGO.

*Montano.* What is the matter?—How now, general?

*Emilia.* O, you are come, Iago? you have done well,
That men must lay their murders on your neck.

*Gratiano.* What is the matter?

*Emilia.* Disprove this villain, if thou be'st a man;
He says, thou told'st him that his wife was false;
I know thou didst not, thou art not such a villain;
Speak, for my heart is full.

*Iago.* I told him what I thought; and told no more
Than what he found himself was apt and true.
*Emilia.* But did you ever tell him she was false?
*Iago.* I did.
*Emilia.* You told a lie; an odious, damned lie;
Upon my soul, a lie, a wicked lie:—
She false with Cassio!—Did you say with Cassio?
*Iago.* With Cassio, mistress. Go to, charm your tongue.
*Emilia.* I will not charm my tongue, I am bound to speak;
My mistress here lies murder'd in her bed.
*All.* O heavens forefend!
*Emilia.* And your reports have set the murder on.
*Othello.* Nay, stare not, masters; it is true, indeed.
*Gratiano.* 'Tis a strange truth.
*Montano.* O monstrous act!
*Emilia.* Villainy, villainy, villainy!—
I think upon 't,—I think,—I smell 't;—O villainy!
I thought so then;—I 'll kill myself for grief.—
O villainy, villainy!
*Iago.* What, are you mad? I charge you, get you home.
*Emilia.* Good gentlemen, let me have leave to speak:
'Tis proper I obey him, but not now.—
Perchance, Iago, I will ne'er go home.
*Othello.* O! O! O! [*Hanging over his wife.*
*Emilia.* Nay, lay thee down and roar,
For thou hast kill'd the sweetest innocent,
That e'er did lift up eye.
*Othello* (*rising*). O, she was foul!—
I scarce did know you, uncle: there lies your niece,
Whose breath, indeed, these hands have newly stopp'd:
I know, this act shows horrible and grim.
*Gratiano.* Poor Desdemona! I am glad thy father 's dead.

Thy match was mortal to him, and pure grief
Shore his old thread in twain : did he live now,
This sight would make him do a desperate turn,
Yea, curse his better angel from his side,
And fall to reprobation.

*Othello.* 'Tis pitiful : but yet Iago knows
That she with Cassio hath the act of shame
A thousand times committed ; Cassio confess'd it ;
And she did gratify his amorous works
With that recognizance and pledge of love
Which I first gave her ; I saw it in his hand ;
It was a handkerchief, an antique token
My father gave my mother.

*Emilia.* O heaven ! O heavenly powers !

*Iago.* Come, hold your peace.

*Emilia.* 'Twill out, 'twill out :—I hold my peace, sir? No;
I will speak as liberal as the air ;
Let heaven, and men, and devils, let them all,
All, all, cry shame against me, yet I'll speak.

*Iago.* Be wise, and get you home.

*Emilia.* I will not.

[*Iago offers to stab his wife.*

*Gratiano.* Fye !
Your sword upon a woman !

*Emilia.* O thou dull Moor ! that handkerchief thou speak'st of
I found by fortune, and did give my husband ;
For often, with a solemn earnestness
(More than, indeed, belong'd to such a trifle),
He begg'd of me to steal it.

*Iago.* Villainous whore !

*Emilia.* She give it Cassio ! no, alas, I found it,

And I did give 't my husband.

*Iago.* Filth, thou liest!

*Emilia.* By heaven, I do not, I do not, gentlemen;
O murderous coxcomb! what should such a fool
Do with so good a wife?

[*Iago stabs Emilia, then runs out.*

*Othello.* Are there no stones in heaven,
But what serve for the thunder?—Precious villain!

*Gratiano.* The woman falls; sure, he has kill'd his wife.

*Emilia.* Ay, ay: O, lay me by my mistress' side!

*Gratiano.* He 's gone, but his wife 's kill'd.

*Montano.* 'Tis a notorious villain. Take you this weapon,
Which I have here recover'd from the Moor:
Come, guard the door without; let him not pass,
But kill him rather. I'll after that same villain,
For 'tis a damned slave.

[*Exeunt Montano and Gratiano.*

*Othello.* I am not valiant neither,
But every puny whipster gets my sword:—
But why should honour outlive honesty?
Let it go all.

*Emilia.* What did thy song bode, lady?
Hark, canst thou hear me? I will play the swan,
And die in music:—"Willow, willow, willow."—
Moor, she was chaste; she lov'd thee, cruel Moor;
So come my soul to bliss, as I speak true;
So speaking as I think, I die,—I die. [*Dies.*

*Othello.* I have another weapon in this chamber,
It is a sword of Spain, the ice-brook's temper;—
O, here it is.—Uncle, I must come forth.

*Gratiano.* (*within*). If thou attempt it, it will cost thee dear.

Thou hast no weapon, and perforce must suffer.

*Othello.* Look in upon me, then, and speak with me,
Or, naked as I am, I will assault thee.

*Re-enter* GRATIANO.

*Gratiano.* What is the matter?

*Othello.* Behold! I have a weapon;
A better never did itself sustain
Upon a soldier's thigh: I have seen the day,
That, with this little arm and this good sword,
I have made my way through more impediments
Than twenty times your stop:—but, O vain boast!
Who can control his fate? 'tis not so now.—
Be not afraid, though you do see me weapon'd;
Here is my journey's end, here is my butt,
And very sea-mark of my utmost sail.
Do you go back dismay'd? 'tis a lost fear;
Man but a rush against Othello's breast,
And he retires:—where should Othello go?—
Now, how dost thou look now? O ill-starr'd wench!
Pale as thy smock! when we shall meet at compt,
This look of thine will hurl my soul from heaven,
And fiends will snatch at it. Cold, cold, my girl!
Even like thy chastity.—
O cursed, cursed slave!—Whip me, ye devils,
From the possession of this heavenly sight!
Blow me about in winds! roast me in sulphur!
Wash me in steep-down gulfs of liquid fire!—
O Desdemona! Desdemona! dead?
Dead? O! O! O!

*Enter* LODOVICO, MONTANO, CASSIO, *carried in a chair, and Officers, with* IAGO, *prisoner.*

*Lodovico.* Where is this rash and most unfortunate man?

*Othello.* That 's he that was Othello;—here I am.

*Lodovico.* Where is that viper? bring the villain forth.

*Othello.* I look down towards his feet,—but that 's a fable:
If that thou be'st a devil, I cannot kill thee.

[*Othello wounds Iago.*

*Lodovico.* Wrench his sword from him.

*Iago.* I bleed, sir; but not kill'd.

*Othello.* I am not sorry neither; I 'd have thee live;
For, in my sense, 'tis happiness to die.

*Lodovico.* O thou Othello, that was once so good,
Fall'n in the practice of a cursed slave,
What shall be said of thee?

*Othello.* Why, any thing:
An honourable murderer, if you will;
For naught I did in hate, but all in honour.

*Lodovico.* This wretch hath part confess'd his villainy:
Did you and he consent in Cassio's death?

*Othello.* Ay.

*Cassio.* Dear general, I never gave you cause.

*Othello.* I do believe it, and I ask your pardon.—
Will you, I pray, demand that demi-devil,
Why he hath thus ensnar'd my soul and body?

*Iago.* Demand me nothing: what you know, you know;
From this time forth I never will speak word.

*Lodovico.* What, not to pray?

*Gratiano.* Torments will ope your lips.

*Othello.* Well, thou dost best.

*Lodovico.* Sir, you shall understand what hath befall'n,
Which, as I think, you know not. Here is a letter,
Found in the pocket of the slain Roderigo;
And here another; the one of them imports
The death of Cassio to be undertook
By Roderigo.

*Othello.* O villain!

*Cassio.* Most heathenish and most gross!

*Lodovico.* Now! here 's another discontented paper,
Found in his pocket too; and this, it seems,
Roderigo meant to have sent this damned villain;
But that, belike, Iago in the interim
Came in and satisfied him.

*Othello.* O, the pernicious caitiff!—
How came you, Cassio, by that handkerchief,
That was my wife's?

*Cassio.* I found it in my chamber;
And he himself confess'd, but even now,
That there he dropp'd it, for a special purpose,
Which wrought to his desire.

*Othello.* O fool! fool! fool!

*Cassio.* There is, besides, in Roderigo's letter,
How he upbraids Iago, that he made him
Brave me upon the watch; whereon it came
That I was cast: and even but now he spake,
After long seeming dead,—Iago hurt him,
Iago set him on.

*Lodovico.* You must forsake this room, and go with us;
Your power and your command is taken off,
And Cassio rules in Cyprus. For this slave,—
If there be any cunning cruelty
That can torment him much, and hold him long,
It shall be his. You shall close prisoner rest,

Till that the nature of your fault be known
To the Venetian state. Come, bring him away.

*Othello.* Soft you; a word or two, before you go.
I have done the state some service, and they know it;
No more of that.—I pray you, in your letters,
When you shall these unlucky deeds relate,
Speak of me as I am; nothing extenuate,
Nor set down aught in malice: then must you speak
Of one that lov'd, not wisely, but too well;
Of one not easily jealous, but, being wrought,
Perplex'd in the extreme; of one, whose hand,
Like the base Judean, threw a pearl away,
Richer than all his tribe; of one, whose subdu'd eyes,
Albeit unused to the melting mood,
Drop tears as fast as the Arabian trees
Their medicinal gum. Set you down this;
And say, besides,—that in Aleppo once,
Where a malignant and a turban'd Turk
Beat a Venetian, and traduc'd the state,
I took by the throat, the circumcised dog,
And smote him—thus. [*Stabs himself.*

*Lodovico.* O bloody period!

*Gratiano.* All that 's spoke is marr'd.

*Othello.* I kiss'd thee, ere I kill'd thee:—no way but this,
Killing myself, to die upon a kiss. [*Dies.*

*Cassio.* This did I fear, but thought he had no weapon;
For he was great of heart.

*Lodovico.* O Spartan dog,
More fell than anguish, hunger, or the sea!
Look on the tragic loading of this bed:
This is thy work:—the object poisons sight;
Let it be hid.—Gratiano, keep the house,

And seize upon the fortunes of the Moor,
For they succeed on you.—To you, lord governor,
Remains the censure of this hellish villain;
The time, the place, the torture,—O, enforce it!
Myself will straight abroad; and, to the state,
This heavy act with heavy heart relate.

## AS YOU LIKE IT.

### Act I. Scene II.

*Rosalind.*

HE calls me back: my pride fell with my fortunes:
I 'll ask him what he would:—Did you call, sir?—
Sir, you have wrestled well, and overthrown
More than your enemies.

*Celia.* Will you go, coz?

*Rosalind.* Have with you:—Fare you well.

[*Exeunt Rosalind and Celia.*

*Orlando.* What passion hangs these weights upon my tongue?
I cannot speak to her, yet she urg'd conference.
O poor Orlando! thou art overthrown;
Or Charles, or something weaker, masters thee.

### Scene III.

*Rosalind.* So was I, when your highness took his dukedom;

So was I, when your highness banish'd him:
Treason is not inherited, my lord;
Or, if we did derive it from our friends,
What 's that to me; my father was no traitor:
Then, good my liege, mistake me not so much,
To think my poverty is treacherous.

* * * * *

*Celia.* I did not then entreat to have her stay,
It was your pleasure, and your own remorse;
I was too young that time to value her,
But now I know her; if she be a traitor,
Why so am I; we still have slept together,
Rose at an instant, learn'd, play'd, eat together;
And wheresoe'er we went, like Juno's swans,
Still we went coupled, and inseparable.

* * * * *

*Celia.* No? hath not? Rosalind lacks then the love
Which teacheth thee that thou and I am one:
Shall we be sunder'd? shall we part, sweet girl?
No; let my father seek another heir.
Therefore, devise with me, how we may fly,
Whither to go, and what to bear with us:
And do not seek to take your change upon you,
To bear your griefs yourself, and leave me out;
For, by this heaven, now at our sorrows pale,
Say what thou canst, I 'll go along with thee.
*Rosalind.* Why, whither shall we go?
*Celia.* To seek my uncle.
*Rosalind.* Alas, what danger will it be to us,
Maids as we are, to travel forth so far?
Beauty provoketh thieves sooner than gold.[29]
*Celia.* I 'll put myself in poor and mean attire,
And with a kind of umber smirch my face;

The like do you ; so shall we pass along,
And never stir assailants.
*Rosalind.* Were it not better,
Because that I am more than common tall,
That I did suit me all points like a man?
A gallant curtle-axe upon my thigh,
A boar-spear in my hand ; and (in my heart
Lie there what hidden woman's fear there will),
We 'll have a swashing and a martial outside ;
As many other mannish cowards have,
That do outface it with their semblances.
*Celia.* What shall I call thee, when thou art a man?
*Rosalind.* I 'll have no worse a name than Jove's own page,
And therefore look you call me, Ganymede.
But what will you be call'd?
*Celia.* Something that hath a reference to my state:
No longer Celia, but Aliena.
*Rosalind.* But, cousin, what if we assay'd to steal
The clownish fool out of your father's court?
Would he not be a comfort to our travel?
*Celia.* He 'll go along o'er the wide world with me ;
Leave me alone to woo him : Let 's away,
And get our jewels and our wealth together ;
Devise the fittest time, and safest way
To hide us from pursuit that will be made
After my flight : Now go we in content,
To liberty, and not to banishment.

## Act II. Scene IV.

*Rosalind.* I could find in my heart to disgrace my

man's apparel, and to cry like a woman: but I must comfort the weaker vessel, as doublet and hose ought to show itself courageous to petticoat: therefore, courage, good Aliena.

## ACT III. SCENE II.

*Orlando.* Hang there, my verse, in witness of my love:
And thou, thrice-crowned queen of night, survey
With thy chaste eye, from thy pale sphere above,
Thy huntress' name, that my full life doth sway.
O Rosalind! these trees shall be my books,
And in their barks my thoughts I 'll character;
That every eye, which in this forest looks,
Shall see thy virtue witness'd every where.
Run, run, Orlando; carve, on every tree,
The fair, the chaste, and unexpressive she.

* * * * *

*Rosalind.* From the east to western Ind,
No jewel is like Rosalind.
Her worth, being mounted on the wind,
Through all the world bears Rosalind.
All the pictures, fairest lin'd,
Are but black to Rosalind.
Let no face be kept in mind,
But the fair of Rosalind.

* * * * *

*Rosalind.* I have been told so of many: but, indeed, an old religious uncle of mine taught me to speak, who was in his youth an in-land man; one that knew courtship too well, for there he fell in love. I have heard him read many lectures against it; and I thank God, I am not a woman, to be touch'd with so many giddy offences as he hath generally tax'd their whole sex withal.

*Orlando.* Can you remember any of the principal evils that he laid to the charge of woman?

*Rosalind.* There were none principal; they were all like one another, as half-pence are; every one fault seeming monstrous, till his fellow fault came to match it.

*Orlando.* I pr'ythee, recount some of them.

*Rosalind.* No; I will not cast away physick, but on those that are sick. There is a man haunts the forest, that abuses our young plants with carving Rosalind on their barks; hangs odes upon hawthorns, and elegies on brambles; all, forsooth, deifying the name of Rosalind: if I could meet that fancymonger, I would give him some good counsel, for he seems to have the quotidian of love upon him.

*Orlando.* I am he that is so love-shaked; I pray you, tell me your remedy.

*Rosalind.* There is none of my uncle's marks upon you: he taught me how to know a man in love; in which cage of rushes, I am sure, you are not prisoner.

*Orlando.* What were his marks?

*Rosalind.* A lean cheek, which you have not: a blue eye, and sunken, which you have not: an unquestionable spirit, which you have not: a beard neglected, which you have not;—but I pardon you for that; for, simply, your having in beard is a younger brother's revenue:—Then your hose should be ungarter'd, your bonnet unbanded, your sleeve unbutton'd, your shoe untied, and everything about you demonstrating a careless desolation. But you are no such man; you are rather point-device in your accoutrements; as loving yourself, than seeming the lover of any other.

*Orlando.* Fair youth, I would I could make thee believe I love.

*Rosalind.* Me believe it? you may as soon make her that you love believe it; which, I warrant, she is apter to do, than to confess she does; that is one of the points in the which women still give the lie to their consciences. But, in good sooth, are you he that hangs the verses on the trees, wherein Rosalind is so admired?

*Orlando.* I swear to thee, youth, by the white hand of Rosalind, I am that he, that unfortunate he.

*Rosalind.* But are you so much in love as your rhymes speak?

*Orlando.* Neither rhyme nor reason can express how much.

*Rosalind.* Love is merely a madness; and, I tell you, deserves as well a dark house and a whip, as madmen do: and the reason why they are not so punished and cured, is, that the lunacy is so ordinary, that the whippers are in love too: Yet I profess curing it by counsel.

## Scene V.

*Silvius.* Sweet Phebe, do not scorn me; do not,
Phebe:
Say, that you love me not; but say not so
In bitterness. The common executioner,
Whose heart the accustom'd sight of death makes hard,
Falls not the axe upon the humbled neck,
But first begs pardon; Will you sterner be
Than he that dies and lives by bloody drops?

* * * * *

*Silvius.* So holy, and so perfect is my love,
And I in such a poverty of grace,

That I shall think it a most plenteous crop
To glean the broken ears after the man
That the main harvest reaps : loose now and then
A scatter'd smile, and that I live upon.

*Phebe.* Know'st thou the youth that spoke to me ere while?

*Silvius.* Not very well, but I have met him oft;
And he hath bought the cottage, and the bounds,
That the old carlot once was master of.

*Phebe.* Think not I love him, though I ask for him;
'Tis but a peevish boy:—yet he talks well;—
But what care I for words? yet words do well,
When he that speaks them pleases those that hear.
It is a pretty youth:—not very pretty:—
But, sure, he 's proud; and yet his pride becomes him:
He 'll make a proper man: The best thing in him
Is his complexion; and faster than his tongue
Did make offence, his eye did heal it up.
He is not tall; yet for his years he 's tall:
His leg is but so so; and yet 'tis well:
There was a pretty redness in his lip;
A little riper and more lusty red
Than that mix'd in his cheek; 'twas just the difference
Betwixt the constant red, and mingled damask.
There be some women, Silvius, had they mark'd him
In parcels as I did, would have gone near
To fall in love with him: but, for my part,
I love him not, nor hate him not; and yet
I have more cause to hate him than to love him:
For what had he to do to chide at me?
He said, mine eyes were black, and my hair black;
And, now I am remember'd, scorn'd at me:
I marvel, why I answer'd not again;

But that 's all one; omittance is no quittance.
I 'll write to him a very taunting letter,
And thou shalt bear it; Wilt thou, Silvius?

*Silvius.* Phebe, with all my heart.

*Phebe.* I 'll write it straight;
The matter 's in my head, and in my heart:
I will be bitter with him, and passing short:
Go with me, Silvius.

## Act IV. Scene I.

*Rosalind.* Break an hour's promise in love? He that will divide a minute into a thousand parts, and break but a part of the thousandth part of a minute in the affairs of love, it may be said of him, that Cupid hath clapp'd him o' the shoulder, but I warrant him heart-whole.

* * * * *

*Rosalind.* No, faith, die by attorney. The poor world is about six thousand years old, and in all this time there was not any man died in his own person, *videlicet*, in a love cause. Troilus had his brains dashed out with a Grecian club; yet he did what he could to die before; and he is one of the patterns of love. Leander, he would have lived many a fair year, though Hero had turned nun, if it had not been for a hot midsummer night: for, good youth, he went but forth to wash him in the Hellespont, and, being taken with the cramp, was drowned; and the foolish chroniclers of that age found it was—Hero of Sestos. But these are all lies; men have died from time to time, and worms have eaten them, but not for love.

* * * * *

*Rosalind.* Ay, go your ways, go your ways;—I knew what you would prove; my friends told me as much, and I thought no less:—that flattering tongue of yours won me:—'tis but one cast away, and so,—come, death.—Two o'clock is the hour?

*Orlando.* Ay, sweet Rosalind.

*Rosalind.* By my troth, and in good earnest, and so God mend me, and by all pretty oaths that are not dangerous, if you break one jot of your promise, or come one minute behind your hour, I will think you the most pathetical break-promise, and the most hollow lover, and the most unworthy of her you call Rosalind, that may be chosen out of the gross band of the unfaithful: therefore beware my censure, and keep your promise.

* * * * *

*Rosalind.* O coz, coz, coz, my pretty little coz, that thou didst know how many fathom deep I am in love! But it cannot be sounded; my affection hath an unknown bottom, like the bay of Portugal.

*Celia.* Or rather, bottomless; that as fast as you pour affection in, it runs out.

*Rosalind.* No, that same wicked bastard of Venus, that was begot of thought, conceived of spleen, and born of madness; that blind rascally boy, that abuses every one's eyes, because his own are out, let him be judge, how deep I am in love:—I 'll tell thee, Aliena, I cannot be out of the sight of Orlando; I 'll go find a shadow, and sigh till he come.

*Celia.* And I 'll sleep.

### Scene III.

*Silvius.* My errand is to you, fair youth:—
My gentle Phebe bid me give you this: [*Giving a letter.*

I know not the contents; but as I guess,
By the stern brow, and waspish action
Which she did use as she was writing of it,
It bears an angry tenour: pardon me,
I am but as a guiltless messenger.
*Rosalind.* Patience herself would startle at this letter,
And play the swaggerer; bear this, bear all;
She says I am not fair; that I lack manners;
She calls me proud; and, that she could not love me
Were man as rare as phœnix: Od's my will!
Her love is not the hare that I do hunt;
Why writes she so to me?—Well, shepherd, well,
This is a letter of your own device.
*Silvius.* No, I protest, I know not the contents;
Phebe did write it.
*Rosalind.* Come, come, you are a fool,
And turn'd into the extremity of love.
I saw her hand: she has a leathern hand,
A freestone-colour'd hand; I verily did think
That her old gloves were on, but 'twas her hands;
She has a huswife's hand; but that 's no matter;
I say, she never did invent this letter;
This is a man's invention, and his hand.
*Silvius.* Sure, it is hers.
*Rosalind.* Why, 'tis a boisterous and cruel style,
A style for challengers: why, she defies me,
Like Turk to Christian: woman's gentle brain
Could not drop forth such giant-rude invention,
Such Ethiop words, blacker in their effect
Than in their countenance:—Will you hear the letter?
*Silvius.* So please you, for I never heard it yet;
Yet heard so much of Phebe's cruelty.

ACT V. SCENE II.

*Rosalind.* O, I know where you are:—Nay, 'tis true; there was never any thing so sudden, but the fight of two rams, and Cæsar's thrasonical brag of—I came, saw, and overcame: For your brother and my sister no sooner met, but they looked; no sooner looked, but they loved; no sooner loved, but they sighed; no sooner sighed, but they asked one another the reason; no sooner knew the reason, but they sought the remedy: and in these degrees have they made a pair of stairs to marriage, which they will climb incontinent, or else be incontinent before marriage: they are in the very wrath of love, and they will together; clubs cannot part them.

* * * * *

*Rosalind.* I will weary you no longer then with idle talking. Know of me then (for now I speak to some purpose) that I know you are a gentleman of good conceit: I speak not this, that you should bear a good opinion of my knowledge, insomuch I say I know you are; neither do I labour for a greater esteem, than may in some little measure draw a belief from you, to do yourself good, and not to grace me. Believe then if you please, that I can do strange things; I have, since I was three years old, conversed with a Magician, most profound in his art, and yet not damnable. If you do love Rosalind so near the heart, as your gesture cries it out, when your brother marries Aliena, shall you marry her; I know into what straits of fortune she is driven; and it is not impossible to me, if it appear not inconvenient to you, to set her before your eyes to-morrow, human as she is, and without any danger.[30]

*Orlando.* Speakest thou in sober meanings?

# ALL'S WELL THAT ENDS WELL.

## Act I. Scene I.

*Helena.*

O, WERE that all!—I think not on my father;
And these great tears grace his remembrance more
Than those I shed for him. What was he like?
I have forgot him: my imagination
Carries no favour in it, but Bertram!
I am undone; there is no living, none,
If Bertram be away. It were all one,
That I should love a bright particular star,
And think to wed it, he is so above me:
In his bright radiance and collateral light
Must I be comforted, not in his sphere.
The ambition in my love thus plagues itself;
The hind, that would be mated by the lion,
Must die for love. 'Twas pretty, though a plague,
To see him every hour; to sit and draw
His arched brows, his hawking eye, his curls
In our heart's table—heart too capable

Of every line and trick of his sweet favour;
But now he 's gone, and my idolatrous fancy
Must sanctify his relicks. Who comes here?

(*Enter* PAROLLES.)

One that goes with him: I love him for his sake;
And yet I know him a notorious liar,
Think him a great way fool, solely a coward;
Yet these fix'd evils sit so fit in him
That they take place, when virtue's steely bones
Look bleak in the cold wind: withal, full oft we see
Cold wisdom waiting on superfluous folly.

* * * * *

*Helena.* Our remedies oft in ourselves do lie
Which we ascribe to heaven: the fated sky
Gives us free scope; only doth backward pull
Our slow designs, when we ourselves are dull.
What power is it, which mounts my love so high?
That makes me see, and cannot feed mine eye?
The mightiest space in fortune nature brings
To join like likes, and kiss like native things.
Impossible be strange attempts to those
That weigh their pains in sense, and do suppose
What hath been cannot be. Who ever strove
To show her merit, that did miss her love?
The king's disease—my project may deceive me,
But my intents are fix'd, and will not leave me.

## SCENE III.

*Countess.* Even so it was with me, when I was young;
If we are nature's these are ours; this thorn
Doth to our rose of youth rightly belong:

Our blood to us, this to our blood is born ;
It is the show and seal of nature's truth
Where love's strong passion is impress'd in youth :
By our remembrances of days foregone,
Such were our faults ; or then we thought them none.
Her eye is sick on 't ; I observe her now.

* * * * *

*Countess.* What 's the matter,
That this distemper'd messenger of wet,
The many-coloured Iris, rounds thine eye ? [31]
Why ?—that you are my daughter ?

* * * * *

*Countess.* Yes, Helena, you might be my daughter-in-law ;
God shield, you mean it not, daughter and mother !
So strive upon your pulse : what, pale again ?
My fear hath catch'd your fondness : now I see
The mystery of your loneliness, and find
Your salt tears' head. Now to all sense 't is gross ;
You love my son, invention is ashamed,
Against the proclamation of thy passion,
To say, thou dost not : therefore tell me true :
But tell me then, 't is so :—for, look, thy cheeks
Confess it, one to the other ; and thine eyes
See it so grossly shown in thy behaviours,
That in their kind they speak it : only sin
And hellish obstinacy tie thy tongue,
That truth should be suspected : speak, is 't so ?
If it be so, you have wound a goodly clue ;
If it be not, forswear 't : howe'er, I charge thee,
As heaven shall work in me for thine avail,
To tell me truly.

*Helena.* Good madam, pardon me !

*Countess.* Do you love my son?
*Helena.* Your pardon, noble mistress.
*Countess.* Love you my son?
*Helena.* Do you not him, madam?
*Countess.* Go not about; my love hath in 't a bond,
Whereof the world takes note; come, come, disclose
The state of your affection; for your passions
Have to the full appeach'd.
*Helena.* Then I confess
Here on my knee, before high heaven and you,
That before you, and next unto high heaven,
I love your son:—
My friends were poor, but honest; so 's my love:
Be not offended; for it hurts not him,
That he is loved of me: I follow him not
By any token of presumptuous suit;
Nor would I have him, till I do deserve him;
Yet never know how that desert should be.
I know I love in vain, strive against hope;
Yet, in this captious and intenible sieve,
I still pour in the waters of my love,
And lack not to lose still: thus, Indian-like,
Religious in mine error, I adore
The sun, that looks upon his worshipper,
But knows of him no more. My dearest madam,
Let not your hate encounter with my love,
For loving where you do: but, if yourself,
Whose aged honour cites a virtuous youth,
Did ever, in so true a flame of liking,
Wish chastly, and love dearly, that your Dian
Was both herself and love; O then give pity
To her, whose state is such, that cannot choose
But lend and give, where she is sure to lose;

That seeks not to find that her search implies,
But riddle-like, lives sweetly where she dies.

### Act II. Scene I.

*Helena.* If I break time, or flinch in property
Of what I spoke, unpitied let me die;
And well deserv'd: Not helping, death 's my fee;
But, if I help, what do you promise me?
*King.* Make thy demand.
*Helena.* But will you make it even?
*King.* Ay, by my sceptre, and my hopes of heaven.
*Helena.* Then shalt thou give me, with thy kingly hand,
What husband in thy power I will command:
Exempted be from me the arrogance
To choose from forth the royal blood of France;
My love and humble name to propagate
With any branch or image of thy state:
But such a one, thy vassal, whom I know
Is free for me to ask, thee to bestow.
*King.* Here is my hand; &c.

### Scene III.

*Helena.* Now, Dian, from thy altar do I fly;
And to imperial love, that God most high,
Do my sighs stream.—Sir, will you hear my suit?

* * * * *

### Scene V.

*Helena.* I am not worthy of the wealth I owe;
Nor dare I say, 'tis mine; and yet it is;
But, like a timorous thief, most fain would steal

What law does vouch mine own.

*Bertram.* What would you have?

*Helena.* Something; and scarce so much:—nothing, indeed.—
I would not tell you what I would: my lord—'faith, yes;—
Strangers and foes, do sunder, and not kiss.

*Bertram.* I pray you, stay not, but in haste to horse.

*Helena.* I shall not break your bidding, good my lord.

### Act V. Scene III.

*Lafeu.* This I must say,—
But first I beg my pardon,—The young lord
Did to his majesty, his mother, and his lady,
Offence of mighty note; but to himself
The greatest wrong of all: he lost a wife,
Whose beauty did astonish the survey
Of richest eyes; whose words all ears took captive;
Whose dear perfection, hearts that scorn'd to serve,
Humbly call'd mistress.

# TAMING OF THE SHREW.

## ACT I. SCENE I.

*Tranio.*

I PRAY, sir, tell me,—Is it possible
That love should of a sudden take such hold?

*Lucentio.* O Tranio, till I found it to be true,
I never thought it possible, or likely;
But see! while idly I stood looking on,
I found the effect of love in idleness;
And now in plainness do confess to thee,—
That art to me as secret, and as dear,
As Anna to the queen of Carthage was,—
Tranio, I burn, I pine, I perish, Tranio,
If I achieve not this young modest girl:
Counsel me, Tranio, for I know thou canst;
Assist me, Tranio, for I know thou wilt.

* * * * *

*Tranio.* Master, you look'd so longly on the maid,
Perhaps you mark'd not what 's the pith of all.

*Lucentio.* O yes, I saw sweet beauty in her face,

Such as the daughter of Agenor had,
That made great Jove to humble him to her hand,
When with his knees he kiss'd the Cretan strand.

*Tranio.* Saw you no more; mark'd you not how her sister
Began to scold; and raise up such a storm,
That mortal ears might hardly endure the din?

*Lucentio.* Tranio, I saw her coral lips to move,
And with her breath she did perfume the air;
Sacred, and sweet, was all I saw in her.

### Act IV. Scene V.

*Katharina.* Forward, I pray, since we have come so far,
And be it moon, or sun, or what you please:
And if you please to call it a rush candle,
Henceforth I vow it shall be so for me.

*Petruchio.* I say, it is the moon.

*Katharina.* I know it is.

*Petruchio.* Nay, then you lie; it is the blessed sun.

*Katharina.* Then, God be bless'd, it is the blessed sun:—
But sun it is not, when you say it is not;
And the moon changes, even as your mind.
What you will have it nam'd, even that it is;
And so it shall be so, for Katharine.

*Hortensio.* Petruchio, go thy ways; the field is won.

* * * * *

*Katharina.* Pardon, old father, my mistaking eyes,
That have been so bedazzled with the sun,
That everything I look on seemeth green:[32]
Now I perceive, thou art a reverend father;
Pardon, I pray thee, for my mad mistaking.

ACT V. SCENE II.

*Petruchio.* Katharine, I charge thee, tell these headstrong women
What duty they do owe their lords and husbands.

* * * * *

*Katharina.* Fye, fye! unknit that threat'ning unkind brow;
And dart not scornful glances from those eyes,
To wound thy lord, thy king, thy governor:
It blots thy beauty, as frosts do bite the meads;
Confounds thy frame, as whirlwinds shake fair buds;
And in no sense is meet, or amiable.
A woman mov'd, is like a fountain troubled,
Muddy, ill seeming, thick, bereft of beauty;
And, while it is so, none so dry or thirsty
Will deign to sip, or touch one drop of it.
Thy husband is thy lord, thy life, thy keeper,
Thy head, thy sovereign; one that cares for thee,
And for thy maintenance: commits his body
To painful labour, both by sea and land;
To watch the night in storms, the day in cold,
While thou liest warm at home, secure and safe;
And craves no other tribute at thy hands,
But love, fair looks, and true obedience;—
Too little payment for so great a debt.
Such duty as the subject owes the prince,
Even such a woman oweth to her husband:
And, when she 's froward, peevish, sullen, sour,
And, not obedient to his honest will,
What is she, but a foul contending rebel,

And graceless traitor to her loving lord?—
I am asham'd, that women are so simple
To offer war, where they should kneel for peace;
Or seek for rule, supremacy, and sway,
When they are bound to serve, love, and obey.
Why are our bodies soft, and weak, and smooth,
Unapt to toil and trouble in the world;
But that our soft conditions and our hearts,
Should well agree with our external parts?
Come, come, you froward and unable worms!
My mind hath been as big as one of yours,
My heart as great; my reason, haply, more,
To bandy word for word, and frown for frown:
But now, I see our lances are but straws;
Our strength as weak, our weakness past compare,—
That seeming to be most, which we least are.
Then vail your stomachs, for it is no boot;
And place your hands below your husband's foot:
In token of which duty, if he please,
My hand is ready, may it do him ease.

## WINTER'S TALE.

### ACT II. SCENE I.

*Hermione.*

THERE'S some ill planet reigns:
I must be patient, till the heavens look
With an aspect more favourable.—Good my lords,
I am not prone to weeping, as our sex
Commonly are; the want of which vain dew,
Perchance, shall dry your pities; but I have
That honourable grief lodg'd here, which burns
Worse than tears drown: 'Beseech you all, my lords,
With thoughts so qualified as your charities
Shall best instruct you, measure me;—and so
The king's will be perform'd!

*Leontes.* Shall I be heard? [*To the Guards.*

*Hermione.* Who is 't that goes with me?—'Beseech your highness,
My women may be with me; for, you see,
My plight requires it. Do not weep, good fools;

There is no cause; when you shall know your mistress
Has deserv'd prison, then abound in tears,
As I come out: this action, I now go on,
Is for my better grace.—Adieu, my lord:
I never wish'd to see you sorry; now,
I trust, I shall.—My women, come; you have leave.

SCENE II.

*Emilia.* As well as one so great, and so forlorn,
May hold together: on her frights and griefs
(Which never tender lady hath borne greater),
She is, something before her time, deliver'd.
*Paulina.* A boy?
*Emilia.* A daughter; and a goodly babe,
Lusty, and like to live; the queen receives
Much comfort in 't; says, My poor prisoner,
I am innocent as you.
*Paulina.* I dare be sworn:
These dangerous unsafe lunes o' the king! beshrew them!
He must be told on 't, and he shall: the office
Becomes a woman best; I 'll take 't upon me:
If I prove honey-mouth'd, let my tongue blister;
And never to my red-look'd anger be
The trumpet any more:—Pray you, Emilia,
Commend my best obedience to the queen;
If she dares trust me with her little babe,
I 'll show 't the king, and undertake to be
Her advocate to th' loudest: we do not know
How he may soften at the sight o' the child;
The silence often of pure innocence
Persuades, when speaking fails.
*Emilia.* Most worthy madam,

Your honour, and your goodness, is so evident,
That your free undertaking cannot miss
A thriving issue; there is no lady living,
So meet for this great errand: Please your ladyship
To visit the next room, I 'll presently
Acquaint the queen of your most noble offer;
Who, but to-day, hammer'd of this design;
But durst not tempt a minister of honour,
Lest she should be denied.

*Paulina.* Tell her, Emilia,
I 'll use that tongue I have: if wit flow from it,
As boldness from my bosom, let it not be doubted
I shall do good.

*Emilia.* Now be you blest for it!
I 'll to the queen: Please you, come something nearer.

*Keeper.* Madam, if 't please the queen to send the babe,
I know not what I shall incur, to pass it,
Having no warrant.

*Paulina.* You need not fear it, sir:
The child was prisoner to the womb; and is,
By law and process of great nature, thence
Freed and enfranchis'd; not a party to
The anger of the king; nor guilty of,
If any be, the trespass of the queen.

*Keeper.* I do believe it.

*Paulina.* Do not you fear; upon
Mine honour, I will stand 'twixt you and danger.

## Scene III.

*Paulina.* Good my liege, I come,—
And, I beseech you, hear me, who profess
Myself your loyal servant, your physician,
Your most obedient counsellor; yet that dare

Less appear so, in comforting your evils,
Than such as most seem yours :—I say, I come
From your good queen.

*Leontes.* Good queen !

*Paulina.* Good queen, my lord, good queen : I say, good queen ;
And would by combat make her good, so were I
A man, the worst about you.

*Leontes.* Force her hence.

*Paulina.* Let him, that makes but trifles of his eyes,
First hand me : on mine own accord, I 'll off ;
But, first, I 'll do my errand.—The good queen,
For she is good, hath brought you forth a daughter ;
Here 'tis ; commends it to your blessing.

* * * * *

*Paulina.* It is yours ;
And, might we lay the old proverb to your charge,
So like you, 'tis the worse.—Behold, my lords,
Although the print be little, the whole matter
And copy of the father ; eye, nose, lip,
The trick of his frown, his forehead ; nay, the valley,
The pretty dimples of his chin, and cheek ; his smiles ;
The very mould and frame of hand, nail, and finger :—
And thou, good goddess nature, which hast made it
So like to him that got it, if thou hast
The ordering of the mind too, 'mongst all colours
No yellow in 't ; lest she suspect, as he does,
Her children not her husband's !

## Act III. Scene II.

*Hermione.* Since what I am to say, must be but that
Which contradicts my accusation ; and

The testimony on my part, no other
But what comes from myself; it shall scarce boot me
To say, Not guilty: mine integrity,
Being counted falsehood, shall, as I express it,
Be so receiv'd. But thus,—If powers divine
Behold our human actions (as they do),
I doubt not then, but innocence shall make
False accusation blush, and tyranny
Tremble at patience.—You, my lord, best know
(Who least will seem to do so), my past life
Hath been as continent, as chaste, as true,
As I am now unhappy; which is more
Than history can pattern, though devis'd,
And play'd, to take spectators: For behold me,—
A fellow of the royal bed, which owe
A moiety of the throne, as great king's daughter,
The mother to a hopeful prince,—here standing
To prate and talk for life, and honour, 'fore
Who please to come and hear. For life, I prize it
As I weigh grief, which I would spare: for honour,
'Tis a derivative from me to mine,[33]
And only that I stand for. I appeal
To your own conscience, sir, before Polixenes
Came to your court, how I was in your grace,
How merited to be so; since he came,
With what encounter so uncurrent I
Have strain'd, to appear thus: if one jot beyond
The bound of honour; or, in act, or will,
That way inclining; harden'd be the hearts
Of all that hear me, and my near'st of kin
Cry, Fye upon my grave!

*Leontes.* I never heard yet,
That any of these bolder vices wanted

Less impudence to gainsay what they did,
Than to perform it first.
*Hermione.* That 's true enough;
Though 'tis a saying, sir, not due to me.
*Leontes.* You will not own it.
*Hermione.* More than mistress of,
Which comes to me in name of fault, I must not
At all acknowledge. For Polixenes
(With whom I am accus'd), I do confess,
I lov'd him, as in honour he requir'd;
With such a kind of love, as might become
A lady like me; with a love, even such,
So, and no other, as yourself commanded:
Which not to have done, I think, had been in me
Both disobedience and ingratitude,
To you, and toward your friend; whose love had spoke,
Even since it could speak, from an infant, freely,
That it was yours. Now, for conspiracy,
I know not how it tastes; though it be dish'd
For me to try how: all I know of it,
Is, that Camillo was an honest man;
And, why he left your court, the gods themselves,
Wotting no more than I, are ignorant.
*Leontes.* You knew of his departure, as you know
What you have underta'en to do in his absence.
*Hermione.* Sir,
You speak a language that I understand not:
My life stands in the level of your dreams,
Which I 'll lay down.

* * * * *

*Paulina.* What studied torments, tyrant, hast for me?
What wheels? racks? fires? What flaying? boiling
In leads or oils? what old, or newer torture

Must I receive; whose every word deserves
To taste of thy most worst? Thy tyranny
Together working with thy jealousies,—
Fancies too weak for boys, too green and idle
For girls of nine!—O, think, what they have done,
And then run mad, indeed; stark mad! for all
Thy by-gone fooleries were but spices of it.
That thou betray'dst Polixenes, 'twas nothing;
That did but show thee, of a fool, inconstant,
And damnable ungrateful: nor was 't much,
Thou would'st have poison'd good Camillo's honour,
To have him kill a king; poor trespasses,
More monstrous standing by: whereof I reckon
The casting forth to crows thy baby daughter,
To be or none, or little; though a devil
Would have shed water out of fire, ere done 't;
Nor is 't directly laid to thee, the death
Of the young prince; whose honourable thoughts
(Thoughts high for one so tender) cleft the heart
That could conceive, a gross and foolish sire
Blemish'd his gracious dam: this is not, no,
Laid to thy answer: But the last,—O, lords,
When I have said, cry, woe!—the queen, the queen,
The sweetest, dearest creature 's dead; and vengeance for 't
Not dropp'd down yet.

*Lord.* The higher powers forbid!

*Paulina.* I say, she 's dead: I 'll swear 't: if word, nor oath,
Prevail not, go and see; if you can bring
Tincture, or lustre, in her lip, her eye,
Heat outwardly, or breath within, I 'll serve you
As I would do the gods.—But, O thou tyrant!
Do not repent these things, for they are heavier

Than all thy woes can stir; therefore betake thee
To nothing but despair. A thousand knees
Ten thousand years together, naked, fasting,
Upon a barren mountain, and still winter
In storm perpetual, could not move the gods
To look that way thou wert.

## Act IV. Scene III.

*Florizel.* Thou dearest Perdita,
With these forc'd thoughts, I pr'ythee, darken not
The mirth o' the feast: Or I 'll be thine, my fair,
Or not my father's; for I cannot be
Mine own, nor any thing to any, if
I be not thine: to this I am most constant,
Though destiny say, no. Be merry, gentle;
Strangle such thoughts as these, with any thing
That you behold the while. Your guests are coming:
Lift up your countenance; as it were the day
Of celebration of that nuptial, which
We two have sworn shall come.
*Perdita.* O lady fortune,
Stand you auspicious!

*Enter* Shepherd *and others.*

*Florizel.* See, your guests approach;
Address yourself to entertain them sprightly,
And let's be red with mirth.
*Shepherd.* Fye, daughter! when my old wife liv'd, upon
This day, she was both pantler, butler, cook;
Both dame and servant; welcom'd all, serv'd all;
Would sing her song, and dance her turn; now here,

At upper end o' the table, now i' the middle ;
On his shoulder, and his ; her face o' fire
With labour ; and the thing she took to quench it,
She would to each one sip : You are retir'd,
As if you were a feasted one, and not
The hostess of the meeting : Pray you, bid
These unknown friends to us welcome : for it is
A way to make us better friends, more known.
Come, quench your blushes ; and present yourself
That which you are, mistress o' the feast : Come on,
And bid us welcome to your sheep-shearing,
As your good flock shall prosper.

*Perdita.* Welcome, sir !
It is my father's will, I should take on me
The hostesship o' the day.—You 're welcome, sir !
Give me those flowers there, Dorcas.—Reverend sirs,
For you there 's rosemary, and rue ; these keep
Seeming, and savour, all the winter long :
Grace, and remembrance, be to you both,
And welcome to our shearing !

*Polixenes.* Shepherdess
(A fair one are you), well you fit our ages
With flowers of winter.

*Perdita.* Sir, the year growing ancient,—
Not yet on summer's death, nor on the birth
Of trembling winter,—the fairest flowers o' the season
Are our carnations, and streak'd gilliflowers,
Which some call nature's bastards : of that kind
Our rustic garden 's barren ; and I care not
To get slips of them.

*Polixenes.* Wherefore, gentle maiden,
Do you neglect them ?

*Perdita.* For I have heard it said,

There is an art, which, in their piedness, shares
With great creating nature.
*Polixenes.* Say, there be;
Yet nature is made better by no mean,
But nature makes that mean: so, o'er that art,
Which, you say, adds to nature, is an art
That nature makes. You see, sweet maid, we marry
A gentler scion to the wildest stock;
And make conceive a bark of baser kind
By bud of nobler race; This is an art
Which does mend nature,—change it rather: but
The art itself is nature.
*Perdita.* So it is.
*Polixenes.* Then make your garden rich in gilliflowers,
And do not call them bastards.
*Perdita.* I'll not put
The dibble in earth to set one slip of them:
No more than, were I painted, I would wish
This youth should say, 'twere well; and only therefore
Desire to breed by me.—Here 's flowers for you;
Hot lavender, mints, savory, marjoram;
The marigold, that goes to bed with the sun,
And with him rises weeping; these are flowers
Of middle summer, and, I think, they are given
To men of middle age: You are very welcome.
*Camillo.* I should leave grazing, were I of your flock,
And only live by gazing.
*Perdita.* Out, alas!
You 'd be so lean, that blasts of January
Would blow you through and through.—Now, my fairest friend,
I would I had some flowers o' the spring, that might
Become your time of day; and yours, and yours;

That wear upon your virgin branches yet
Your maidenheads growing:—O Proserpina,
For the flowers now, that, frighted, thou let'st fall
From Dis's waggon! daffodils,
That come before the swallow dares, and take [34]
The winds of March with beauty; violets, dim,
But sweeter than the lids of Juno's eyes,
Or Cytherea's breath; pale primroses,
That die unmarried, ere they can behold
Bright Phœbus in his strength, a malady
Most incident to maids; bold oxlips, and
The crown-imperial; lilies of all kinds,
The flower-de-luce being one! O, these I lack
To make you garlands of; and, my sweet friend,
To strew him o'er and o'er.

*Florizel.* What! like a corse?

*Perdita.* No, like a bank, for love to lie and play on;
Not like a corse: or if,—not to be buried,
But quick, and in mine arms. Come, take your flowers:
Methinks, I play as I have seen them do
In Whitsun' pastorals: sure, this robe of mine
Does change my disposition.

*Florizel.* What you do,
Still betters what is done. When you speak, sweet,
I'd have you do it ever; when you sing,
I'd have you buy and sell so; so give alms;
Pray so; and for the ordering your affairs,
To sing them too: When you do dance, I wish you
A wave o' the sea, that you might ever do
Nothing but that; move still, still so, and own
No other function. Each your doing
So singular in each particular,
Crowns what you are doing in the present deeds,

That all your acts are queens.
*Perdita.* O Doricles,
Your praises are too large: but that your youth,
And the true blood, which fairly peeps through it,
Do plainly give you out an unstain'd shepherd;
With wisdom I might fear, my Doricles,
You woo'd me the false way.
*Florizel.* I think, you have
As little skill to fear, as I have purpose
To put you to 't.—But come; our dance, I pray;
Your hand, my Perdita; so turtles pair
That never mean to part.
*Perdita.* I 'll swear for 'em.
*Polixenes.* This is the prettiest low born lass, that ever
Ran on the green-sward: nothing she does or seems,
But smacks of something greater than herself,
Too noble for this place.

* * * * *

[*Here a dance of Shepherds and Shepherdesses.*

*Polixenes.* Pray, good shepherd, what
Fair swain is this, which dances with your daughter?
*Shepherd.* They call him Doricles; and he boasts himself
To have a worthy feeding; but I have it
Upon his own report, and I believe it;
He looks like sooth: He says, he loves my daughter,
I think so too; for never gaz'd the moon
Upon the water, as he 'll stand, and read,
As 'twere, my daughter's eyes; and, to be plain,
I think there is not half a kiss to choose
Who loves another best.
*Polixenes.* She dances featly.

*Shepherd.* So she does any thing; though I report it,
That should be silent; if young Doricles
Do light upon her, she shall bring him that
Which he not dreams of.

* * * * *

*Florizel.* Old sir, I know
She prizes not such trifles as these are:
The gifts, she looks from me, are pack'd and lock'd
Up in my heart; which I have given already,
But not deliver'd,—O, hear me breathe my life
Before this ancient sir, who, it should seem,
Hath sometime lov'd: I take thy hand; this hand,
As soft as dove's down, and as white as it,
Or Ethiopian's tooth, or the fann'd snow,
That 's bolted by the northern blasts twice o'er.

*Polixenes.* What follows this?
How prettily the young swain seems to wash
The hand, was fair before!—I have put you out:—
But to your protestations; let me hear
What you profess.

*Florizel.* Do, and be witness to 't.

*Polixenes.* And this my neighbour too?

*Florizel.* And he, and more
Than he, and men; the earth, the heavens, and all,
That, were I crown'd the most imperial monarch,
Thereof most worthy; were I the fairest youth
That ever made eye swerve; had force, and knowledge,
More than was ever man's,—I would not prize them
Without her love: for her, employ them all;
Commend them, and condemn them, to her service,
Or to their own perdition.

*Polixenes.* Fairly offer'd.

*Camillo.* This shows a sound affection.

*Shepherd.* But, my daughter,
Say you the like to him?
*Perdita.* I cannot speak
So well, nothing so well: no, nor mean better:
By the pattern of mine own thoughts I cut out
The purity of his.
*Shepherd.* Take hands, a bargain;
And, friends unknown, you shall bear witness to 't;
I give my daughter to him, and will make
Her portion equal his.
*Florizel.* O, that must be
I' the virtue of your daughter: one being dead,
I shall have more than you can dream of yet;
Enough then for your wonder: But, come on,
Contract us 'fore these witnesses.

* * * * *

*Camillo.* This is desperate, sir.
*Florizel.* So call it; but it does fulfil my vow;
I needs must think it honesty. Camillo,
Not for Bohemia, nor the pomp that may
Be thereat glean'd; for all the sun sees, or
The close earth wombs, or the profound seas hide
In unknown fathoms, will I break my oath
To this my fair belov'd: Therefore, I pray you,
As you have ever been my father's honour'd friend,
When he shall miss me (as, in faith, I mean not
To see him any more), cast your good counsels
Upon his passion: Let myself and fortune
Tug for the time to come. This you may know,
And so deliver:—I am put to sea
With her, whom here I cannot hold on shore;
And, most opportune to our need, I have
A vessel rides fast by, but not prepar'd

For this design. What course I mean to hold
Shall nothing benefit your knowledge, nor
Concern me the reporting.

* * * * *

*Camillo.* A course more promising
Than a wild dedication of yourselves
To unpath'd waters, undream'd shores; most certain,
To miseries enough: no hope to help you:
But, as you shake off one, to take another:
Nothing so certain as your anchors; who
Do their best office, if they can but stay you
Where you 'll be loath to be: Besides, you know,
Prosperity 's the very bond of love;
Whose fresh complexion and whose heart together
Affliction alters.

*Perdita.* One of these is true;
I think, affliction may subdue the cheek,
But not take in the mind.

*Camillo.* Yea, say you so?
There shall not, at your father's house, these seven years,
Be born another such.

*Florizel.* My good Camillo,
She is as forward of her breeding, as
I' the rear of birth.

*Camillo.* I cannot say, 'tis pity
She lacks instructions; for she seems a mistress
To most that teach.

*Perdita.* Your pardon, sir, for this;
I 'll blush you thanks.

*Florizel.* My prettiest Perdita.—
But, O, the thorns we stand upon! Camillo,
Preserver of my father, now of me:

The medicine of our house !—how shall we do?
We are not furnish'd like Bohemia's son ;
Nor shall appear in Sicily.—
*Camillo.* My lord,
Fear none of this : I think, you know, my fortunes
Do all lie there : it shall be so my care
To have you royally appointed, as if
The scene you play were mine. For instance, sir,
That you may know you shall not want,—one word.
[*They talk aside.*

ACT V. SCENE III.

*Leontes.* Let be, let be.
'Would I were dead, but that, methinks, already—
What was he that did make it ?—See, my lord,
Would you not deem it breath'd? and that those veins
Did verily bear blood?
*Polixenes.* Masterly done :
The very life seems warm upon her lip.
*Leontes.* The fixture of her eye has motion in it.
As we are mock'd with art.
*Paulina.* I 'll draw the curtain ;
My lord 's almost so far transported, that
He 'll think anon it lives.
*Leontes.* O sweet Paulina,
Make me to think so twenty years together;
No settled senses of the world can match
The pleasure of that madness. Let 't alone.
*Paulina.* I am sorry, sir, I have thus far stirr'd you : but

I could afflict you further.
*Leontes.* Do, Paulina;
For this affliction has a taste as sweet
As any cordial comfort.—Still, methinks,
There is an air comes from her: what fine chisel
Could ever yet cut breath? Let no man mock me,
For I will kiss her.
*Paulina.* Good my lord, forbear;
The ruddiness upon her lip is wet;
You 'll mar it, if you kiss it; stain your own
With oily painting. Shall I draw the curtain?
*Leontes.* No, not these twenty years.
*Perdita.* So long could I
Stand by, a looker on.
*Paulina.* Either forbear,
Quit presently the chapel: or resolve you
For more amazement: if you can behold it,
I 'll make the statue move indeed; descend
And take you by the hand; but then you 'll think
(Which I protest against) I am assisted
By wicked powers.
*Leontes.* What you can make her do,
I am content to look on: what to speak,
I am content to hear; for 'tis as easy
To make her speak, as move.
*Paulina.* It is requir'd,
You do awake your faith: then, all stand still;
Or those, that think it is unlawful business
I am about, let them depart.
*Leontes.* Proceed;
No foot shall stir.
*Paulina.* Musick; awake her: strike.—
'Tis time; descend; be stone no more: approach,

Strike all that look upon you with marvel. Come;
I 'll fill your grave up: stir; nay, come away;
Bequeath to death your numbness, for from him
Dear life redeems you.—You perceive, she stirs.
[*Hermione comes down from the Pedestal.*
Start not; her actions shall be holy, as
You hear, my spell is lawful; do not shun her,
Until you see her die again; for then
You kill her double: Nay, present your hand:
When she was young, you woo'd her; now, in age,
Is she become the suitor.

*Leontes.* O, she 's warm! [*Embracing her.*
If this be magic, let it be an art
Lawful as eating.

*Polixenes.* She embraces him.

*Camillo.* She hangs about his neck;
If she pertain to life, let her speak too.

*Polixenes.* Ay, and make 't manifest where she has liv'd,
Or, how stol'n from the dead?

*Paulina.* That she is living,
Were it but told you, should be hooted at
Like an old tale; but it appears, she lives,
Though yet she speak not. Mark a little while.—
Please you to interpose, fair madam; kneel,
And pray your mother's blessing.—Turn, good lady,
Our Perdita is found.
[*Presenting Perdita, who kneels to Hermione.*

*Hermione.* You gods, look down,
And from your sacred vials pour your graces
Upon my daughter's head!—Tell me, mine own,
Where hast thou been preserv'd? where liv'd? how found

Thy father's court? for thou shalt hear, that I,—
Knowing by Paulina, that the oracle
Gave hope thou wast in being—have preserv'd,
Myself to see the issue.

# NOTES.

## Note, Page 16.

"*Thou know'st the mask of night is on my face.*"] This speech of Juliet's shows the perfect refinement and delicacy of Shakespeare's conception of the female character.

## Note 1, Page 24.

"*O God! I have an ill divining soul.*"] This miserable prescience of futurity I have always regarded as a circumstance particularly beautiful. The same kind of warning from the mind Romeo seems to have been conscious of, on his going to the entertainment at the house of Capulet:—

"My mind misgives,
Some consequence yet hanging in the stars
Shall bitterly begin his fearful date
From this night's revels."—Stevens.

## Note 2, Page 58.

The character of Cleopatra is a master-piece. What an extreme contrast it affords to Imogen! One would think it almost impossible for the same person to have drawn both.

The Egyptian is voluptuous, ostentatious, conscious, boastful of her charms, haughty, tyrannical, fickle. Her luxurious pomp and gorgeous extravagance are displayed in all their force and lustre, as well as the irregular grandeur of the soul of Mark Antony. Take only the first four lines that they speak, as an example of the regal style of love-making;—

"*Cleopatra.* If it be love indeed, tell me how much."

The rich and poetical description of her person beginning,

"The barge she sat in, like a burnish'd throne,"

seems to prepare the way for, and almost to justify the subsequent infatuation of Antony, when in the sea-fight at Actium he leaves the battle, and "like a doating mallard," follows her flying sails.

This play is full of that pervading comprehensive power, by which the Poet always seems to identify himself with time and circumstance. It presents a fine picture of Roman pride and Eastern magnificence, and in the struggle between the two, the Empire of the world seems suspended like the swan's-down feather,

"That stands upon the swell at full of tide,
And neither way inclines."

THE COMPILER.

Meanwhile Plutarch, that writer of antiquity, says that Cleopatra certainly possessed the virtues of fidelity, love of country, and natural affection in a very eminent degree. She had several opportunities of betraying Antony, could she have been inclined to it either by fear or ambition. Her tenderness for her children is always superior to her self-love; and she had a greatness of soul which Augustus Cæsar never knew. It is not so much a matter of surprise that Antony lost the government of half the civilized world owing to the fascinations of this Queen; she met the Triumvir at an age when beauty, in its full perfection, called in the maturity of the understanding to its aid; her voice was moreover delightfully melodious, and had the same variety of modulation as an instrument of many strings. She spoke many languages, and there was but few of the foreign ambassadors whom she answered by an interpreter. She died at the age of thirty-nine, having reigned twenty-two years, the fourteen last in conjunction with Antony. THE COMPILER.

### NOTE 3, PAGE 61.

"*Her tongue will not obey her heart.*"] This sentence is considered the most beautiful simile in all our author's works.

### NOTE 4, PAGE 61.

"*Is she as tall as me.*"] This scene, says Dr. Greg, is a manifest allusion to the questions put by Queen Elizabeth to Sir James Melville concerning his mistress, the Queen of Scots. Whoever will give himself the trouble to consult his memoirs may probably suppose the resemblance to be more than accidental.

## NOTE 5, PAGE 65.

"*And it is great.*"] The difficulty of the passage, if any difficulty there be, arises only from this, that the act of suicide and the state which is the effect of suicide are confounded. Voluntary death, says she, is an act which "bolts up change;" it produces a state

> "Which sleeps, and never palates more the dung,
> The beggar's nurse and Cæsar's;"

which has no longer need of the gross and terrene sustenance in the use of which Cæsar and the beggar are on a level. The speech is abrupt, but perturbation in such a state is surely natural.

JOHNSON.

## NOTE 6, PAGE 73.

"*Sweets to the sweet: farewell.*"] Nothing can be more affecting or beautiful than the Queen's apostrophe to Ophelia on throwing flowers into the grave. Shakespeare was thoroughly a master of the mixed motives of human character, and he here shows us the Queen, who was so criminal in some respects, not without sensibility and affection in other relations of life. Ophelia is a character almost too exquisitely touching to be dwelt upon.

HAZLITT.

## NOTE 7, PAGE 76.

The pathos in Cymbeline is not violent or tragical, but of the most pleasing and amiable kind. A certain tender gloom overspreads the whole. Posthumus is the ostensible hero of the piece, but its greatest charm is the character of Imogen.

Posthumus is only interesting from the interest she takes in him, and she is only interesting herself from her tenderness and constancy to her husband. It is the peculiar characteristic of Shakespeare's heroines, that they seem to exist only in their attachment to others. They are pure abstractions of the affections. We think as little of their persons as they do themselves, because we are let into the secrets of their hearts, which are more important.

We are too much interested in their affairs to stop to look at their faces, except by stealth and at intervals. No one ever hit the true perfection of the female character, the sense of weakness leaning on the strength of its affections for support, as well as Shakespeare; no one ever so well painted natural tenderness free from affectation and disguise; no one else ever so well showed how delicacy and timidity, when driven to extremity, grow romantic and extravagant; for the romance of his heroines (in which they abound) is only an excess of the habitual prejudices of their sex, scrupulous of being false to their vows, truant to their affections, and taught by the force of feeling when to forego the forms of propriety for the essence of it.

His women are in this respect exquisite logicians, for there is nothing so logical as reason. They know their own minds exactly; and only follow up a favourite idea, which they are sworn to with their tongues, and which is engraven on their hearts, into its untoward consequences. They are the prettiest little set of martyrs and confessors on record.

We have almost as great an affection for Imogen as she had for Posthumus; and she deserves it better. Of all Shakespeare's women she is perhaps the most tender and the most artless.

Her incredulity in the opening scene with Iachimo, as to her husband's infidelity, is much the same as Desdemona's backwardness to believe Othello's jealousy. Her answer to the most distressing part of the picture is only, "My lord, I fear, has forgot Britain." Her readiness to pardon Iachimo's false imputations and his designs against herself is a good lesson to prudes, and may show that where there is a real attachment to virtue, it has no need to bolster itself up with an outrageous or affected antipathy to vice.

HAZLITT.

## NOTE 7*, PAGE 78.

"*Overbuys me*
*Almost the sum he pays.*"

"The most minute portion of his worth would be too high a price for the wife he has acquired."

## NOTE 8, PAGE 79.

"*I durst attempt it against any lady in the world.*"] Our poet's object in writing this play was a noble one—the vindication of the character of woman from the aspersions of thoughtless and unprincipled men.

It is not Imogen alone whom the Italian profligate, Iachimo, slanders, it is her whole sex ; of his attempt upon her chastity, he says to her husband, "I durst attempt it against any lady in the world." Impossible as it may appear to pure and innocent minds, men still live who are ignorant and sensual enough to make the same vile boast. Among the pleasure-seeking gallants of the Elizabethan age, when seduction and duelling were by a large number of that class considered mere venial vices, if not graceful accomplishments, such unbelievers of the purity of woman were, perhaps, not uncommon, and in this play the bard read them a stern reproof from the stage.

Villiers, the second Duke of Buckingham, has thus alluded to this custom and privilege of the dramatists :—

> "When Shakespeare, Jonson, Fletcher ruled the stage,
> They took so bold a freedom with the age,
> That there was scarce a knave or fool in town,
> Of any note, but had his picture shown."

Imogen is a personification of woman ; woman enthroned in the holy temple of her pure and chaste affections, rejecting the tempter of her honour with the bitterest scorn and loathing, and enduring wrong and suffering with the most touching patience and sweetness. The gentler sex should be always grateful to the memory of our great Shakespeare, for his genius did sweet homage to their character ; he invests his female creations with all that is most pure and generous in humanity, picturing them, indeed, as beautiful to the eye, but a thousand times more acceptable to the heart. There is a moral dignity about his women, a holy strength of affection, which neither suffering nor death can pervert, that elevates them above the sterner nature of man, placing them on an equality with angels.

The adventures of Imogen are like a beautiful romance ; her flight after her banished husband, her wretchedness and forlorn condition when informed that he believes her false and has given order for her death : her assumption of boy's attire, in which disguise she wanders among the mountains, at point to perish of hunger ; her meeting with her disguised brothers in the cave ; her supposed death and recovery, and, finally, her discovery of her repentant husband, and throwing herself without any reproach upon his bosom, are all beautifully portrayed. Imogen is, indeed, a pattern of connubial love and chastity. HALLIWELL.

### NOTE 9, PAGE 82.

"*I' the bottom of a cowslip.*"] This simile contains the smallest out of a thousand proofs that Shakespeare was an observer of nature, though in this instance no very accurate describer of it, for the drops alluded to are of a deep yellow.

STEEVENS.

### NOTE 10, PAGE 95.

"*Is breach of all.*"] Keep your daily course uninterrupted ; if the stated plan of life is once broken confusion follows.

### NOTE, PAGE 98.

"*We scarce are men, and you are gods.*"] With the exception of the remorse expressed by Enobarbus in "Antony and Cleopatra," these lines have no equal in poignant grief.

### NOTE, PAGE 100.

"*Think, that you are upon a rock ; and now*
*Throw me again.*"

For a poet to attempt any further delineation of the female heart would be

"To gild refined gold, to paint the lily,
To throw a perfume on the violet,
To smoothe the ice, to add another hue
Unto the rainbow, or with taper light
To seek the beauteous eye of heaven to garnish,
Is wasteful and ridiculous excess."

*King John*, Act iv. Scene 2.

### NOTE 11, PAGE 110.

"*Upon thy wedding day.*"] The poet in these lines has unconsciously placed in the mouth of the Dauphin's bride the genius of the present age, by so vivid an expression of the horrors of war ! It would be well for suffering humanity if the enlightened women of all civilized nations were to follow Professor Ruxton's earnest advice to go into mourning, on the reverberation of the first shot fired with the intention of defacing the precious image of our dear Redeemer.—In the "Times" of May 30th, 1874, the following graphic account was written by a lady traveller of her ascent to the crater of Killanea in the Island of Hawaii, the largest of the Sandwich Archipelago :—

"We stood on the high bank of an irregular lake of liquid fire, which was seething and rolling to and fro, glowing with exceeding great heat, and sending up vast columns of smoke; the bottom of the cliff was fringed with fire, the shore-line of lava looked like blood, compared with the black cliff above it; a cascade of fire was playing in the centre of the lake, boiling up, rolling downward, bubbling, tossing up jets of molten lava and scattering fiery spray all around it; then for a few minutes it subsided, and the lake cooled over on top a thin crust of gray and black, but it soon heaved up slowly in the centre, and spouted up a fiery geyser, 30 or 40 feet high, that played like a colossal fountain several minutes, flinging out showers and clots of lava and dashing up red billows against the cliffs with a sound resembling surf on a rocky shore, only that it had something indescribably hellish and diabolical in it that filled me with an awful shudder; that swashing, self-conscious sound, now faint, now loud, was to me far the most impressive part. I think I should go mad if I had to listen to it long, and realize that it was caused by the restless, surging sea of fire that seemed the very lake of perdition."

Such vivid sensations of horror might with truth be applied to a battle-field, as the compiler has had sad occasion to witness.

"When, after battle, I the field have seen,
Spread o'er with ghastly shapes which once were men."

YOUNG'S *Night Thoughts.*

Few women, if any, have seen the human form, made in the image of the Creator, after having been struck with a round shot—it is indescribably shocking to gaze at! Now hear what an artillery officer of no mean reputation writes of the shock the poor soul must endure on being hurled into the presence of the Almighty.

"But over the crest poured incessantly the resistless cannon-shot, in whose rush there seems something vindictive, as if each were bestridden by some angry demon, crashing through men and horses, and darting from the ground on a second course of mischief. The musket-ball, though more deadly and directed to an individual mark, bears nothing appalling in its sound, and does not mutilate or disfigure when it strikes. But fronting uncovered and inactive a range of guns, which hurl incessantly those iron masses over and around you, while on all sides are seen their terrible traces, it is difficult to stave off the thought, that in the next instant your arm or leg may be dangling from your body a crushed and bloody mass, or your spirit driven rudely through a hideous wound across the margin of the undiscovered country."—HAMLEY'S *Crimea.*

O ! that some great and good lady of the land at the head of society would commence a crusade to obliterate war from the face of this beautiful world ! May Great Britain inherit the glory of initiating the movement ! her name would be handed down to generations as yet unborn, and for ever remove the reproach that women have hitherto done nothing to excite the gratitude of mankind. How was duelling in England for ever voted uncivilized and a remnant of the dark ages? By a clever leading article in the "Times," turning the custom into ridicule. And shall it be said that the Thunderer accomplished by a stroke of his pen more than the gentle influence of women had ever attempted since the world began?

It is in vain to look to the Church for aid; its ministers are imbued with too much of the policy of the monastery and the nunnery, whose inmates cared nothing for suffering humanity in their selfish desire to gain Paradise for themselves; although we know Christianity condemns war, both in its motives and character, it is admitted on all sides by those who know anything about our sublime and divine religion—indeed, many Christians of the first and second century suffered martyrdom as soldiers of the Roman army sooner than disobey the divine precept, "Thou shalt not kill."

Let all remember the lines in Hamlet :—

> "While to my shame, I see
> The immediate death of twenty thousand men
> That, for a fantasy and trick of fame,
> Go to their graves like beds;"

and in the prologue to Henry V. :—

> "Then should the warlike Harry like himself
> Assume the port of Mars, and, at his heels
> Leash'd in, like hounds, should famine, sword, and fire
> Crouch for employment."

Rubens, if he had painted it, would not have improved upon this simile.

It is time for women to interfere, men have made such a sad mess of things.

> "O, but man, proud man,
> Drest in a little brief authority,

*  *  *  like an angry ape,
Plays such fantastic tricks before high Heaven
As make the angels weep."  THE COMPILER.

NOTE 12, PAGE 168.

"*To weep at what I am glad of.*"] This is one of those touches of nature that distinguish Shakespeare from all other writers. It was necessary, in support of the character of Miranda, to make her appear unconscious that excess of sorrow and excess of joy find alike their relief from tears; and as this is the first time that consummate pleasure had made any near approaches to her heart, she calls such a seeming contradictory expression of it folly.—STEEVENS.

NOTE 13, PAGE 170.

"*The more thou dam'st it up, the more it burns.*"] If Shakespeare had only written this beautiful piece of poetry, he would almost have deserved Milton's praise of him:—

"And sweetest Shakespeare, Fancy's child,
Warbles his native wood-notes wild."

But as it is he deserves rather more praise than this.
HAZLITT.

"Triumph, my Britain, thou hast one to show
To whom all scenes of Europe homage owe.
He was not of an age, but for all time!

*  *  *  *

"Sweet Swan of Avon! What a sight it were
To see thee in our waters yet appear,
And make those flights upon the banks of Thames
Which so did take Eliza and our James."—BEN JONSON.

"When Learning's triumph o'er her barbarous foes
First reared the stage, immortal Shakespeare rose;
Each change of many-coloured life he drew;
Exhausted worlds and then imagined new;
Existence saw her spurn her bounded reign,
And panting time toiled after him in vain.
His powerful strokes presiding truth impressed,
And unresisted passion stormed the breast."—DR. JOHNSON.

The birthdays of such men as Shakespeare ought to be kept, in common gratitude and affection, like those of the friends whom we love.—LEIGH HUNT.

### NOTE 14, PAGE 175.

"*O thou that dost.*"] It is hardly possible to point out four lines in any of the plays of Shakespeare more remarkable for ease and elegance.—STEEVENS.

### NOTE 15, PAGE 177.

"——— *let it be his fault,*
*And not my brother.*"

*i. e.* let his fault be condemned, or extirpated, but let not my brother himself suffer.

### NOTE 16, PAGE 178.

"*And mercy then will breathe within your lips*
*Like man new made.*"

As amiable as a man come fresh out of the hands of his Creator; or as tender-hearted and merciful as the first man was in the days of innocence, immediately after his creation.

### NOTE 17, PAGE 185.

"Mr. Chalmers assigns the date of this play to 1613, a year when the fashion of duelling was so rife. Shakespeare evidently was bent on placing its practice in a ridiculous light, knowing well the power of ridicule often exceeded that of the law, and in the combat between the valiant Sir Andrew Aguecheek and the disguised Viola he has placed the custom in an eminently absurd situation.

Sir Francis Bacon had lamented in the House of Commons the great difficulty of redressing the evil of duels owing to the corruption of man's nature. King James tried to effect what Parliament had despaired of effecting, and in 1613 issued 'an Edict and Censure against Private Combats' conceived with great vigour and expressed with decisive force."—HALLIWELL.

NOTE 18, PAGE 186.

"*Mine eye too great a flatterer for my mind.*"] I think the meaning is, I fear that my eyes will seduce my understanding, that I am indulging a passion for this beautiful youth, which my reason cannot approve.—MALONE.

NOTE 19, PAGE 189.

"*A blank, my Lord; she never told her love.*"] Shakespeare alone could describe the effect of his own poetry:—

"Oh, it came o'er the ear like the sweet south
That breathes upon a bank of violets,
Stealing and giving odour."

NOTE 20, PAGE 191.

"*Blame not this haste of mine: If you mean well.*"] This is a passage of impassioned sweetness; Olivia in her address to Sebastian whom she supposes to have already deceived her in a promise of marriage. HAZLITT.

NOTE 21, PAGE 196.

"*For look where Beatrice, like a lapwing, runs.*"] There is something delightfully picturesque in the manner in which Beatrice is described as coming to hear the plot which is contrived against herself.

NOTE 22, PAGE 197.

"*Taming my wild heart to thy loving hand.*"] This image is taken from falconry. She had been charged with being as wild as haggards of the rock; she therefore says, that wild as her heart is, she will tame it to the hand. JOHNSON.

NOTE 23, PAGE 200.

"*You have staid me in a happy hour; I was about to protest I loved you.*"] Many a lady might learn a winning lesson from this delightful frankness. Schlegel aptly observes: "Their witty vivacity does not even abandon them in the avowal of love; and their behaviour only assumes a serious appearance for the purpose of defending the slandered hero. This is exceedingly well imagined; the lovers of jesting must fix a point beyond which they are not to indulge in their humour, if they would not be mistaken for buffoons by trade."

It is worthy of notice that the most valuable synthetic criticism of our poet's works should have proceeded from the pen of a German—Augustus Schlegel—from one speaking a foreign language, one who had to break down the strong barriers of divers speech and customs before he could become in the least degree acquainted with the works of our national Poet. But Schlegel did this, nor this alone; he cast aside all prejudices in favour of the bards of his fatherland; and they were men of lofty intellectual rank, profound thinkers, whose deep thoughts went forth in the garb of loveliness, and found a sympathetic vibration in the hearts of their countrymen, from the courtly peer to the almost solitary peasant in the beauty-clad valley, bowing in reverence: still he passed beyond them, and laid his garland at the feet of Shakespeare. HALLIWELL.

### NOTE 24, PAGE 221.

The reconciliation between the lovers and their sweethearts is very good, and the penance which Rosalind imposes on Biron before he can expect to gain her consent to marry him full of propriety and beauty.

### NOTE 25, PAGE 240.

"*Ye men of Cyprus.*"] These pretty lines, so complimentary to beauty and excellence, were unwittingly repeated when the Governor of Paris, a courtier of the old school, received Marie Antoinette at the barriers; pointing with his sword to the crowd, he said, "Lovely daughter of Maria Theresa, behold one hundred thousand lovers at your feet." THE COMPILER.

### NOTE 26, PAGE 260.

The celebrated Dr. Johnson, although no very great admirer of Shakespeare, used to admit that the perusal of this scene made him suffer intense emotion, and where is there a young person who has not shed hot tears over it? The compiler translated it *vivâ voce* to a few unlettered Maharatta chiefs on one of the hill forts of the Western Ghats of India. They all went to their homes more or less affected; the next day, in the hyperbolical language of the East, they told him that their livers had burst with anguish at the story, but they added, they did not know which to pity most, Othello or Desdemona.

THE COMPILER.

### NOTE 27, PAGE 262.

"*A murder which I thought a sacrifice.*"] The passage probably bears the following meaning :—Thou dost harden thy heart, and so force me to send thee out of the world in the state of the murdered, without preparation for death, when I intended that thy punishment should have been a sacrifice atoning for thy crime.

HALLIWELL.

### NOTE 28, PAGE 265.

"*Nay, had she been true.*"] How beautifully these lines express his unbounded love for his wife; the practical Emilia, in the former scene, weighs the value of the world in comparison with a "small vice," but here the poor, doting, simple-minded Moor prefers his wife's love to the possession of unbounded power and wealth, and in like manner, a few hours before, Desdemona was rejecting the world for her husband's love. No wonder Dr. Johnson felt so acutely when reading this play! a soft heart had the great lexicographer, be witness the scene one night in Fleet Street, so feelingly told by the Laird Boswell.

### NOTE 29, PAGE 276.

"*Beauty provoketh thieves sooner than gold.*"] This idea is beautifully expressed in one of Moore's Irish melodies :—

"Rich and rare were the gems she wore,
And a bright gold ring on her wand she bore;
But oh! her beauty was far beyond
Her sparkling gems or snow-white wand.

"'Lady! dost thou not fear to stray,
So lone and lovely, through this bleak way?
Are Erin's sons so good or so cold
As not to be tempted by woman or gold?'

"'Sir knight! I feel not the least alarm;
No son of Erin will offer me harm,
For though they love women and golden store,
Sir knight! they love honour and virtue more!'

"On she went, and her maiden smile
In safety lighted her round the Green Isle.
And blest for ever is she who relied
Upon Erin's honour and Erin's pride."

### NOTE 30, PAGE 285.

"*Human as she is.*"] That is, not a phantom, but the real Rosalind, without any of the danger generally conceived to attend the rites of incantation. JOHNSON.

### NOTE 31, PAGE 288.

"*The many-colour'd Iris rounds thine eye.*"] There is something exquisitely beautiful in this representation of that suffusion of colours which glimmers round the sight when the eye-lashes are wet with tears. HENLEY.

### NOTE 32, PAGE 293.

"*That everything I look on seemeth green.*"] Shakespeare's observations on the phenomena of nature are very accurate. When one has sat long in the sunshine, the surrounding objects will often appear tinged with green. BLACKSTONE.

### NOTE 33, PAGE 300.

"'*Tis a derivative from me to mine.*"] This sentiment, which is probably borrowed from Ecclesiasticus iii. 11, cannot be too often impressed on the female mind; "the glory of a man is from the honour of his father; and a mother in dishonour is a reproach unto her children." STEEVENS.

### NOTE 34, PAGE 306.

"*Daffodils*
*That come before the swallow dares.*"

These lines seem enamoured of their own sweetness.

HAZLITT.